A Responsible Congress

A Responsible Congress: The Politics of National Security

BY ALTON FRYE

PUBLISHED FOR THE COUNCIL ON FOREIGN RELATIONS

McGRAW-HILL BOOK COMPANY

New York   St. Louis   San Francisco   Düsseldorf
London   Mexico   Sydney   Toronto

Library of Congress Cataloging in Publication Data

Frye, Alton.
    A responsible Congress.

    Includes index.
      1. United States.   Congress.   2. United States—National security.   I. Title.
JK1051.F79   328.73'07'4   74–31498

ISBN 0–07–022600–8

1 2 3 4 5 6 7 8 9 0 BPBP 7 4 3 2 1 0 9 8 7 6 5

The editors for this book were Thomas H. Quinn and Cheryl Love, the designer was Ellen Seham, and the production supervisor was Milton Heiberg.
It was set in Garamond by National ShareGraphics, Inc.

Printed and bound by the Book Press.

To Andrew and Emily,
joys of another congress

Contents

Preface

Perhaps we have reached the time when books, like other potentially hazardous products, should be properly labeled. "Caution: The following study is of unproven therapeutic value and is sold exclusively for the purpose of ventilating one man's views." Such a warning is peculiarly appropriate to studies of the Congress, for the legislature may well be our most perplexing institution. No one should claim a comprehensive or authoritative insight into its workings. To treat so complex a body and the hundreds of vivid personalities who compose it is to encounter an endless succession of contradictions, reminiscent of that ancient logical dilemma "Every statement is false, including this one." Not every statement about the Congress is false, but each is likely to capture only a fraction of a truth which is but partially ascertainable.

Having discounted the dependability of studies of Congress, one may wonder whether anybody should bother to write them, much less read them. The writer's own justification for imposing words on pages, and pages on readers, is rather simple: It is as necessary as it is difficult to develop an informed discourse about the American Congress and its contemporary operations. Surprisingly for a creature that speaks with such volume and variety, Congress has difficulty articulating a shared perspective on its own experience and functions. To compensate for the atomization inherent in an institution of 535 equals, members of Congress and those who serve with them need to become more self-conscious about their individual and collective activities.

It is in the search for that kind of self-consciousness that I have written this volume. It comprises some history and reflections about the recent experience of Congress in addressing a number of crucial policy areas. Here one will find a modest sense of achievement and a measure of frustration, a number of arguable opinions and a dose of impatient concern—but no "Hobbeservations," those cynical views of the American Congress as a nasty, brutish, or irretrievably inept institution. A realistic appraisal of the national legislature must do more than amplify the many criticisms of Congress; it must also acknowledge the ways, sometimes subtle and subterranean, in which many members of Congress are groping to cure their institutional afflictions.

A senator once rebuked a witness critical of the executive branch by saying, "You are making progress more difficult by refusing to recognize its achievement." The same observation is often apt in regard to comments on Congress. Wholesome and little-noticed changes are percolating through the Capitol. These changes are measured less by procedural and organizational developments than by a more assertive mood and a shifting focus of attention on issues of public policy. Cumbersome though the processes are, members of Congress have been steering them increasingly toward grave questions which too long suffered legislative neglect. Strategic weapons choices, establishment of basic objectives for arms control negotiations, more explicit participation in decisions on the disposition and employment of military forces—these and a host of comparable concerns have been ascending in the hierarchy of congressional priorities. These newfound interests have induced few formal innovations in Congress, but they have certainly aroused new life in the existing structure.

This book testifies to that new life. Without fawning or frowning upon the Congress, we need to take note of this budding rejuvenation and to nurse it further. For nothing is more essential to the enduring vitality of our body politic than a vigorous and creative legislature. In the faith that a responsible Congress can be the noblest achievement of American politics, I offer these pages.

Acknowledgments

Even modest books acquire immodest obligations. No author could have incurred a happier set of debts than I acquired in the course of this study.

This work began to germinate during the mid-sixties when I was a research associate of the Harvard University Center for International Affairs, then directed by Professor Thomas Schelling, a friend and colleague whose fascinating mind is the source of endless stimulation to all who know him. Many of the concepts and notions explicated here were forged and tested in the years 1968 to 1971, when I served as legislative and administrative assistant to the junior Senator from Massachusetts, Edward W. Brooke. As his associates in Congress have come to appreciate, collaboration with Ed Brooke is an education in that brand of public service which blends rational policy with robust politics.

In its final form the book materialized during my tenure as International Affairs Fellow of the Council on Foreign Relations and fellow of the Woodrow Wilson International Center for Scholars, a joint appointment which I was privileged to hold during 1971–1972 To John Temple Swing, then director of the Council's International Affairs Fellowship program, and to Benjamin H. Read, the first director of the Woodrow Wilson International Center, I am deeply grateful for psychological and intellectual sustenance far beyond my powers to describe, much less to repay.

Portions of the study have benefited from discussion in a variety of forums. Chapter 2 builds on a presentation to the annual meeting of the American Political Science Association. An earlier version of Chapter 4 was delivered to the annual convention of the American Society of Public Administration. Chapter 5 grows out of papers prepared for the Carnegie–Columbia University project on accountability and a brief study published by the Wilson Center in its International Affairs series. My article entitled "Congress: The Virtues of Its Vices" (*Foreign Policy*, Summer 1971) anticipates some of the analyses developed in Chapter 7.

In completing the book I have had the good fortune of reviewing the entire work with a joint study group assembled by the Council and the Woodrow Wilson Center. There could have been no more cheerful and provocative critics, and any author would have found their discussions exhilarating and instructive. Chaired by the Honorable Paul C. Warnke, the group included Congressman John B. Anderson, Congressman Leslie Aspin, J. Brian Atwood, William J. Baroody, Jr., T. Edward Braswell, Jr., Senator Thomas F. Eagleton, Terry Emerson, Congressman Dante B. Fascell, Richard L. Garwin, Meg Greenfield, Thomas A. Halsted, Richard C. Holbrooke, Townsend W. Hoopes, Thomas L. Hughes, Samuel P. Huntington, Edward A. Kolodziej, David W. MacEachron, David E. McGiffert, Albert Meisel, Jonathan Moore, Andrew Pierre, Lawrence I. Radway, Benjamin H. Read, Thomas C. Schelling, John H. Sullivan, John Temple Swing, and Senator Robert Taft, Jr. I am also indebted to W. Richard Smyser, former fellow of the Woodrow Wilson Center and now a member of the National Security Council staff, for timely comments during the crucial phase of revisions; and to John S. Saloma III, for helping to cultivate our mutual interest in Congress through many years.

As the work neared completion, Richard H. Ullman, the Council's Director of Studies, applied his lucid editorial skills to the clear benefit of the manuscript. William P. Bundy extended both encouragement and criticism in those happy proportions which stimulate rather than stymy an author's final efforts, as did Gordon J. F. MacDonald, who shared his rich perspective on a number of the technological issues discussed in the book.

To my wife, Patricia, I gladly make the ultimate concession—the other readers agreed with her on almost every comment.

Like other authors before me, I have searched in vain to find a scapegoat among this long list of creditors. Alas, there is none. The flaws which linger are my own.

A Responsible Congress

I. *Advocate and Overseer: Congress and American Security*

One of Washington's notable raconteurs, the Reverend Howard
Stone Anderson, tells of a lady visitor to the nation's capital who
took one of the familiar guided tours of the city. When the bus
driver pointed out the discreetly styled Hay-Adams Hotel, the lady timidly
inquired, "Oh, was that Sherman Adams?" The amused driver explained,
"No, m'am, it's named after Henry Adams, the famous writer." At Ward
Circle, the lady again raised her hand and asked, "Could that be Montgomery
Ward?" Once again the guide cleared up the confusion by answering that
the circle was actually dedicated to Artemus Ward, the well-known humor-
ist. Similar episodes occurred at almost every landmark until at last the bus
drew up before a fine old building in Georgetown where the driver announced, "And this is historic Christ Church." There was a long silence.
Finally a voice from the rear of the bus called out, "Go ahead, lady, you can't
miss 'em all."

As a symbol of ineptitude that little lady compares with an institution
more commonly portrayed in political humor as a crotchety old man—the
Congress of the United States. By 1974 survey data showed that in the view
of the American public, the competence and performance of congressmen
ranked somewhere south of trash collectors. These findings caused understandable chagrin at the Capitol, as well they should in every quarter concerned with representative government. For "the erosion of public esteem,"
as Congressman John Anderson of Illinois phrased it, fundamentally weak-
ens the capacity of Congress to fulfill its constitutional duties. Yet these
public appraisals of Congress are rooted in slender and filtered knowledge of
the legislature's actual workings. Like Woodrow Wilson at the time he
wrote his famous treatise *Congressional Government,* most Americans have
never visited Congress or had an opportunity to observe its labors.

1

When one studies Congress more intimately, it is apparent that ordinary citizens could scarcely be more dissatisfied with its modern record than are many of its own members. Over the past decade this popular and official discontent has bred the first stirrings of a new vitality in the legislature. Just as the crisis of confidence in Congress antedates the travesty of Watergate, so too does the movement in Congress to establish the basis for future confidence in the institution's diligence and effectiveness.

In no area has this movement been more essential than in the field of national security policy. Here lies perhaps the gravest dilemma of contemporary statecraft: In an age of nuclear weapons, when issues of war and peace require an executive capable of prompt and vigorous action, they also pose risks far too great for the nation to vest decision-making authority in the hands of one man or a few men at the pinnacle of executive power. It is the task of Congress to resolve this dilemma by maintaining an institutional balance of power which disciplines the President without paralyzing him.

The quest for this new balance represents an acknowledgment by many members of Congress that the legislature's long-standing habit of extreme deference to the Chief Executive in national security matters has cost the nation many of the benefits normally associated with the separation of powers. Particularly during the Cold War, when militant anticommunism reigned on Capitol Hill, Congress tended to reinforce the prevailing inclinations of the executive branch rather than to temper them by exploring alternative policies. For many years this was especially true of strategic weapons policy. Whatever proposals the President advanced Congress inclined to enlarge rather than to refine.

The very vocabulary of nuclear strategy has argued against a more discriminating legislative role. "Assured destruction," "counterforce," "damage-limiting capability," "catalytic war," "pre-emptive strike," "CEP," "MIRV"—the lexicon is arcane, the concepts are often complex. The field of strategic analysis suffers from what Athelstan Spilhaus tartly labels "acronymphomania." The issues of nuclear strategy are not common topics in everyday discourse. Nor have they been regular and familiar matters of debate in the Congress.

Yet few questions pose so grave a challenge and so essential a duty for the legislative body. For embedded in decisions on force postures and strategic policy are some of the most profound expressions of national values, both moral and political. The strategic plans and weapons systems a nation adopts as its own reflect judgments about the requirements of national survival and the worth of human lives, reckoned in the tens of millions. Ends and means become entangled in Gordian knots neither Aristotle nor Alexander could unravel.

Granted that problems of military strategy and technology are immensely complicated and mind-numbing affairs, the root questions are ethical and political in nature. Whether and under what circumstances the United States should threaten to destroy another society is scarcely a matter to be left to mere executive pragmatism. It calls for the kind of collective moral judgment which might better be expressed through the most broadly representative device available to a people. In truth, however, the nation's legislative representatives have seldom approached such fundamental issues. Congress has not usually produced coherent debate on nuclear strategy. Those members and committees that have involved themselves in one or another aspect of the subject have performed valuable service, but the operating solutions have fallen to the executive branch to design and implement, and Congress has customarily picked up the bill without objection.[1]

An important distinction needs to be made, of course, between broad decisions regarding the structure of strategic forces and the doctrines for their employment, and the immediate decisions for actual use of the forces in an emergency. The former decisions require years to conceive and carry out, and they deserve the most careful deliberation of which the community is capable. Congress both can be and ought to be involved in examining the far-reaching implications of such issues. For the latter class of decisions the opportunity and feasibility of congressional participation are obviously more limited. It is in the supervision of force posture and doctrine that Congress can achieve maximum influence on the urgent decisions which may be taken in moments of crisis. Action on the former class of issues defines the options available at the time the President is faced with a decision to use the forces. To assert that the President should have a reasonable and flexible range of strategic options and that only the President can act for the nation in the ultimate crises to which nuclear weapons are related is not to say that the Commander-in-Chief should be provided every strategic option or absolute discretion in the use of the nation's arsenal.

There is an understandable degree of tension between the need for sophisticated understanding of intricate technologies and strategies and the need for improved participation by the lay members of Congress in policy-making. Somewhat paradoxically, many sensitive and knowledgeable members of the defense community have taken the lead in stressing to congressmen that the central questions of nuclear strategy concern political and ethical values rather than technical judgments. Some of the experts have been among the first to insist that other citizens and their representatives should assume the burden of decisions on broad strategic policy, rather than leave it to the

---

[1] To qualify this generalization, Arnold Kanter demonstrates that congressional committees have often had significant influence on defense programs by relatively modest budgetary adjustments in key categories. See his "Congress and the Defense Budget, 1960–1970," *American Political Science Review*, vol. 66, March 1972, pp. 129–143. See also Samuel P. Huntington, *The Soldier and the State* (New York: Vintage Books, 1964), pp. 400–428, as well as the excellent studies by Huntington, *The Common Defense* (New York: Columbia, 1961), and Edward A. Kolodziej, *The Uncommon Defense and Congress, 1945–1963* (Columbus, Ohio: Ohio State University Press, 1966).

monopoly of an elite. Certain members of Congress, however, including some of the keenest students of national security, have been reticent about increasing the congressional role.[2] They have been apprehensive that sound strategy might not be served by the type of political rationality and the bargaining and balancing acts which are common in Congress.

One ought to respect this concern. Irresponsibility and irrationality are not alien—or unique—to Congress. Public clamor and critical events can set off tidal waves in the legislature, sweeping aside the most thoughtful and valid considerations and elevating the plausible and unwise. But the inescapable task for a responsible Congress is to frame the appropriate questions for its own consideration. One cannot expect a vote of congressmen—or of scientists—to determine whether a weapon will work or not, any more than one could use a referendum to decide whether the law of gravity will apply in Cucamonga.

But one can expect the Congress to assess the more fundamental choices of risk, preference, and value. To what degree should the national posture emphasize deterrence, to what degree defense? What risks should the United States be willing to accept in the interests of promoting strategic arms control? What should be the governing policies with regard to strategic targeting, e.g., countervalue or counterforce targets, people or weapons, cities or silos? Should the United States ever contemplate reliance on so-called "launch on warning" procedures, or should we invest whatever is required to insure that none of our strategic missiles is so vulnerable it cannot ride out a possible attack?

These and countless similar issues crop up, sometimes eccentrically, in congressional deliberations. They are rarely recognized for what they are, profound tests of national values. Such choices are not the exclusive prerogative of Congress, but neither should the Congress allow them to fall exclusively to the executive. They, like many other issues of foreign policy and security, are properly the shared responsibility of the two branches. Belatedly, some members of Congress are seeking to accept this responsibility. Perhaps this trend is best understood by relating it to earlier congressional efforts in this field and to the broader context of strategic discussion in the country.

DOCTRINE BECOMES DOGMA: THE CONGRESSIONAL FAITHFUL

Hurrying from a conference on the 1971 defense authorization, the late L. Mendel Rivers, chairman of the House Armed Services Committee,

---

[2] This concern persists today, but it was quite evident in the voluminous interviews of congressmen conducted by Lewis Anthony Dexter two decades ago. See Dexter, "Congressmen and the Making of Military Policy," in Robert L. Peabody and Nelson W. Polsby (eds.), *New Perspectives on the House of Representatives* (Chicago: Rand McNally, 1963), pp. 305–324.

phrased his view tersely: "Congressmen don't understand these military things. My members rely on me, and I know who to rely on. I'd rather have one general who knows this business than a hundred senators who don't."

Chairman Rivers typified those congressional leaders who build their claim to expertise on presumed knowledge of which experts to consult. The principle has much intrinsic merit; a reputation for ability to choose wise counselors has always been a prized quality among high policy-makers. In the strategic field, the counsel on which Chairman Rivers and most overseers of U.S. military policy have relied has tended to be the doctrinal product of the executive hierarchy. One may agree that this doctrine has generally been sophisticated and often quite sound, and still conclude that it would have been wise to explore more fully the implications and likely consequences of particular doctrines and to examine possible alternatives.

It is perhaps not surprising that many members of Congress, seared by memories of the blood and treasure expended in the Second World War, seemed almost insensitive to the change of scale in warfare signified by Hiroshima and Nagasaki. There was no discernible congressional opposition to the early American drift into heavy reliance on the threat of nuclear retaliation as the keystone of national strategy. After all, the Soviets had not accepted the generous American proposals of the Acheson-Lilienthal plan. Given the fact of U.S. demobilization on a massive scale and the brief continuance of nuclear monopoly by this country, the threat to use the bomb seemed a natural option. There was great anxiety over the possibility the Soviet Union would acquire nuclear weapons, but congressional assessment of the prospect was too vague to permit concrete analysis of the changes in policy which an end to our monopoly would logically dictate.

Even after the Soviets broke the U.S. nuclear monopoly, the explicit formulation of the "massive retaliation" doctrine in the early nineteen-fifties was absorbed by Congress with scarcely a murmur. In some respects it played on the wishful thinking of economy-minded legislators, who hoped that the threat of nuclear retaliation at the time and place of our choosing would effectively deter local aggressions by the Soviet bloc. If it worked, this form of "cheap deterrence" could save billions that might otherwise be spent on maintaining conventional forces, a dubious course anyway to congressmen convinced of Russian and Chinese manpower advantages. But could massive retaliation deter, and what if the threat failed?

The critiques which showed that "massive retaliation" was obsolete at birth, at least so far as deterring a nuclear-capable Soviet Union was concerned, did not originate in Congress. One might have thought that at least some members would want to consider the consequences of allowing a conventional conflict to trigger massive retaliation upon a state on the verge of a capability to respond in kind against Washington, New York, or other U.S. cities. The retreat from the more extreme formulations of the doctrine began almost immediately in the executive branch, indeed in the remarks of Secretary Dulles himself, but not under the spur of congressional pressure.

On the contrary, the fierce and hostile rhetoric of anticommunism persisted throughout the fifties and much of the sixties in Congress, modified slightly if at all by an awareness that the Soviet Union was coming to hold millions of Americans hostage to its own nuclear weapons. Congressional debates and reports still hinted that, under some circumstances, the United States might be able to undertake a nuclear strike against the Soviet Union.

Beginning in 1961, the sobering testimony of Secretary of Defense Robert McNamara indicated that nuclear war would mean mutual devastation of the Soviet Union and the United States. Yet certain members of Congress continued to flirt with technological fixes; some military officers promised they could maintain the U.S. option to use nuclear weapons against the Soviet Union. Although open advocacy of preventive war could and did cost a general officer his job, more subtle suggestions still circulated that the United States might sometime have to initiate a nuclear strike.

McNamara's attempts to rationalize U.S. strategy and posture by advocating a so-called "full spectrum" capability of conventional and nuclear forces, to be employed under a new doctrine known as flexible response, did not entirely preclude this contingency. In fact, while the McNamara programs would undoubtedly be costly, the House and Senate Armed Services committees were receptive to efforts to maintain and exploit overwhelming nuclear superiority, which they hoped would flow from the planned strategic expansion of the sixties. This interest was fed by the belligerent rocket rattling of Soviet Premier Khrushchev, who nourished the worst fears of many Americans by timing metaphorical threats to "bury" the West with shrill exploitation of what appeared to be an emerging missile gap. Khrushchev's political aggressiveness contributed significantly to congressional demands that the United States increase its arsenal.

Given the growth of Soviet forces, a good many congressmen were now attracted to the need to create an American counterforce capacity to deny the Soviet Union the opportunity to strike the United States if war should break out. In this respect men like Senators Goldwater and Symington, always inclined to emphasize the advantages of a superior offense, were highly sympathetic to the "counterforce damage-limiting" operations alluded to by Secretary McNamara. The Secretary expounded these possibilities most notably in his famous speech at Ann Arbor, Michigan, on June 16, 1962, declaring that should war come, the United States would initially use its own strategic forces, not against Soviet cities, but against suitable military installations. This speech clearly sought to convey a signal to the Russians in hopes of eliciting reciprocal restraint on their part in support of a "no cities" strategic strike plan, at least in the opening phase of a potential conflict.

The Ann Arbor formulation seemed a plausible and humane policy, designed to bolster deterrence but also to insure that the costs of its failure would be moderated. Targeting U.S. aircraft and missiles against Soviet forces seemed to make sense, although the vast disparity in numbers of weapons possessed by the two countries made it hard to see how the Soviet Union could apply similar standards. In this period Moscow could not hope to reduce American forces below a level sufficient to wipe out every likely target in the Soviet Union. If it exhausted its own strategic forces against U.S. bases and weapons, how could it then hope to deter later attacks on its cities? What served U.S. interests in the Ann Arbor doctrine was less suitable to Soviet requirements.

The mismatch between Soviet and American strategic requirements should have been evident at the time to alert congressmen and citizens. Only subsequent experience revealed the Ann Arbor doctrine's more profound defects, one political and one strategic.

Politically, the notion of damage-limiting through counterforce strikes sustained the false hopes of many congressmen and other Americans that the United States could somehow deny or greatly limit the Soviet Union's power to do this country untold harm. It declared that nuclear superiority was really meaningful in an operational military sense. Thus it tended to perpetuate the existing congressional tendency to proceed on the illusory assumption that more weapons were obviously better, that security could still be pursued in the ancient fashion of accumulating hardware, that the chilling fact of a vulnerable America did not have to be faced. It was an utterly human instinct to avoid the disturbing reality that the United States could not escape unacceptable damage in any nuclear exchange with the Soviet Union. The uncritical reception accorded the counterforce damage-limiting policy reveals how eager congressmen were to believe that this nation could buy its way out of the excruciating dilemma of nuclear insecurity.

But what was politically palatable was strategically unsettling. The Ann Arbor posture proved to be less stabilizing than desired. The posture sought to exploit the numerical advantage in weapons enjoyed by the United States in the early sixties. Furthermore, anticipating a steady growth in Soviet capabilities, the maintenance of a counterforce damage-limiting option required a rapid expansion of U.S. land- and sea-based missile forces, an expansion which in hindsight came to appear excessive, even to its advocates in the upper reaches of the Defense Department.

The net effect was probably to postpone serious attempts at stabilizing strategic relations between the superpowers. Until mutual vulnerability was acknowledged and mutual deterrence recognized as the only realistic basis for the Soviet-American strategic balance, at least in the short run, the two sides were condemned to a futile and expensive competition in armaments. In fact the ephemeral advantages of strategic superiority were paid for in heightened insecurity on both sides, as the escalated deployment of weapons of mass destruction multiplied the levels of damage each could inflict on the other. Potential damage levels soared well beyond those most reasonable men would consider necessary for deterrence.

In fairness one needs to recall that the political context of the period did not invite an effort to persuade Congress that the United States would have to learn to live with mutual deterrence as a maximum strategic goal. The Berlin crisis of 1961, the threatening Soviet feats in space and military technology, the adamant Soviet stands in various international forums, and the Cuban missile adventure all suggested Moscow's hostile intentions and strong forward momentum in many fields.

Thus what may not seem wise in retrospect is nonetheless understandable. Just as in the aftermath of Sputnik Congress pressed for a vigorous U.S. response to the Soviet challenge, so in the sixties many key members were pressing the executive to intensify its defensive efforts. The House Appropriations Committee and the Joint Committee on Atomic Energy had been emphatic in pressing the Department of Defense to accelerate the Polaris submarine program, having added funds well beyond those requested for the program in the fiscal 1959 budget. Frequently thereafter congressmen would hark back to the apparent wisdom of their action on Polaris, which became recognized as the most invulnerable component of the American second-strike capability. Time and again congressmen would cite the Polaris example in pressing executive branch officials to accept additional funds and legislative guidance to pursue a favored weapon system.

As a general principle, congressmen all but universally shared the feeling that if the country was to make a mistake, it should "err on the side of safety." This conviction was, of course, the political equivalent of what strategic analysts came to call "worst case" analysis, i.e., adopting as the governing standard for U.S. force design the highest reasonable estimate of the possible enemy threat. The result of this attitude was a strong and virtually unquestioned consensus on the Hill in favor of a "high hedge" against destabilizing breakthroughs by the Soviet Union. While the responsible committees often were reducing the defense budget in specific areas, they tended to be uniformly openhanded when it came to starting or expediting new strategic weapons programs.

The sense of peril was keen and enduring, spurred in part by the visible technological triumphs of the Soviet space program. In this atmosphere expenditures on what later proved to be redundant programs occasioned only mild, retrospective regret. Such was the case in the field of intercontinental missiles, where a proliferation of efforts had persisted after the nineteen-fifties. After the first-generation American ICBM, the Atlas, was deployed, a sizeable number of larger Titan missiles were installed, only to be phased out with the introduction of the smaller and more reliable solid-fuel Minuteman missile, which in its successive versions became the backbone of the U.S. land-based forces. Belatedly, congressmen and Defense Department officials came to realize that the $12 billion investment in Titan was a dubious expense for so brief service and that a wiser course might have been to go directly from Atlas to Minuteman. (By 1971 only fifty-four Titans remained in the inventory, although many such rockets had seen duty in the space program.) But no one in Congress had argued at the time that it might be prudent to forgo Titan, and there was no serious recrimination for Congress's failure to examine this option more thoroughly.

This pattern of legislative behavior and attitudes appeared in instance after instance, as powerful members and committees of the Congress repeatedly pressed the executive to do more. In 1962 a classic confrontation between Carl Vinson of the House Armed Services Committee and Secretary McNamara grew out of the B-70 supersonic bomber program, which Vinson fought adamantly to fund at a higher level. Though smoothed over by White House intervention, the B-70 dispute left lingering scars and fed a rising strain in relations between the House committee and the Secretary.

Other members argued for a more vigorous program of exploratory development of military space technology. While reiterating their support for restricting the use of space to peaceful purposes, many congressmen and senators were alarmed at reports of Soviet military space efforts and determined to deter hostile use of the newly opened environment. In 1962 Senator Thomas Dodd called for the appointment of a military officer to head the entire U.S. space program, which was widely perceived on the Hill as justified primarily by its technological benefits to national security.

More mundane controversies found congressmen contesting the Department of Defense decision to build the TFX aircraft, the hotly debated multiservice and multipurpose plane which became the centerpiece in a continuing battle between McNamara and the Senate Permanent Subcommittee on Investigations. Senator John McClellan and others doubted that a single plane could be built to perform the missions of both Navy and Air Force; they were especially critical of the manner in which the TFX contract was awarded to the General Dynamics Corporation, contrary to the recommendations of the military evaluators, who preferred a proposal of the Boeing Company.[3] Much of the Senate committee's critique carried a thrust toward building the higher-performance (and higher-risk) aircraft favored by the military but rejected by McNamara as unnecessarily "gold-plated," or loaded with nonessential technical features. In the House, the Appropriations Committee attacked the venture from another direction, earmarking funds in the 1964 budget for a mach 3 (three times the speed of sound) plane rather than the mach 2.5 design approved by the Department of Defense for the TFX. At virtually every juncture congressmen, dealing in the general weapons concepts more than in detailed technical evaluations of system feasibility and cost effectiveness, inclined in the direction of the more ambitious program.

Indeed, to many the very term "cost effectiveness" came to symbolize a willingness on the part of Secretary McNamara's Pentagon to take risks with

---

[3] A full exposition of this lingering episode is Robert J Art, *The TFX Decision: McNamara and the Military* (Boston: Little, Brown, 1968).

the nation's security rather than bear the risks of more adventurous development and deployment programs across the spectrum of strategic weapons. Given their evident dispositions on the nature of the threat faced by the country, it was not surprising that Chairman Rivers and like-minded members of Congress would be acutely concerned at what they considered false economy and misguided constraints imposed by the new Department of Defense. Congressional displeasure also flowed from what critics considered immaturity and excessive zeal on the part of the youthful corps of systems analysts recruited by McNamara. Senior legislators were simply offended, as senior military officers often were, by what seemed to them overbearing and insensitive intrusions by civilian systems analysts into the realms traditionally reserved for "professional military judgment." These personal frictions sometimes made it more difficult to focus on the merits of analyses and decision. They undoubtedly amplified the policy differences which earned Secretary McNamara widespread hostility in Congress before his lengthy tenure ended.

Precisely because the congressional mood consistently favored greater strategic preparedness, McNamara's pronouncements at Ann Arbor and in his annual posture statements were read by a number of legislators in a spirit different from the one he intended. If McNamara sought to convey in the "no cities" policy a call for mutual restraint, members of the key congressional committees tended to respond by demanding an intensified program to make it possible to avoid striking cities by perfecting weapons able to attack Soviet weapons. The Secretary's stated intention to avoid attacks on cities in the early phases of a nuclear exchange may have meant only that he was contemplating a limited counterforce employment of existing U.S. weapons to diminish somewhat Soviet capacity to destroy our population centers. To congressmen unprepared to accept the fact that the Soviet Union could attack the United States with nuclear weapons, the Secretary's attempt to compromise with the harsh facts of our own vulnerability was an invitation to press for a decisive counterforce capability sufficient to disarm enemy strategic forces by attacking them first. As one representative phrased it in an unguarded moment, "this committee [House Appropriations] has been on record since 1961 in favor of a first-strike posture under certain conditions . . . ."

Mr. McNamara tried to dissuade the Congress from exaggerated expectations in this regard. In his 1963 presentation on the defense budget, he stressed that "we have not found it feasible, at this time, to provide a capability for insuring the destruction of any very large portion of the fully hard ICBM sites, if the Soviets build them in quantities, or of missile-launching submarines. Fully hard ICBM sites can be destroyed but only at great cost in terms of the numbers of offensive weapons required to dig them out." That invulnerability was, of course, the reason the United States had chosen to bury a major fraction of its own retaliatory forces in silos. Yet what was impracticable to the Secretary was not necessarily undesirable to the people's elected spokesmen in Congress.

Tensions between Congress and the Secretary mounted, as a number of influential members came to fear that the United States was not doing enough to maintain its strategic superiority. These tensions were rooted not only in the political sensitivity of congressmen to the loss of the American nuclear advantage; they also grew out of the legislators' misplaced confidence that, given enough resources, technology could solve almost any technological problem. In a sense they shared the enthusiasms of those military officers who were infatuated with one or another potential breakthrough, perhaps in outer space, which some commentators depicted as the "high ground" in the war of the future. The deep fears of Soviet aggression in a program for world domination sought relief in the kind of technological escapism represented by certain advanced weapons concepts. Many congressmen were receptive to briefings on highly speculative approaches to denying an enemy the capability to strike the United States, possibly by erecting a "truly effective" missile defense, or by designing methods to destroy another country's submarines, or by perfecting means to disarm an enemy's land-based bombers and missiles. Driven near to desperation by an unwonted menace to the nation's heartland, they clung to the hope that it could be thwarted by dint of our own effort. The earth had shrunk, and technology had robbed America of the security long afforded by her isolation between two oceans; perhaps technology would yet restore what it had rent.

Attempts to steer the nation's strategic policy by pumping more money into this or that weapons system proved futile, as had previous efforts to use the appropriations process as an affirmative control over executive behavior. The executive branch consistently interpreted increases in funds as, in President Kennedy's phrase, "only a ceiling, not a mandate to spend." The result was that Congress had no direct mechanism for imposing its will in such cases, even though it had a powerful constitutional claim to a right to do so. Those congressmen who had hoped to influence national strategy and force posture through this device found themselves utterly frustrated. As Representative Glenard P. Lipscomb glumly remarked in early 1967, "Adding on to what we feel is necessary is getting to be a rather ineffective action."

Theoretically, one might suppose, Congress could have asserted its preferences by denying funds for the strategic programs proposed by the executive and authorizing money only for those favored on the Hill. But that kind of sledgehammer technique is politically comparable to the use of nuclear weapons in war: because the power is too awesome to employ for constructive purposes, the powerful often appear to be impotent. Furthermore, in the context of legislative-executive relations, such drastic action is feasible only when there is a sharp dichotomy between program choices. Hypothetically, for example, if both branches wanted to build an additional aircraft carrier, Congress favoring nuclear power and the Department of Defense inclined toward conventional power for the vessel, the legislative preference might be made to prevail through a ban on spending for a conventional power plant. But instances of this sort are relatively rare and are hardly the most decisive aspects of national security policy.

In the larger decisions connected with U.S. strategic programs of the nineteen-sixties, the Congress found itself in no position to say no to the executive's major weapons recommendations, for the good reason that it felt the executive was already doing too little in crucial areas. To the central legislative critics of these years the problem was how to trigger greater and more varied strategic effort, how to improve the mix in U.S. forces, how to coax the Department of Defense to do more—not how to veto the Department's allegedly modest initiatives.[4] Congressmen pressing for a more vigorous defense effort would not have found it congenial to cut back on the Department of Defense proposals. Some members may even have suspected, in their wary attitude toward what they considered "go slow" civilian management in the Pentagon, that Secretary McNamara and friends would welcome some further trimming of the Department's plans. Their wariness was matched by the widespread perception in the Department that "the problem with Congress" was getting it to accept the Secretary's own cutbacks on service requests, e.g., in the Department's reduction of the planned Minuteman deployment from a total of more than 2,000 missiles urged by the Air Force to the 1,000 eventually approved by the office of the Secretary of Defense. The many players in the legislative-executive contest recognized that Congress, during these years, was "stickier on the downside than on the up."

Taking account only of the expressed views and desires of the legislative leaders customarily at the center of defense policy-making, one might have expected that the turn of the decade would find increasing pressures for yet more substantial investment in strategic programs. The threat would seem to warrant it, in the minds of the members of the Armed Services and Appropriations committees. China was acquiring a nuclear capability. Russia, after long years of straining upward, was approaching nuclear parity, while the

---

[4] I have stressed here the policy considerations involved in congressional pressure for greater strategic spending; for the most part, I believe that policy concerns are far more important to members' judgments on defense issues than the often-cited pork-barrel considerations. Some of the most systematic analyses of the relationship between defense spending in a member's state and a member's votes on defense matters reinforce this view. Bruce Russett reports no relationship between defense contract awards and Senate voting, although he detects a modest correlation between direct military payroll expenditures in a state and the voting patterns of senators from that state. See Russett, *What Price Vigilance?* (New Haven, Conn.: Yale, 1970), pp. 56–90. Previous studies reported no clear relationships at all in this regard; see Charles Gray and Glenn Gregory, "Military Spending and Senate Voting: A Correlational Study," *Journal of Peace Research*, no. 1, 1969, pp. 44–54; and Stephen Cobb, "Defense Spending and Foreign Policy in the House of Representatives," *Journal of Conflict Resolution*, vol. 13 (September 1969), pp. 358–369.

United States appeared almost to be treading water, allowing the Soviet Union to overtake it in numbers of long-range missiles and submarines. If popular opinion in and out of Congress retained its traditional conviction that "more is better," there would likely be a "gut reaction" in support of expanding the U.S. arsenal. And if the Chief Executive failed to recommend such expansion, he must contend with visions of a new missile-gap controversy in the next presidential sweepstakes.

Yet the attitudes and actions of the more vocal congressional participants in the national security process did not give an accurate picture of the broader and more diverse spectrum of opinion which had been evolving in Congress during these years. As the President was to discover in proposing an anti-ballistic missile system, one could no longer rely upon "gut reaction" on the Hill to produce overwhelming support for a new weapons deployment. Suddenly and somewhat surprisingly, strategic issues had become a salient concern to a wider public. The debut of the Sentinel ABM system, recommended by the Johnson Administration in late 1967, met a congressional audience not so much critical of its adequacy as dubious of its necessity.

II. *Strategy Meets Politics: The Anti-Ballistic Missile System*

With past experience and early signals as one's guide, one would
have expected that the proposal to deploy an anti-ballistic missile
defense system would elicit a prompt surge of congressional
approval. The Joint Chiefs of Staff, which had potent influence among
congressmen and senators, had been urging an ABM deployment since 1960.
Even before that time, Congress had added $137 million to President
Eisenhower's 1957 budget request to spur development of the Nike-Zeus
system. The last budget submitted by Mr. Eisenhower had sought $287
million for continued ABM research, but the President explicitly cautioned
against any premature commitment to deploy such weapons.

Through the sixties, as we have seen, key members of Congress were
pressing the Kennedy and Johnson administrations to do more in general
and to deploy an ABM system in particular. The visible currents of legislative sentiment were reflected in the Senate Armed Services Committee's
April 1966 decision to add $167.9 million to the fiscal year 1967 budget for
preproduction activities on an ABM system. The senators commented that
after nine years of research and development on the Nike-X (as it was by
then called), the committee believed the system could provide significant
protection against many types of missile attack and that it might well save
millions of American lives. Thus, the committee's authorization of $585
million, including the $417 million asked by the Department of Defense for
continued research and development (R & D), was justified as "reasonably
priced insurance" which could cut the eventual lead time for deployment by
a full year. At this juncture there there was no serious challenge in Congress
to the committee's intimation that an ABM deployment was probably wise
and necessary.

By late 1966 the emerging impatience for an ABM of members like Richard Russell had received what might have seemed a decisive boost: the Soviet Union was installing an ABM defense around Moscow.[1] For years the defense community had been racked by anxiety and argument over whether certain radars and missiles in the Soviet Union might be useful against missiles as well as aircraft. That dispute had focused on installations across northern Russia and had resulted, somewhat inconclusively, in the operating assumption that Soviet air defenses were not in fact "ABM-capable." But the evidence of the new construction around the Soviet capital was less ambiguous. In November 1966 Secretary McNamara revealed that the Russians had begun an ABM deployment, using large and long-range missiles later known to Western intelligence circles as "Galosh" rockets.

Coupled with the Congress's action in adding unbudgeted funds for pre-production work on a U.S. ABM, the 1966 intelligence created a complex political problem for President Johnson. It was not the American custom to allow the Soviet Union to gain a unique advantage in any area of strategic weaponry. Habit alone would have dictated that if the Soviets had an ABM, so should the United States. But the executive branch was seriously divided on the feasibility and desirability of such a deployment. The Joint Chiefs now revived their pressure for a heavy, nationwide deployment to maximize protection against a possible Soviet strike on the American population. The Defense Department's civilian leadership viewed such a thick deployment as technically useless, since it could be overwhelmed by increasing Soviet offensive forces, and strategically foolish, since it would predictably induce an intensification of the arms race. Yet Secretary McNamara fully comprehended the President's political problem and tried to put forward a plan to meet it. With the support of the Secretary of State, McNamara urged the President to postpone any immediate start on deployment until a full exploration could be made of possible negotiations for a mutual ban on ABM systems. President Johnson accepted the compromise, but, though hopeful that arms control talks could begin, he felt obliged to meet the congressional demands for action by requesting standby financing for ABM deployment should the negotiating effort prove barren.[2]

Under the circumstances this was a plausible course and the one which appeared to have the fewest political risks. An overture to the Soviets for mutual restraint would be joined with preparation for national action.

President Johnson put the matter directly to Premier Kosygin in a letter of January 21, 1967:

---

[1] Soviet Premier Khrushchev and Defense Minister Malinovskii had repeatedly claimed that the Soviet Union had solved the problem of defending against missile attacks. See the editorial notes to the RAND Corporation translation of V. D. Sokolovskii, *Soviet Military Strategy* (Englewood Cliffs, N.J.: Prentice-Hall, 1963), pp. 315–316.

[2] An informed appraisal of the executive branch decision-making is Morton H. Halperin, "The Decision to Deploy the ABM: Bureaucratic and Domestic Politics in the Johnson Administration," *World Politics*, vol. 25, October 1972, pp. 62–95. See also Halperin's *Bureaucratic Politics and Foreign Policy* (Washington: Brookings, 1974), pp. 1–7, 297–311.

I think you must realize that following the deployment by you of an anti-ballistic missile system I face great pressures from the Members of Congress and from public opinion not only to deploy defensive systems in this country, but also to increase greatly our capabilities to penetrate any defensive systems which you might establish.[3]

Mr. Johnson anticipated that the ensuing arms race would impose colossal costs on both countries "without substantially enhancing the security of our own peoples or contributing to the prospects for a stable peace in the world."

The President no doubt respected the counsel of his Cabinet advisers in resisting a hasty move toward deployment, but he also shared many of the perspectives of Senator Russell and other Hill colleagues, particularly the conviction that negotiations with a determined Soviet adversary would be facilitated by a clear demonstration that the United States was prepared to take suitable unilateral action if necessary. "We arm to parley" was nearly universal gospel in the Congress, and one doubts that Lyndon Johnson had cast off the faith on succession to the Presidency. Even if he had acquired certain doubts about the tactic—and his support of the many measures of strategic restraint advocated by McNamara and others suggests the possibility—knowledge that the Soviets were deploying a missile defense net made the moment most inopportune for attempting to persuade the Congress that U.S. strategic restraint was the soundest basis for seeking a negotiated stabilization of the arms balance. And the President, being less sensitive to the strategic consequences of an ABM deployment than some of his advisers, probably felt that if the Soviets would not talk, it would be useful to have an ABM.

In short the situation in early 1967 was very much bent in favor of some kind of recommendation to proceed with ABM deployment. The contingency scheme offered in Mr. Johnson's State of the Union message was more modest than one might have expected. While the $712.3 million provided for ABM in the fiscal year 1968 budget included some funds for procurement, the President in no way specified the nature of a possible deployment or the scale and pace of his likely action. The flexibility requested by the President was easily granted by the Congress; and there was no significant legislative controversy in 1967 over the larger questions—the relationship between ABM and the stable deterrence on which national security had come to rest, the impact of such weapons on the arms race, the assumption that diplomatic success in limiting strategic arms hinged upon U.S. readiness to persist in further deployments.

The President's half-step toward a commitment to deploy left him, as he must surely have known, at the mercy of events. They proved merciless. In the summer of 1967 two developments left the President with no apparent

[3] Lyndon Baines Johnson, *The Vantage Point: Perspectives of the Presidency, 1963–1969* (New York: Holt, 1971), pp. 479–480.

alternative to moving forward with the ABM system. At Glassboro, New Jersey, the summit meeting between Mr. Johnson and Soviet Premier Kosygin found the Russian leader, though extensively instructed by Secretary McNamara on the hazards of an ABM competition, singularly uninterested in heading off ABM deployments. The Premier echoed the familiar Soviet doctrine that ABM systems were purely "defensive" weapons and hence unobjectionable; he betrayed no awareness at this time of the likelihood that, in the novel context of nuclear deterrence, installation of such defensive systems might threaten the very foundations of strategic stability and compel both sides to take costly countermeasures in their offensive forces in order to maintain an assured capacity to retaliate. Mr. Kosygin either did not grasp or did not choose to admit that he grasped the fact that ABM systems, if deployed on a large scale, threatened deterrence. Perhaps the Premier was feigning indifference in order to extract some diplomatic advantage from what he may have considered a Soviet lead in ABM. Only later—one must acknowledge, after the United States began to deploy an ABM—did Soviet writers and officials come to stress the dangers of a contest in missile defenses. In June 1967 the Soviet Premier rebuffed the President's attempt to engage him in talks aimed at forestalling such a contest.

A second event amplified the effects of the cool Soviet attitude toward strategic arms talks: the Chinese detonation of a hydrogen device, years ahead of the schedule anticipated by many Western experts. This breakthrough seemed to point toward accelerated achievement of a Chinese thermonuclear capability which, if matched by progress in delivery systems, would presumably place the United States in early jeopardy from another quarter. Talks seemed to be out, the threat seemed to be rising. Having asked and obtained standby authority to deploy an ABM, the President was bound to go forward. Elementary mind-reading—the kind generally involved in speculations about the behavior of decision-makers—suggests that both Mr. Johnson's own instincts and his appraisal of the political dynamics of the ABM issue, in and out of Congress, persuaded him this was the right thing to do.

Still, the President's decision to build an ABM left open many questions about what kind of system to install. Evidently the essential thing for the President was to have something started; the exact character of the ABM system was not a matter to which he addressed himself. An intriguing study by Morton H. Halperin indicates that Secretary McNamara, having lost a rear-guard action to avoid ABM deployment, nevertheless retained broad authority from his chief to define the type of deployment to execute. The manner in which he did so, in a famous speech in San Francisco on September 18, 1967, left no doubt whatsoever of the Secretary's principal fear. His lengthy description of the perils, costs, and infeasibility of a heavy defense against the Soviet Union prefaced the announcement that the Administration would recommend a "thin" nationwide defense against possible Chinese attacks and against potential inadvertent launches. The troubled Defense Secretary explicitly warned against any illusion that, given the known and projected state of technology, the United States could build substantial protection against the large and growing Soviet missile forces. And his warning was geared specifically to a profound concern that the "mad momentum" of the arms race might be spurred by even so modest a deployment, since it might appear to the Soviets as a first step toward the denser ABM system which could diminish their confidence in their capacity to retaliate.

McNamara did not bother to veil his apprehension that, once begun, the ABM system would be driven to larger and larger scale by the political eddies already stirring in the military bureaucracy and in Congress. As he said at San Francisco, he was worried that there would be "strong pressure from many directions to procure and deploy the weapon out of all proportion to the prudent level required."The Secretary's remarkable statement, transparently designed to dampen the rousing political demands for ABM, was probably the most tepid endorsement of any weapons deployment in U. S. history. Obviously, the mounting heat on the President and the habitual tendency of the United States to "hedge on the high side" by procuring weapons in superabundance had convinced McNamara that the gravest problem was to cool an inflated public and legislative market for ABM, not to heat up a depressed one. It is interesting to note a certain parallel between Administration conduct on this occasion and in regard to the unhappy course of the Vietnam war. In both instances the executive branch betrayed a deep-seated fear that it had to proceed with the utmost caution, lest the public fever rise rapidly and trigger much more drastic action. The Administration's desire to move gradually and prudently on complex and risky matters, without enlisting the strong popular emotions lurking so near the surface, can be viewed either as a sorry verdict on its attitude toward democratic processes or as a high tribute to its sense of responsibility. No doubt it was a bit of both.

Through late 1967 and early 1968 the Secretary's reticent support for ABM was warranted. His revelation in November that the Soviet Union was developing an orbital bombardment capability heightened congressional perception of a growing menace. Testimony that month before the Joint Committee on Atomic Energy, meeting to consider ABM prospects and options in general, gave great attention to the so-called FOBS (fractional orbital bombardment system), which Senator Henry Jackson and others considered a violation of the spirit, if not the letter, of the recently concluded treaty banning the stationing of weapons of mass destruction in outer space. This development knocked another chink in the feeble wall of international trust; congressmen and citizens who were inclined to suspect the Soviets of the most hostile intent would derive little comfort from McNamara's declaration that "I am not concerned" about FOBS. Responding to the committee's alarm, the Director of Defense Research and Engineering, Dr. John Foster, testified that yes, the planned ABM system could be modified to cope with a potential FOBS attack.

American analysts hypothesized that the orbital weapon (which the United States had not considered worth developing) might be intended primarily for possible surprise attacks against U. S. strategic bomber bases, since such weapons were not likely to be accurate or cost-effective enough for strikes against missile silos and they were certainly superfluous for targeting cities. The Secretary and other officials pointed out that new radar capabilities for "over the horizon" detection of FOBS or ICBM launchings would defeat any attempt to gain the advantage of surprise and would afford ample time for the United States to get its bomber fleet airborne in any future crisis. Committee members, however, mirrored the opinion widely held on Capitol Hill. Radar warning was nice to have, but they also were extremely interested in active defense against FOBS and Soviet missiles.

Thus, scarcely six weeks after McNamara's heavily qualified announcement of a light ABM deployment against expected Chinese missile capabilities, congressional discussion was looking toward additional missions to cope with the vastly greater Soviet strategic forces. Many members of Congress, not to mention officers of the Joint Staff and others in the Defense Department, welcomed the decision to deploy the light Sentinel system as the opening wedge in ultimate construction of the larger, anti-Soviet system envisaged by the nation's senior military leaders. Whether Sentinel was called an anti-Chinese system or not, pro-ABM congressmen openly admitted that they saw the program as providing the infrastructure for an ABM shield of the American population against the Soviet Union. They were quite willing to allow McNamara to have his rhetoric about the necessity to keep the deployment limited so long as they got the resources to begin the more ambitious program to which they aspired.

All in all, as Robert McNamara prepared to depart the Pentagon in late 1967, initial reactions to the proposed Sentinel system confirmed his worst fears that the influential congressional advocates of preparedness would push vigorously to expand the defense network. The sympathetic exchanges between his successor, Clark Clifford, and the Senate Armed Services Committee during Mr. Clifford's confirmation hearing in January 1968 indicated that the new Secretary was dedicated to American strategic superiority. These magic words promised to remove the tension over strategic weapons policy which had marked legislative-executive relations during McNamara's tenure. If tradition prevailed, the incipient ABM deployment would now have smooth sailing, politically at least. But tradition did not prevail.

ABM CONTRETEMPS: A HIDDEN MOOD SURFACES

"It was the only occasion since World War II on which a substantial part of the public and their representatives in Congress questioned the wisdom of the Defense Department on a major weapons issue."[4] *Congressional Quarterly's* judgment suffices. Beneath the vocal congressional support for ABM was lurking a potential coalition of opposition.

It began to take shape during 1968, mainly in Senate deliberations on the Sentinel proposal. A growing number of members suddenly realized that their private doubts about the wisdom of ABM deployment were shared by other colleagues. This realization was not the product of a concerted campaign by any organized lobby or by aroused members of the Senate itself. Indeed, the organized activity was in behalf of the ABM deployment and flowed through the traditional channels of committee consideration. True to form the House ratified its Armed Services Committee's recommendation to authorize the deployment and the Senate committee filed a favorable report, albeit over the objections of a small number of senior members, most notably including Margaret Chase Smith of Maine and Stuart Symington of Missouri. Senator Smith was simply unpersuaded that the Sentinel technology was worth anything. Senator Symington doubted that the ABM would be effective, but most importantly, he was by this time highly aroused over the exorbitant costs of new weapons, and, with the staggering burden of Vietnam war expenditures very much on his mind, he feared that the American economy was being overtaxed by defense programs. Despite their reservations, the action by the full Senate committee seemed to herald relatively routine approval by the Senate, where Chairman Russell's personal prestige was legendary.

Yet the minor skirmish in the committee during the spring of 1968 was the prelude to a major battle which was to extend over several years and to become the symbol of a drastic legislative shift toward critical review of major weapons programs. The factors which account for the ABM imbroglio were disparate in depth and scale. Certainly the psychological by-products of the Vietnam experience were at the center of the case, with some members feeling that military judgments on new weapons systems were likely to be no better than what they considered their proven misjudgments on the course of the war. There was a heightened concern in these months over the apparent tendency of modern weapons to grow ever more costly and ever less reliable. But the issue of cost overruns, though already raised by such programs as the F-111 aircraft, was to acquire its special salience later, as revelations regarding the giant C-5 transport aircraft provoked heated congressional and public discussion.

Even in 1968, when the budding coalition against the ABM first became aware of itself, a new strategic perception, at once vague and profound, lay

    [4] *Congress and the Nation*, vol. II (Washington: Congressional Quarterly Service, 1969), p. 869.

at the heart of the changing Senate mood. There was a mounting skepticism about whether, in a nuclear age, more arms automatically meant more security. In retrospect one is tempted to conclude that Secretary McNamara's missionary zeal in pointing out the hazards of ABM deployment in the context of the Soviet-American strategic equation had won more converts than he expected. Other influences were at work as well, including a number of "exiles" with executive branch experience who had come to serve as staff assistants to senators dealing with foreign affairs and national security. Several of these men and women were familiar with at least portions of the extensive strategic literature which dealt with the pros and cons of ABM and with the broader aspects of strategic arms control. Thus, filtering into the Senate consciousness by 1968 was an unprecedented awareness of the fact there there was another side to the argument concerning a major weapons system, a side richly and thoughtfully documented by the very Secretary who had proposed the Sentinel network.

Senator John Sherman Cooper of Kentucky, together with such other colleagues on the Foreign Relations Committee as Senators Fulbright, Case, Church, Mansfield, and Clark, had come to feel that, while every reasonable measure of national preparedness should be undertaken, the time had come to see whether an endless, frustrating, and reckless arms race could be curbed by negotiations between the superpowers. Similar views were held by others in the Senate, notably Philip Hart, Gaylord Nelson, Edward Brooke, and Jacob Javits. The impulse of these men and others who would join with them was not grounded in technical objections to the proposed ABM system, as Mrs. Smith's committee position had been, or in the economic considerations which had played such a large part in bringing Senator Symington to oppose the system. While both technical and economic arguments would be marshaled to support their case, these senators were acting on the basis of a high-level political judgment that the United States could best serve its long-term security interests through attempts to negotiate a standstill in the strategic arms race.

The emergence of these instincts in the Senate amounted to a revival of politics in the field of national security after a generation in which technology had dominated policy. Indeed, one of the most troubling problems was the way in which political judgments had come to be subordinated to a primitive kind of technological determinism. The events of 1968 demonstrated that senators were distressed and even angered by the automaticity with which national security policy was being shaped by technical developments. There had long been smouldering doubt and resentment at the habitual tendency to act on the premise that a weapon that could be built should be built. As senators and their fellow citizens came to perceive that a vast and diversified nuclear arsenal did not provide either the fact or the feeling of greater security—that in fact the arms race had brought a clear and absolute decline in the relative physical security of the United States—the path was cleared for a more discriminating political assessment of the value of various weapons.

Among the hazards of mobilizing opposition to the ABM deployment was the possibility that an antitechnology bias would disconnect the debate from realistic moorings fully as much as the protechnology bias had done previously. At times in the subsequent debates this tendency reared its head and senators ventured far afield from a judicious appreciation of the technological factors of which sensible policy had to take account. This was true, however, on both sides of the issue. Proponents sometimes made extravagant claims about the system's potential for protecting against ballistic missile attack. Opponents sometimes offered exaggerated charges that the system could be easily defeated by an enemy's innovations in missile design or mode of attack. Nevertheless, the Senate deliberations did not usually stray beyond the range of reasonable technical opinion, which itself accommodated quite a spread of views. Most senators could and did cite informed technical authorities in support of their positions, whether for or against deployment.

It is hard to resist the conclusion that a credible political challenge to the ABM was in fact possible only because the system was open to technical dispute.[5]   Had the system been a sure-fire success, even in the limited mission proposed for it, it is not likely that there would ever have been a great debate over ballistic missile defense. Precisely because distinguished scientists and engineers with long experience in the defense field were skeptical of the feasibility and value of an ABM, it became possible to make the issue a matter of extended public discussion. It is no reassuring compliment to democratic politics but probably a necessary dose of sobriety to reflect that if the engineers had been agreed, the politicians might never have had a meaningful crack at the issue. And this is probably true in spite of the fact that the strategic and political questions posed by ABM deployment far transcended the issue of whether the system would work or not.

The episode had its ironic aspects. A principal critique of the McNamara administration of the defense establishment, and one voiced on Capitol Hill, concerned the practice of studying weapons to death, as some would have put it. The Armed Services committees were especially insistent on speeding up the number of new weapons starts. By this time complaints about cost overruns and redundant weapon systems were less numerous than demands that the Department ought to be getting more weapons off paper and into

[5] Anne Cahn, *Eggheads and Warheads: Scientists and the ABM* (Cambridge, Mass.: M.I.T. Center for International Studies, 1971), especially pp. 54–99 and 122–173. Interesting samples of the technical-strategic debate during this period are D. G. Brennan and Johan J. Holst, *Ballistic Missile Defence: Two Views,* The Institute for Strategic Studies (London), Adelphi Paper no. 43, November 1967; and Jeremy J. Stone, *The Case against Missile Defences,* The Institute for Strategic Studies (London), Adelphi paper no. 47, April 1968.

the field. Here was a system which, while directed toward an admittedly complex problem (once capsuled misleadingly as "hitting a bullet with a bullet"), had gone through one of the lengthiest and most expensive development programs in history. Advocates might have been able to bolster their colleagues' confidence and muster their support by pointing to the intensive development effort that preceded a recommendation to deploy.

Under some circumstances that could have been a winning ploy. This time, however, the recurrent debates over the ABM had familiarized many senators with the extraordinary difficulty and complexity of the task such a system would face. In other words the very fact that the ABM technology had been evolving through an unusually long development cycle meant that would-be senatorial skeptics had ample time to nourish their doubts. Instead of inspiring confidence that the bugs had been worked out, the prolonged R & D effort had helped confirm the suspicions of those increasingly inclined to doubt that such complicated machines should be relied upon as the major foundation of the country's security programs.

In justice to the remarkable accomplishments of those who had devoted years to the quest for an effective defense against missiles, one ought to acknowledge that some congressional critics of ABM did not realize the extent to which specific engineering advances—in phased-array radars, high-performance missiles, and other areas—had made a substantial ABM defense feasible against a fair spectrum of threats. The same point was made at various times in the debate by the Director of Defense Research and Engineering, Dr. Foster, who described the most prominent technical opponents of the deployment as men who had not been directly involved in the immediate ABM program during recent years. Many of the critiques relied upon analysis of the macroscopic difficulties faced by the ABM system rather than a microscopic examination of the particular technology contemplated for Sentinel. Specific details were often inaccessible or too esoteric for political digestion anyway. But if one faults the anti-ABM forces for being ungenerous to the impressive technical feats being performed in the program, one must charge pro-ABM spokesmen in both the executive and the Congress with being overly sanguine in their view of the likelihood of technical solutions to the myriad problems faced by such a deployment.

Caution and agnosticism were the reasonable stances to take toward the technological claims and counterclaims, but such stances were rarely adopted—the dynamics of controversy seldom indulge such intellectual niceties. A degree of distortion undoubtedly occurred in the presentations of the technological features of the proposed deployment, and a kind of dialogue of the deaf occasionally ensued. For instance, a central technical criticism from the beginning of the debate was the general assertion that the system could never be adequately tested and hence could not be depended on to operate reliably. Almost lost in the fierce exchanges of 1968–1970 was the fact that the initial phases of ABM deployment were intended to meet that very concern by permitting full-scale operational tests of deployed hardware (although necessarily relying on simulated runs of missile firings). Indeed, the more moderate proponents of ABM deployment stressed that they viewed the initial steps toward deployment as explicitly experimental, with a final deployment decision to await the outcome of extensive test procedures on the assembled radars, computers, and other hardware at the first sites.

Yet there were sound reasons for fearing that this more modest conception of how to proceed would be lost in the shuffle. The military services had in the missile age come to rely heavily upon the practice of concurrency in high-priority programs—and the "DX priority" of the ABM system was the highest accorded any weapon program. Under the doctrine of concurrency, relatively higher risks were taken regularly by procuring and deploying the elements of a weapon system even before the development effort passed certain critical milestones. Early availability was favored over maximum confidence that the system would meet its performance specifications. This deployment model had been followed most notably in the initial Atlas ICBM program, when the urgent need to prevent an intercontinental missile gap had governed. First-generation missiles were then retrofitted after deployment with the modifications and components which the nearly simultaneous development program produced. Understandably, ABM critics who were knowledgeable about defense procurement procedures feared that elements of a relatively unproven and highly expensive missile defense network would spread across the landscape in advance of the elaborate development and test program they knew to be necessary.

Had the original ABM proposals been couched in terms emphasizing that an initial site or two would be fully exploited as test beds for operational development of the system before a commitment to wider deployment would be made—a theme which the Nixon Administration sounded belatedly in defense of its revised program in 1969—some of those opposed to deployment might have been disarmed. Obviously, the context of the debate would have been altered significantly. It would have been awkward for critics to contend that the planned ABM system had been inadequately tested and then to oppose an Administration request to conduct such testing. However, the program described by Secretary McNamara in September 1967 and recommended by President Johnson in January 1968 bore all the earmarks of a final decision to proceed with installation of at least several radar, computer, and missile complexes, not of a tentative go-ahead for operational development of technology then only partially proven.

In this respect the political action on the ABM proposal illustrates a perennial deficiency of decisions on weapons and other complicated issues. The manner in which the executive branch presented the plan to the Congress tended to elide the conditional and contingent aspects of the program. However many uncertainties, qualifications, and constraints the operating agencies may themselves recognize in deciding to proceed with such efforts, they tend to block out such embroidery when they package their recommendations to the Congress. Even the ABM decision, though uniquely displayed with many of the warts upon it, was not conveyed to Congress and the country with a full appreciation of the technical and strategic uncertainties involved. This is surely not surprising, since an executive which habitually revealed all the contradictory and conditional factors which qualified its recommendations might well undermine its whole case before the Congress.

Beyond the fact that ingrained concepts of leadership lead the executive branch to feel that it must announce and argue its recommendations with a degree of decisiveness which seldom makes adequate allowance for the complexity of the issues, a sense of intellectual superiority is at work. Knowing that it disposes of the greater analytic resources, the executive is prone to believe that it has already done the best analyses possible and that it would be counterproductive to reopen all the complexities to reconsideration in the more volatile and presumably less objective setting of Congress. Aggressive executives recognize that to do so is to risk losing the initiative in a program, a prospect especially obnoxious to a rationalist like Robert McNamara. McNamara's personal attitude toward ABM, damned with faint praise in his San Francisco statement that there were "marginal" grounds for concluding that deployment was "prudent," was uniquely lukewarm for him, but his successor followed the normal pattern of advocacy in his firmer and less qualified endorsements of Sentinel.

Given this customary tendency to obscure uncertainties in connection with programs recommended by the executive, Congress is often predisposed to treat issues like the ABM more starkly than is wise. Arguments acquired more black and white contrast than was reasonable. The system would or would not work, it was said, when the truth was that it might or might not. Deployment would speed an end to the arms race by inducing negotiations; or it would preclude negotiations by speeding up the arms race. In the give and take of debate, judgments were asserted with more confidence than they deserved. The complexity of the ABM issue was not always given its due. Sometimes it was cited as sufficient grounds for deferring to the more "expert" judgment of the executive branch. Furthermore, once senators began to take positions for or against deployment, it became difficult to incorporate new complexities and new information, whether technical or political, which did not accord with the member's public commitment. In other words, the ABM debate exemplified the difficulties of coping with uncertainty and complexity in the collective decision-making process which is the Congress.

Yet even an unsympathetic commentator would have to observe that in the course of the repetitive debates on ABM, Congress succeeded in raising most of the relevant technical, strategic, and political issues.[6] Such a com-

---

[6] Alton Frye, "ABM: Inner Debate Narrows While Issues Begin to Broaden," *Ripon*

mentator might complain that much irrelevant and misleading material entered the record, and that the more committed opponents and proponents of deployment made highly selective use of the information at their disposal, as advocates will do. As the controversy grew intense and popular interest awakened, some members were undoubtedly influenced as much by constituent pressure as by a reasoned examination of the case. Nevertheless, the overall process was more than creditable. Many "swing" senators took a decidedly nonideological and detached approach to the question. Experts might lament the haphazard and disorderly character of the discussion and the fact that few members grasped all the important details of the program. Still, the implications of the proposal were ferreted out and explored in incomparable depth. The principal technical and strategic features were examined. The risks of delaying deployment were weighed against the risks of immediate deployment. The Senate assessed a number of strategic options, including alternative ABM deployments and offensive innovations that might be deployed instead of a defensive network. And most importantly the Senate demonstrated a newfound realization that these questions were essentially political in nature, involving not merely "scientific" solutions to "objective" problems, but political values and preferences among a variety of approaches to promoting the nation's security interests.

This realization was scarcely evident in the initial Senate vote on the Sentinel system. On April 18, 1968, only seventeen senators supported Senator Gaylord Nelson's amendment to delete from the military procurement authorization $342.7 million for the program. That same day, however, Senator Cooper offered the first of what would become a series of amendments to various bills in which he sought to delay deployment of the system, while continuing full support for development of the technology. In formulating his proposal, Senator Cooper was highlighting for the Senate a crucial distinction with much political promise, for it promised to permit senators to lend discriminating support for additional work on ABM without committing themselves to actual deployment. Thus the Cooper amendment and its successors were not posing for the Senate a choice between killing ABM and not killing it, but raising the more comfortable prospect of postponing the hard decision until more information was available on the weapon's practicability and likely costs. Senator Cooper's measure was defeated by the surprisingly small margin of 31 to 28, the first real suggestion that substantial opposition to deployment might emerge.

Still the temperature of the Senate on ABM was not rising rapidly during these months, and on several additional votes later in the year the margin for support for Sentinel was larger, including an absolute majority of the Senate membership. On June 25 an attempt to delay a start on construction for one year was defeated 52 to 34, the peak expression of opposition in 1968. The deployment was being pressed strongly by the Armed Services Committee, and as he had revealed to the Senate in a letter of June 18, Secretary Clifford was quite opposed to any delay, stating the country could "no longer rely merely on contined R & D but should proceed with actual deployment of an operating system." Though he and his legislative allies carried the day, the Secretary stirred even deeper concern among opponents by hinting that experience with an "operating system" might teach the U. S. how to deploy a still larger and more effective system—perhaps not only against the Chinese.

To be sure, the Deputy Secretary of Defense, Paul Nitze, had focused his testimony before the Senate committee on the prospect that the Sentinel deployment would be able to deny China the capability of inflicting damage on the continental United States for more than a decade. But always lurking in the background was the veiled intimation that the initial deployment might actually be a foot in the door for the ambitious schemes fostered by the Joint Chiefs of Staff. Nitze's own predecessor, Cyrus Vance, together with former Presidential Science Advisor Jerome Wiesner and others, had underscored the difficulties of adapting current defensive technology to meet changing future threats, particularly insofar as the varied Soviet forces were concerned; they noted that if the Nike-Zeus system originally proposed in the early sixties had been installed, it would have been obsolete by the time it was operational. These skeptics thought the same fate was in store for Sentinel, certainly if there were an attempt to extend it to an anti-Soviet mission.

Such cautions were frequently overlooked, however, by the congressional advocates of the system. Richard Russell made little secret of his own expectation that this was the beginning of an effort to obtain a more comprehensive strategic defense against the main menace, Soviet Russia, and Henry Jackson commented that people should not take the Sentinel rationale too literally. Few implications could have been better calculated to alarm and stiffen the backs of the men who were beginning to see the ABM as one more dubious and massive commitment which, once under way, would create intense and perhaps irresistible pressure for its own expansion. An exasperated John Sherman Cooper asked his colleagues on the Senate floor, "Is it our purpose to install a 'thin' system at an estimated cost of $6.5 billion, or is it to lay a foundation to install what has been admitted to be an ineffective system against the Soviet Union at a minimum cost of $40 billion?" No convincing answer was heard, and Majority Leader Mike Mansfield charged flatly that the "thin" system was just the first installment on a "thick" one. It was increasingly evident that many influential senators shared McNamara's anxiety that it would be nearly impossible to keep the deployment limited.

These early rumblings of senatorial opposition enlisted the interest of a number of scientific and technical professionals who had worked on various aspects of ABM programs for some years. Not only Dr. Wiesner but other distinguished figures such as Hans Bethe, Wolfgang Panofsky, and George Rathgens began to make known to senators their disagreement with the decision to proceed with ABM. Through letters to individual members, conversations with legislative assistants, and otherwise, the division of opinion within the technical community became ever more clear. These technical disputes—although they often turned less on strictly engineering judgments than on implicit strategic and political considerations—gradually came to be the center of the debate, providing the occasion for some senators to oppose the system and the opportunity for them to seek the votes of colleagues who were worried about investing in what might turn into a white elephant.

This preoccupation with technological assessments of the system was a mixed blessing for the quality of legislative action. Obviously, if opponents could demonstrate that the system would not work, they would have established the most conclusive case against deployment, just as proponents would gain by a credible exposition of the system's technical promise. At the same time, however, inordinate attention to strictly technological considerations inevitably had the effect of distracting members and the public from the even more important political and strategic criteria which activated most of the senators. The ABM debate suffered consistently from a tendency to resolve a political decision on technical grounds—and this was hardly less true of those who aspired to break the historical pattern of technological determinism in U. S. strategic policy than of those with whom they contended. Thus the campaign to rescue politics from the tyranny of technology proceeded with extraordinary obeisance to the tyrant. If the ABM system had not been under attack technically, it would have been virtually impossible to attack it politically.

The technical critiques of Sentinel had gained sufficient force by the fall of 1968 for the opponents to seek a closed session of the Senate to present certain sensitive information. Although executive sessions of the full body were rare, attendance was moderately poor; the national political campaign was well advanced, and many impatient legislators were already on the hustings. Following a closed-door review of classified data on the program, a motion to delay deployment failed once again, this time by a vote of 45 to 25. Superficially, a glance at the numbers seemed to indicate that the anti-ABM battle was getting nowhere. However, on previous votes during the year, sixteen of the absentee senators had cast their votes against deployment. Close reading of the tallies showed that a total of forty-one senators could now be counted as opposed to deployment.

The unexpected voting trend in the Senate was accompanied by some unexpected political reactions across the country. The grass roots were sprouting some unanticipated flowers of opposition. Here was another irony. In the original planning for the ABM system one of the toughest questions related to the selection of which areas would receive initial defenses. The theory of many in the ABM program was that citizens in unprotected regions would be distressed, possibly irate, that their locales were not on the priority list of areas to be defended. Indeed, some planners, particularly in the Army ballistic missile defense staff, welcomed this prospect as a likely lever for forcing more widespread deployment; others feared it for the same reason.

Through the latter part of 1968 citizen outrage over the choice of initial sites did resound in several areas of the nation—but not in the regions omitted from the deployment plan. The complaints came from areas scheduled to be defended by the first sites—Boston, Chicago, Seattle—where many vocal residents were unhappy that giant radars and nuclear-tipped missiles would soon be their neighbors. It was not just a matter of property values, though some people did think that the nearby deployment would damage the immediate real estate market. A far deeper fear was at work, one which percolated miles beyond the vicinity of the planned sites. Stimulated by citizen-technicians who charged that the system was not dependable, voters in Massachusetts and elsewhere began to conclude that the system would afford no real protection at all. Worse, since the radars would be prime strategic targets if nuclear war ever occurred, they saw the ABM sites as gigantic magnets for attack, inviting even greater destruction than the area would otherwise suffer. In short the psychological calculus of the Sentinel planners had backfired. Instead of constituent demands for wider deployment, voters were insisting that the weapons be moved away.

These political storms swirled into the early months of 1969 and helped to precipitate a thorough review of the ABM program by the new Administration. Simultaneously, the strategic context to which the defensive system was presumably addressed had been altered. The Chinese were making no noticeable progress toward an intercontinental delivery capability, while developments in Soviet offensive missile systems were arousing greater concern, specifically over the danger that large SS-9 missiles might eventually pose a threat to the U. S. force of land-based missiles. On March 14, 1969, responding to what he described as a changed threat and attempting to meet the concerns of those who feared that a small ABM would inevitably grow into a large one, President Nixon reoriented the program. More explicitly than any previous Chief Executive, Mr. Nixon's press conference and supporting statement revealed his understanding that there was no feasible way to protect the American population against a Soviet attack and that the nation's security necessarily depended on deterrence of a nuclear strike.[7] To serve that mission, the President shifted the program away from an initial anti-Chinese defense of cities and toward a focus on protecting Minuteman

---

[7] The President's Safeguard statement is conveniently reprinted in American Enterprise Institute, *The Safeguard ABM System: Special Analysis* (Washington, 1970), pp. 9–21.

silos against a possible Russian counterforce strike. The new "Safeguard" program would use the same technology and would retain the option of gradual growth into a thin nationwide screen against China, though one designed to be less ambiguous and provocative to the Soviets. Moreover, the President outlined a phased deployment and promised annual reviews to determine if additional phases would be needed.

Much of the President's strategic rationale was judicious and admirable. He had made a conscientious effort to meet some of the principal objections of congressional and citizen critics. One would have expected the revamped program to dampen some of the opposition. But there remained important criticisms of the deployment, including the debatable use of expensive hardware conceived primarily for city defense as the means of protecting hardened missile silos. Furthermore, the anti-ABM forces had acquired a certain momentum, and if moving the ABM away from the complaining cities weakened some of their grass-roots strength, they nonetheless retained a sense of common purpose in questioning the deployment. The coalition of critics did not dissolve in the wake of the Safeguard announcement.

ABM had become a symbol, a test of many values—national priorities, attitudes toward arms limitation, the balance of power between Congress and the executive. To some opponents, like Senator Albert Gore of Tennessee, the shifting rationale and direction of the ABM program only proved that it was "a weapon in search of a mission." Particularly in the Senate but also with rising force in the lower chamber, the ABM remained under fire. Petitions and letters continued to pour into congressional offices, indeed in increasing numbers. Once people came to oppose Sentinel, their hostility to any deployment persisted, no matter how Safeguard might be modified and relabeled.

Unprecedented open hearings before the Senate Armed Services Committee, now chaired by John Stennis of Mississippi, as well as proceedings in the Foreign Relations Committee, provided major forums for the public exploration of the Safeguard program.[8] Normally, the committee had examined such issues only in closed session and with testimony limited to members of the executive branch and an occasional interested member of Congress. This time, however, advocates like Albert Wohlstetter and Paul Nitze, no longer in government, contended before the Armes Services Committee and the public with opposition spokesmen like Wolfgang Panofsky and Herbert York. Whether the exchanges were fully digested by many senators or not, the committee built a richly detailed record and undoubtedly made a distinct

[8] Hearings before the Committee on Armed Services, U. S. Senate, *Authorization for Military Procurement, Research and Development, Fiscal Year 1970, and Reserve Strength*, Part 2, Apr. 22 and 23, 1969, pp. 1109–1456a. Also see the Hearings before the Subcommittee on International Organizations and Disarmament Affairs, Committee on Foreign Relations, U. S. Senate, *Strategic and Foreign Policy Implications of ABM Systems*, Mar. 6, 11, 13, 21, and 28, 1969.

contribution to the strategic education of the Congress and the country.

Pro-Safeguard spokesmen emphasized the developing threat to the U. S. retaliatory forces; the Soviet Union was gaining an overall lead in the number of ICBMs and, particularly in view of the large size of some of its weapons, might achieve a capability to destroy large fractions of the Minuteman force by the mid-seventies unless the United States deployed an active defense of the silos. Wohlstetter, among others, stressed that defending the silos was the least destabilizing response the United States could make, far preferable to adopting a so-called "launch on warning" policy for the Minuteman force or to expanding the offensive forces on land or at sea.

Critics of Safeguard acknowledged that under some circumstances—notably a later failure of strategic arms talks coupled with increases and qualitative improvements in Soviet missiles—it might be sensible to defend the silos. They disputed the argument that the deployment had to begin now and that the proposed technology was suitable for the mission. Instead they favored vigorous pursuit of negotiations with the Soviets to ban ABM systems and simultaneous work on developing an improved, hard-point defense technology for later installation if necessary. Technically, the most telling criticisms of Safeguard concerned the relative vulnerability of the large and incredibly costly radars which were the heart of the system and which, if neutralized by a Soviet attack, would paralyze the entire defense; and the uncertainty that the complex, multiprocessor computers could actually be built, programmed, and operated with adequate reliability. Strategically, Panofsky and other witnesses pointed out that there was no known way for the Soviets simultaneously to destroy all elements of the American deterrent—missiles, planes, and submarines—and that even the modified ABM system might appear to the Soviet Union as a start on a thick system which could jeopardize its capacity to retaliate against the United States; hence, using area defense components of Sentinel for the Safeguard mission might have an adverse impact on the arms race as the Soviets further multiplied their delivery vehicles to maintain their confidence that they could penetrate any possible U. S. defenses. Finally, leading opponents made much of Panofsky's calculation that even if Safeguard worked perfectly, it would add very little to the survivability of Minuteman and could be overcome easily by a few additional months' missile production in the Soviet Union—points hotly contradicted by defense officials and such other Safeguard proponents as the recently formed Committee to Maintain a Prudent Defense Policy, chaired by none other than Dean Acheson.

Defense authorities like Dr. Foster granted that important technical difficulties would have to be overcome, including those associated with the overall integration of this most complex system ever constructed. They insisted that such obstacles could only be surmounted through actual deployment and operational testing of Safeguard, as proposed. Department of Defense testimony indicated that comparable computers and software routines had already been devised for use in the vast A.T. & T. telephone-switching network and that similar phased-array radars were then working, citing the space-tracking facility at Eglin Air Force Base, Florida. While they acknowledged that a better system might later be devised, specifically geared to hard-point defense of missile silos, they asserted that only Safeguard technology could be deployed in time to meet the incipient threat and that they had high confidence in the design. Some proponents commented that whatever imperfections Safeguard might have, Soviet strategic planners would have to assume that it worked and would be deterred by that assumption. Thus both sides had come to diametrically opposed formulations of an "I win, you lose" case: critics claimed that even if the system worked perfectly, it would not afford meaningful protection, to which proponents replied that even if it didn't work at all, it would provide a meaningful deterrent.

Many additional points were raised and argued before the committee, in the press, and on the Senate floor, but this brief discussion illustrates the central items of contention. In the midst of this fierce controversy, the Senate groped for a consensus on what, next to Vietnam, had become the most divisive question in contemporary national security policy. For senators, confronted with disagreement among the experts, it sometimes became a matter of whom to believe. Members frequently inclined to place their personal faith and credit in scientists with thom they had previously worked or in whom they had confidence on other issues. Thus the technical views of various scientists acquired weighted political values in different quarters. Dr. Edward Teller's endorsement of ABM was more influential with Thomas Dodd than with Clifford Case. Dr. Harold Agnew's support for deployment held special importance for Henry Jackson and other members of the Joint Committee on Atomic Energy who had admired his work at the Los Alamos Laboratory. Conversely, Senator Philip Hart and other major opponents of Safeguard were more hospitable to the arguments of Herbert York, George Rathgens, and scientists prominently associated with the Council for a Livable World or the Federation of American Scientists, both politically active organizations of scientists and engineers.[9] Ideological and personal alignments between politicians and technicians appeared in the Senate, often

---

[9] The ABM controversy generated deep and bitter disagreements in the technical communities. The disputes did not cease when the Operations Research Society of America, in an attempt to evaluate the performance of scientists in the public debate, issued a report faulting some of the participants. See ORSA Ad Hoc Committee on Professional Standards, "Guidelines for the Practice of Operations Research," *Operations Research*, vol. 19, September 1971, pp. 1123–1146, also appendixes III and IV regarding the Safeguard and Minuteman vulnerability disputes, pp. 1175–1257.

Two books capture some of the contending rationales: Abram Chayes and Jerome B. Wiesner, *ABM: An Evaluation of the Decision to Deploy an Antiballistic Missile System* (New York: Harper, 1969), and Johan J. Holst and William Schneider, Jr. (eds.), *Why ABM?* (Elmsford, N.Y.: Pergamon, 1969).

based on connections quite remote from the specifics of the ABM decision. As the Senate moved toward a climactic ABM vote in the summer of 1969, the game of "pick your scientist" proceeded apace.

The Senate's technological preoccupations were reflected in the character of the amendments on ABM which were offered in 1969. There were three principal proposals aimed at restricting the Safeguard deployment, and all of them hinged on the technical challenge to the system. The first of these was developed in the Armed Services Committee itself, where Senator Thomas McIntyre of New Hampshire was acquiring an increasingly active role as chairman of a new ad hoc Subcommittee on Research and Development. With the assistance of freshman Senator Edward W. Brooke, McIntyre devised a compromise scheme to reconcile the many conflicting views by denying funds for deployment of ABM missiles but authorizing an operational test of Safeguard radars and computers at the first two sites recommended by the Administration. The New Hampshire Senator argued forcefully that if the operational testing demonstrated the system's effectiveness and if the threat continued to develop, his proposal would cause no significant delay in eventual deployment but would retain congressional control over any decision to "weaponize" the system by adding the requisite defensive missiles. It was essentially a half-step toward deployment, but clearly limited the program to developmental status. Nevertheless, Senator McIntyre's earnest attempt to find a moderate solution to the ABM quandary proved unavailing in committee and again on the floor, where many of the most ardent Safeguard opponents considered it too generous to the system.

The crucial Senate vote came on another proposal by Senators Cooper and Hart, who had collaborated the previous year and earned the right to lead the floor fight. The 1969 Cooper-Hart amendment was the product of the most wide-ranging consultation in the Senate. In the weeks leading up to the decisive votes on August 6, Cooper, Hart, and their allies were in contact repeatedly, formulating language designed to maximize the ABM opponents' strength, canvassing prospects with more thoroughness than ever before in a debate on weapons.

An important innovation was the active staff caucus which had begun meeting in the Senate early in the year and which formed a continuing conference of the interested offices opposed to deployment. This staff network, led informally but effectively by William Miller of Senator Cooper's staff and Muriel Ferris of Senator Hart's, was a promising vehicle for building and maintaining *esprit de corps* among ABM opponents in more than thirty Senate offices. These periodic sessions, which became quite regular during July and early August, first raised and then reinforced the prospect of real victory as participants came to feel the wide and intense sentiment on the issue. This staff operation was invaluable as an intelligence device, alerting the leading senators to possible defections and potential recruits. It would continue through the following year as well, while nothing comparable emerged among the system's supporters, who relied instead on the customary mechanisms of committee leadership.

The Cooper-Hart amendment, offered originally on July 9 and modified two weeks later, sought to mute the confrontation with the President by leaving all Safeguard funds in the bill but restricting their use to continued R & D on the system. The intent was to preclude any construction of system components at probable deployment sites and to confine development work to existing test centers, particularly Kwajalein atoll in the Pacific, where radars, computers, and missiles were already being checked out against intercontinental missiles launched from the U. S. west coast. The Cooper-Hart amendment's strong appeal made the outlook extremely close, and only the most intensive efforts by pro-Administration senators staved off the challenge, defeating the proposal by the razor-thin margin of 51 to 49.

The final hours of debate on Cooper-Hart turned frantic when Senator Smith of Maine, who seemed to hold the key to victory and who had not committed herself to her colleagues' proposal, filed an amendment of her own. Unlike Cooper and Hart's, Mrs. Smith's language barred all funds for Safeguard and limited ABM work to more advanced technology. Her letter to other senators described her thoughts with typical forthrightness: "I have no confidence in the Safeguard ABM system and if one has no confidence in it then I cannot see the logic or justification in voting for research and development of it." After an initial quick defeat (89 to 11) of the Smith formula, fast drafting on the floor modified the amendment and persuaded Senators Cooper and Hart to support the senior Senator from Maine. On this modified Smith amendment, opposition to Safeguard reached its peak, the Senate dividing evenly, 50 to 50, but the amendment still failed to pass.

The next day, August 7, the McIntyre amendment went down to defeat, 70 to 27. Had the Cooper-Hart coalition held, the additional votes picked up by Senator McIntyre's proposal would have carried the day and explicitly limited the ABM program to developmental activities. Some senators went against the McIntyre formula on the grounds, privately stated, that they would rather have a live issue than what they judged a hollow victory. With the Senate so closely divided, the failure to accept a healing compromise insured that the issue would remain lively for many months.

MISSILE DEFENSE AND MISSILE DIPLOMACY: CONSTANT CONUNDRUM

Among the deepest philosophical tensions stirred by the debates over ABM is one which centers on the relationship between weapons systems and the diplomacy of arms control. Both the Johnson and Nixon administrations proceeded with ABM on the ancient thesis that successful negotiations must proceed from strength. The executive regularly contended that an ongoing

ABM program was a valuable bargaining chip and that a legislative repudiation of Sentinel/Safeguard would gravely undermine the possibilities of negotiated arms limitation. Lurking behind the overt technological challenge to the ABM system—and a more fundamental factor in the opposition of many senators—was a direct challenge to this diplomatic hypothesis.

Among the Cooper-Hart forces were many, including the leaders, who judged the outlook for diplomacy to be improved if the United States exercised restraint in regard to ABM deployment. Their central objective was not to prevent the installation of a missile defense system, but to facilitate the strategic arms negotiations which these senators, more than any others, had come to consider essential to future U. S. security. In and out of Congress men of this persuasion—including some who initially supported ABM deployment, like former Assistant Secretary of Defense Paul Warnke—voiced a common theme regarding the new generation of strategic weapons: The *threat* of deployment might energize diplomacy, but the *fact* of deployment would defeat it. The atom's unimagined power of mass destruction had rendered obsolete the notion or bargaining from strength, at least so far as the control of nuclear weapons was concerned.

On the other hand, the most articulate legislative spokesmen for ABM fully shared the belief of the Presidents' men, namely, that the soundest approach to bargaining with the Russians was to undertake a substantial ABM deployment which, if diplomacy failed to produce mutual controls over strategic weapons, would be a valuable increment to national defense. This was the repeated argument of ABM advocates. Senator Russell saw the system as a "very strong card" for American diplomats, and Senator John Stennis seconded him by declaring, "I have never heard a more absurd way in which to approach negotiations with the Soviets than by announcing in advance that we will remove a big part of bargaining strength from the agenda by not going forward with the ABM program." By this reasoning, it was less vital that the system be seen as a confident military enterprise than that it be perceived by the Russians as an ongoing program that could get better.

The repeated Soviet charges that the United States would destroy the basis for negotiations if it persisted in attempts to bargain from strength only convinced many ABM proponents that they had correctly gauged the situation, for they saw growing Russian criticisms of American ABM deployment as a sure sign of the system's bargaining value. Why would Moscow be complaining, they wondered, if it was not feeling the pressure of the incipient U. S. missile defense network? The root question, of course, was whether this pressure would bring the Soviet Union to the conference table or drive it into additional weapons deployments to match or surpass the United States. Would the Soviets perceive the ABM as a threat or an inducement?

One can best construe the differing perspectives on this difficult question as ideological preferences or political hunches. Neither the most learned scholar nor the most insightful politician could formulate an objective, immutable rule on the relationship between strategic deployments and successful diplomacy. Circumstances and opportunities differ, the personalities of decision-makers differ, technological and historical factors differ—and the prudent observer must vary his judgment to fit the particular case. We will never know whether the Strategic Arms Limitation Talks (SALT) would have begun, or how far they would have progressed, if the United States had abstained from an ABM program. This kind of restraint could have helped—or hindered—the negotiations. Since, however, by 1969 the United States was definitely launched upon a course of limited ABM deployment, one can only evaluate SALT in this context. One may regret that SALT did not move more rapidly, that it did not get to the heart of the strategic issues more promptly, that it did not establish a quick freeze of strategic deployments for the duration of the negotiations. But one cannot demonstrate that the U. S. ABM program actually proved a great impediment to the negotiations. A conclusive assessment must await access to the archives of the Soviet government.

The evidence, such as it is, seems to favor those who argued that the system would be a diplomatic asset. Was it mere coincidence that, a scant two days after the Senate overrode objections to the Sentinel plan in June 1968, the Soviet Union agreed to discuss strategic arms control? Knowledgeable officials of the executive branch believed the Soviets had decided some time before that date to respond favorably, but Moscow's timing almost appeared designed to confirm the arguments of those stressing the system's diplomatic utility. Senator Henry Jackson was especially emphatic in drawing the inference that the U. S. decision to proceed with an ABM had elicited the Soviet Union's expression of willingness to take part in talks aimed at mutual restraint in the arms race.

The inference is plausible. Movement toward serious arms negotiations had been desultory since the mid-sixties. At Glassboro and elsewhere Premier Kosygin had displayed no interest whatsoever when the conversation turned to the issue of ABM limitations. It may be that Soviet planners and political leaders had simply not thought through the implications of such defensive deployments, and that their strategic doctrine was only slowly coming to grips with the fact that unrestricted ABM deployments would force matching increases in an adversary's offensive inventories if the adversary was to retain confidence in his capacity to retaliate and hence to deter.[10] If so, the U. S. initiation of ABM construction may have accelerated the

---

[10] Of interest is Lawrence T. Caldwell, *Soviet Attitudes to SALT,* The Institute for Strategic Studies (London), Adelphi Paper no. 75, February 1971. The Soviet Union was quite attentive to the U. S. strategic discussions of this period; see V. V. Larionov, "The U. S. Strategic Debate," *USA,* no. 3, March 1970, reprinted in *Survival,* vol. 12, August 1970, pp. 263–272.

maturation of Soviet strategic thought by confronting Moscow with a concrete requirement to take account of the military consequences of an American defensive net.

Alternatively, in spite of their historic dedication to dense air defenses, the Soviets may have comprehended quite clearly the interaction between ABM and offensive force requirements; Kosygin's coolness to ABM controls and the continuing insistence of Soviet strategic literature during this period on the superficial notion that missile defenses were unobjectionable and stabilizing may have rested on the hope that the United States would talk itself out of ABM while the U. S. S. R. could gain certain politico-military advantages by continuing a unilateral program. One recalls Khrushchev's early boasting of the Soviet capability to hit a "flyspeck" in space. So long as the United States was not engaged in a competitive ABM effort, the Soviets may have felt no necessity to move toward joint arrangements on ABM until convinced that Congress would not kill the American program. Without intimate details from inside the Kremlin we are limited to speculating about the real Soviet attitudes and incentives in this matter. Nonetheless, the overt evidence fits the hypothesis that the Soviet appetite for the Strategic Arms Limitation Talks was whetted by the U. S. start on ABM, even if many American experts considered the system a very poor beginning. After the tardy start of the SALT talks, the discussions uncovered unwonted Soviet interest in stopping the U. S. ABM deployment.

The Soviet repression of Czechoslovakia chilled the negotiating atmosphere in 1968. In addition the American election campaign diminished the likelihood that substantial arms control discussions could be launched until after the new Administration took office, although President Johnson was eager for them and his Administration had already made extensive preparations for the negotiations. In early 1969 both governments reaffirmed their desire to enter bilateral talks on strategic issues, but the Nixon team devoted most of the year to educating itself in the intricacies of the possible negotiations. When Safeguard completed its first run through the congressional obstacle course in August of that year, the stage was set for preliminary exchanges with Moscow on the tactical basis urged by the President, i.e., with an ongoing U. S. ABM program as a presumed spur to serious diplomacy. Those preliminary explorations finally began in November 1969 in Helsinki and resumed in April of the following year in Vietnam.

The fact that talks were at last under way greatly altered the context in which congressional deliberations on ABM were conducted. The direction the SALT talks would take was unclear, but their very existence shifted the legislative focus from technological to diplomatic evaluations of the ABM issue. This was evident in the 1970 debate. At the outset many congressional critics, staff members, and press commentators expected that in view of the razor-thin margin of the previous year, the Administration's program would be rejected by the Senate. Even the House now had more vocal opponents of deployment, including a small but courageous band of rebels on Chairman Rivers' Armed Services Committee, notably Lucian Nedzi of Michigan and Charles Whalen of Ohio. The staff caucus of anti-ABM senators was alive and flourishing and promised to be a potent force in coordinating a renewed drive to delete ABM funds.

The confidence of the opponents was bolstered by the knowledge that their technological criticisms of Safeguard were gaining strength. Administration officials now acknowledged that the Soviet Union might indeed be able to overwhelm the defense of the Minuteman silos by deploying additional SS-9 missiles beyond those estimated in American threat projections for the mid-seventies. Furthermore, responding to charges that the huge and costly Safeguard radars were too vulnerable, the Department of Defense launched special programs to perfect smaller, harder, and less expensive radars which could be deployed redundantly if the threat to Minuteman exceeded Safeguard's capabilities. Department spokesmen continued to stress, however, that more advanced systems could not be ready on the schedule for Safeguard and would not meet the short-run danger from rapid buildup of the Soviet offensive force. Safeguard, in their opinion, would work and would afford valuable protection to the deterrent, but the modest claims for the system were tacit concessions to the case made by critics in previous months.

Primarily for diplomatic purposes the Administration was anxious to maintain the momentum of ABM deployment. Its 1970 recommendations called for deployment of a third Safeguard site at Whiteman Air Force Base, Missouri, and for surveys and some land acquisition at five additional sites, including a fourth potential site to defend Minuteman silos and four additional sites related to the possible ultimate deployment of a thin area defense against the Chinese. The actual deployment program was modest enough, but there was a certain provocative symbolism in asking Congress to endorse work at a total of eight sites of the planned twelve-site nationwide system. What seemed a minimum prudent program to the President and his advisers seemed an unwarranted and wasteful escalation to confirmed opponents in the House and Senate.

Once again the crucial contest loomed in the Senate, although more than a hundred representatives had joined the opposition in the House. The heightened diplomatic sensitivity of the legislative disposition of the issue now brought key proponents of Safeguard into intense collaboration, searching for a compromise solution which would be acceptable to the Senate. While many offices were involved in one or another of these exercises during the first half of 1970, the most germane efforts took place in the Senate Armed Services Committee. Beginning in February 1970 and continuing for several months thereafter, the staffs of Senators Stennis, Jackson, Brooke, and McIntyre sought repeatedly to define the options that might earn the common support of these senators, who had divided on the question the year before. These lengthy discussions failed to produce a consensus at either a staff or a senatorial level, but they narrowed differences among the four offices and helped to create a sympathetic setting for the full committee's action.

That action was extraordinarily significant, far more so than most observers appreciated. The committee considered two major amendments to the Safeguard authorization for fiscal 1971, one authored by Senator Brooke and the second by Senator Howard Cannon of Nevada in conjunction with Senator Jackson. The Brooke amendment was the more far-reaching, for, while it did not reduce funds for Safeguard, it would have constrained actual deployment to the first two sites already authorized. Not only would this have underscored the limitation of the system to the mission of defending Minuteman silos, but it would have had some significant technical advantages. The special appeal of Senator Brooke's proposal rested on the latter and on the distinctive rationale he developed in that connection. By leaving full funding in the bill but restricting use to two sites, the amendment would have encouraged the Department of Defense to employ a so-called "defense-in-depth" option, providing thicker protection of the Minuteman fields at two locales rather than somewhat thinner defense of more Minutemen at three sites. Particularly important in the defense-in-depth option was the fact that it would have met in part the concern over the vulnerability of the radars by permitting installation of another radar at either Grand Forks, North Dakota, or Malmstrom, Montana. Given such a redundant capability, the system would acquire the option for what is called "preferential defense," a somewhat complicated procedure which, suffice to say, would have required a fourfold increase in the number of attacking warheads to neutralize the defense. In some respects, therefore, the Brooke formula could claim to provide superior protection of the Minuteman force at comparable cost and without expanding the Safeguard deployment to a third site.

Knowing that the Brooke scheme represented a credible alternative to the Administration's recommendation, the pro-Safeguard committee majority felt obliged to make some movement toward accommodation on the issue. The chairman and his allies were aware, of course, that any proposal they sent to the floor would come under attack. But beyond the predictable desire to maximize the area of agreement within the committee and to strengthen their bill's chances of passage in the full chamber, the chairman and Senator Jackson shared the strategic judgment that a start on acquiring sites for an anti-Chinese defense was premature at best and unwise at worst. This view was reinforced by tactical considerations: (1) the shift from Sentinel to Safeguard had already downgraded the emphasis on a defense against the eventual Chinese missile threat and (2) the Administration had reportedly admitted that the Chinese-oriented elements of Safeguard were negotiable in the interests of a suitable strategic understanding with the Soviet Union. These developments did not augur well for selling to their colleagues a bill making provision for portions of the system beyond defense of the deterrent. For the Armed Services Committee leadership, therefore, the palatable middle ground lay with the Cannon amendment, which deleted funds for site surveys and acquisition at the four area defense sites outside the Minuteman fields. This would be coupled with report language expressly defining the mission of Safeguard as defense of the deterrent, not protection against a hypothetical Chinese ICBM.[11] By adopting Senator Cannon's amendment, the committee was able to ward off the more far-reaching Brooke provision and to improve its position for justifying the committee recommendation as a reasonable compromise which did not go as far as the Administration had recommended.

The informed Senate opponents of ABM welcomed the committee's action but were determined to push for still further cuts in the authorization. There was some disagreement among these critics as to how far they should go in floor attacks on the committee bill. A number of those hostile to deployment, notably Harold Hughes of Iowa and Mike Gravel of Alaska, argued that the major floor amendment should seek to strike all authority for deployment, deleting current funds for the initial two sites as well as rejecting an expansion of the system. Senators Brooke and McIntyre, the latter most emphatically, felt that the more promising course lay in a concentrated effort to pass the defense-in-depth formula which the committee had defeated. After much discussion and many soundings among interested members, Senators Cooper and Hart concluded that there was scant chance of killing the program outright, but that they would lead an effort to delete funds for any additional sites beyond the ones approved in 1969. Meeting several times in mid-July in the chambers of the Majority Leader, Mike Mansfield, a dozen leaders of the anti-ABM caucus displayed particular sensitivity to the political delicacy of the position in which opponents found themselves in 1970. A Brooke memorandum of July 31, 1970, circulated at one of those sessions captures the flavor of their concerns and suggests some of the strategems weighed in the caucus:

1. There is a consensus that the most powerful Administration argument is "ABM helps SALT" and that we must meet that argument responsibly.

2. . . . there is a hazard that, should SALT fail after ABM was rejected, those opposing ABM would certainly be blamed. The Administration is already positioned to make such recriminations.

3. On the other hand, even if a relatively generous compromise amendment on ABM is offered and SALT succeeds in curtailing deployment, the money will not be spent and the system we oppose will not be deployed anyway.

[11] Committee on Armed Services, U. S. Senate, *Authorizing Appropriations for Fiscal Year 1971 for Military Procurement, etc.,* 91st Cong., 2d Sess., Report no. 91-1016, July 14, 1970, pp. 18–23, 105.

4. A scheme to cut Phase I [Grand Forks and Malmstrom] in no way can be portrayed as meeting the diplomatic argument; it is a flat contradiction. In fact even a direct assault on Phase II is subject to this charge since it would be described as failing to meet the projected threat and would mean some disruption of the production lines.

Question: Will not a good many Senators perceive that if they oppose ABM and SALT fails, they are in a very risky posture, while if they support ABM and SALT succeeds, they have the best of both worlds (the short-term comfort of supporting the President and the long-term benefit of no ABM to which they can point in coming elections).

I still see no proposal other than the option for defense in depth at Phase I sites which meets our objective of limiting the system and yet is not vulnerable to the charge of completely undercutting the President's diplomacy.

Considering all these factors, I believe a logical sequence for the ABM vote can be constructed this way:

1. Start with a winner, defining *where* ABM activities will take place and follow up with a vote on *what* can be done at the sites approved.

2. The language of the Brooke amendment relates only to the first question. It mentions neither functional nor dollar limitations, and simply specifies that whatever deployment occurs shall take place only at Grand Forks and Malmstrom . . . .this should be our strongest first amendment.

3. The next amendment should be strictly a dollar cut, deleting $350 million if the aim is to kill Phase II and more if the purpose is to cut back on Phase I.

Advantage: This is a minimum risk strategy directed at a victory on limiting the system geographically before we face the controversial tests on cutting the budget for the system. Anyone who favors killing Phase II should at least favor limiting the system to the first two sites; it may be, however, that some will favor limiting the system to the first two sites who will not buy a sharper cutback on Phase I or a reversion to R & D.

Some pro-ABM Senators can logically support this amendment for geographical limitation on the rationale that defense in depth there provides the same protection to the deterrent and comparable diplomatic leverage in SALT. Thus they can vote for the first amendment when they may have to oppose substantial fund cuts.

Other pro-ABM Senators may oppose the geographical limitation, but once it passes, they may support subsequent fund cuts on the ground that sufficient money is available to carry on an adequate program at the first two sites. Also, seeing the victory of the "antis" on the geographical limit, some Senators may wish to cover themselves by supporting fund cuts and we may get a bandwagon effect.

In sum, I believe this plan maximizes our chance for an initial, substantial victory, and possibly enhances the prospects for follow-up wins on direct dollar cuts. At the same time, to the extent this package is sold on the "defense in depth" theme, it is the only vehicle yet proposed for meeting for Administration's key argument on the diplomatic requirements for continued ABM deployment.

The memorandum highlights the fact that diplomatic considerations were now paramount. The power of the President's appeal to senators not to rob him of diplomatic leverage was best measured by the Senate's willingness to disregard the virtually decisive technological critique of the deployment which emerged in the course of floor debate. On August 6 Senator J. William Fulbright published a declassified version of the Defense Department's own Ad Hoc Group on Safeguard, which, under the chairmanship of Dr. Lawrence O'Neill, had submitted its report to the Secretary of Defense on January 27, 1970. The Group's report had served as the basis for the Department's recommended program for fiscal 1971, a program which, it will be recalled, contemplated both additional defense of Minuteman and some steps toward an ultimate anti-Chinese system. Now that the Armed Services Committee had omitted all work on the larger system, however, the Group's technical assessment of Safeguard's contribution to protecting Minuteman reverberated dramatically:

> The group believes that a more cost effective system for the active terminal defense of Minuteman than Phase IIa of Safeguard can be devised. . . . If the only purpose of Safeguard is defined to be to protect Minuteman, Phase IIa as defined in March 1969 should not proceed. Instead, a dedicated system for active defense of Minuteman should replace or, if the need for the MSR [radar] is proved, augment Phase IIa.

If the Senate had been preoccupied with technological criteria, as in 1969, disclosure of the O'Neill panel's analysis should have tipped the balance against the ABM. By now, however, the claims of diplomacy were so dominant that this technological bombshell made little more than a mild ripple in the chamber.

In the event, there were three assaults on the committee's ABM recommendation, a Hughes amendment to cut all funds for Safeguard, which failed 62 to 33; a Cooper-Hart amendment to delete authority and funds for expansion beyond the first two sites, which failed 52 to 47; and the Brooke amendment which allowed full funding but restricted deployment to defense in depth at Grand Forks and Malmstrom, which failed 53 to 45. As in the previous year, a majority of senators voted for one or another of the limiting amendments. The Brooke plan enlisted three votes which had been cast against Cooper-Hart—those of Senators Anderson, Cook, and McIntyre—but five defections from the Cooper-Hart coalition cost the opponents victory. As expected, decisive swing voters like James Pearson of Kansas, a convinced skeptic about the value of Safeguard, explained their support for the ABM proposal largely in terms of the diplomatic requirements stated by the President.

How does one evaluate the results of these months of fierce legislative controversy? Does the tally sheet provide a sufficient indication of the winners and losers? It does not, and it is a cardinal error to interpret issues of this sort in the absolute terms imposed by a call of the yeas and nays on a given vote. That way lies the mythical politics of "good guys versus bad guys," a habit of mind generally and fortunately alien to the American Congress. Legislative politics are what theorists call a "non-zero sum game," that is, a contest in which one's side's gains are not necessarily made at the expense of the other side. In the ABM case the roll calls obscure the fact that both proponents and opponents of Safeguard made important gains and neither suffered intolerable losses. To assess the process, one must look to the substantive policy which eventually issued forth from Capitol Hill. That policy was a measurable improvement over what the executive branch had begun promoting in 1967.

It is true that Congress authorized *an* ABM deployment; but it was not *the* ABM deployment specifically proposed by the President. And even before the first presidential recommendation of any ABM deployment the political environment on Capitol Hill was operating to shape the character and scope of the program. The motley history of the ABM illustrates vividly the way in which Congress functions as much by induction as by direction in guiding policies and programs.

In part to meet what he construed as a requirement of congressional politics, Lyndon Johnson had advanced the Sentinel scheme. Partly in response to the unexpected opposition to Sentinel, Richard Nixon sharply revised the program, revealing a sensitivity not only to a changing strategic threat but to the perceptive demands of domestic critics that the U. S. make every effort to avoid provoking a new round in the arms competition. From its inception the Safeguard program was in fact heavily geared to the strategic rationales of ABM opponents.

The extremely narrow margin in the Senate votes of 1969 left supporters of Safeguard uncertain as to the likely result in 1970 and induced them to modify the Administration's proposals still further. In order to head off more drastic adjustments on the floor, as we have seen, the Senate Armed Services Committee halved the number of proposed sites affected by the fiscal 1971 bill and explicitly limited the mission of Safeguard to defense of the deterrent. A number of anti-ABM senators recognized that this distinction between local defense of Minuteman (at a maximum of four possible sites) and area defense of cities against China (at a total of twelve sites) was the critical front at which the opposition should stand. Just prior to final passage of the fiscal year 1971 bill Senator Thomas Eagleton of Missouri considered offering a motion to instruct the Senate conferees to insist on this limitation of Safeguard to defense of the deterrent, since he feared that the

House approval of additional sites for the more provocative area defense might yet prevail in the final legislation. He refrained from doing so, however, because of assurances already elicited in lengthy colloquys with Senators Stennis, Tower, and Goldwater. In arguing against the Brooke amendment, the chairman had emphatically declared that the Senate conferees would work vigorously in the conference with House members to uphold the Senate's limitations on the system. He expressed confidence that "everyone connected with this matter will be willing to settle on this [i.e., defense of the deterrent] for this year in the Senate bill." While many ABM supporters kept open the possibility that a thin area defense might be desirable at some future date, congressional pressure for more limited deployment combined with developments in the SALT negotiations to diminish markedly the likelihood that there would ever be a nationwide ABM system in the United States.

The following year, 1971, the Administration confined its recommendations to defense of the deterrent, and proposed only a minimal sustaining program in apparent expectation that mutual limits on ABM deployment would be agreed upon shortly. At the same time it accelerated work on the so-called Hardsite technology, looking toward precisely the kind of nonprovocative, local defense long advocated by opponents of Sentinel/Safeguard. Perhaps most surprising of all, on August 4, 1971, the Senate Armed Services Committee constrained the Safeguard deployment still further, reducing its authority to deployment at only two sites and to advance preparation at two more. In this action, justified partly by reported delays in construction, the committee had adopted the essence of the 1970 Brooke amendment.

Thus Congress had been a major influence in the evolution of the American ABM program from its initial conception as a thin nationwide defense against China into a far more modest and stabilizing effort to defend selected portions of the Minuteman force. The protracted engagements over the ABM issue produced no clear-cut roll-call victories for ABM opponents, but their impact on actual policy was real and profound. Though the process was often, in Meg Greenfield's apt phrase, a "ragged non-debate," the outcome was a more sensible and constructive program.

One may best appraise Congress's ultimate impact on the ABM issue by considering the alternative possibility, i.e., a situation in which the legislators had been passive or indifferent to the executive's original proposals in this field. Had there been no congressional reticence toward Sentinel and Safeguard, by 1972 the United States would have been well on its way to a full twelve-site defensive deployment. With such an infrastructure laid out across the country, it would have been exceedingly difficult, if not impossible, to conclude the Moscow Treaty of 1972 limiting ABM installations to negligible levels. And continued congressional skepticism about the value of such weapons had much to do with the follow-on accord of 1974 in which the two governments gave up the option to build a second ABM facility, undertaking to hold deployment to a single site in each country. In this perspective the deliberations of congressmen are seen to have afforded diplomacy maximum opportunity to build a long-term reinforcement for strategic stability. Those who hail the President's notable achievements in the Strategic Arms Limitation Talks should at least reserve a modest round of applause for the Congress.

The ABM debate was a novel congressional experience, honing the legislature's capacity to tackle complex and technologically loaded issues. However flawed its performance may have been, Congress had taken a major step toward a revitalized role in national security policy.

III. *Congress and MIRV: An Exercise in Legislative Catalysis*

Was the ABM debate the exception that proves the rule of
general legislative inattention to strategic issues, or was it the
herald of a new pattern of congressional activity in this field?
The latter, one suspects and hopes. Yet the pattern is not likely to prove
neat, clean, and orderly. Congress is continually sorting out the ways in
which it addresses strategic problems. Even the most momentous issues may
still fall through the cracks of the somewhat ramshackle legislative structure
concerned with national security.

An illustration of this danger was the very belated concern of Congress
for a program whose strategic implications could be graver than those of the
ABM system. This program was the U.S. effort to deploy multiple independently targetable re-entry vehicles (MIRV) as the backbone of the American
retaliatory forces. Failure to scrutinize this deployment may well turn out to
be one of the costliest oversights ever, in terms of the national security goal
of a stable strategic relationship. Barring exceptional restraint on the part of
the Soviet Union and the United States, there is a grim prospect that the two
superpowers may find that the introduction of MIRV generates heavy pressures for large additions to their strategic inventories. The upshot could be
a major upward spiral in arms procurement with diminished real security on
both sides.

Why is this so, and why did the Congress neglect the hazards of MIRV
while exploring the ABM dispute so fully? It is easier to explain the destabilizing potential of MIRV systems than to sketch the reasons why Congress
did so little to guard against it. As its name implies, MIRV is a method of
installing more than one warhead on a single rocket and of directing each
warhead to a separate target. This technology is a radical advance over the

original multiple-warhead systems, exemplified by certain Polaris missiles carried by American submarines, which were designed to place all their warheads in a cluster on a single target. MIRV makes it possible for one rocket to attack several targets, and therein lies the difficulty. Given sufficient accuracy and adequate nuclear yield, it may be feasible for one rocket to destroy several enemy rockets, even those buried deep in hardened silos. So far as fixed, land-based missiles are concerned, MIRV thus threatens to give a distinct advantage to the side which launches its weapons first in a counterforce strike against the adversary's ICBMs.[1]

All this is in the future and will require substantial continued advances in MIRV technology, but to the extent that such capabilities enter either or both sides' arsenals they will undermine a cardinal principle of stability, namely, the requirement that in order to deter rather than invite attack, strategic weapons should be invulnerable. One hastens to add that even should MIRV attain such a capacity, there would remain immense difficulties in devising plans for simultaneous attacks on an adversary's bomber force, not to mention the submarine fleets which both sides now possess and which many analysts consider ample deterrents in themselves. And there are conceivable responses to MIRV deployment which could overcome the impending threats to ICBMs; e. g., the land-based missiles might be made mobile or based deceptively in such a manner as to preclude effective targeting of them. But these hypothetical cures for the destabilizing impact of MIRV have their own negative consequences; quite apart from the substantial economic costs involved, they share with MIRV the quality of making the so-called "counting problem" more severe. That is, with MIRVs or mobile ICBMs or deceptive basing it becomes more difficult for either side to know with confidence how many warheads the other side may have deployed.

This uncertainty can undermine stability by obliging a country to hedge against a possible error in its intelligence on the other nation's capabilities. Such a hedge is likely to take the form of additional deployments of its own, which in turn may prompt the other state to increase its forces, and so on in a process of escalating and counterproductive increments to the two sides' forces. Plausible calculations suggest that if the United States and the Soviet Union actually get caught up in such a process and each is determined to guarantee the survivability of its land-based missile deterrent by enlarging it (as opposed to defending it actively by an ABM system), the competition is not likely to reach a stable position until both countries have spent tens of billions of dollars and have fielded extravagant numbers of ICBMs. In short the advent of MIRV *may*—not will—portend an unprecedented intensification of the strategic arms race.[2]

[1] Leo Sartori, "The Myth of MIRV," *Saturday Review*, Aug. 30, 1969, pp. 10–15, 32.
[2] See my analysis presented to the Senate in the executive session discussions of the

The potential counterforce uses of MIRV have long been recognized in the defense community. Indeed for some senior officers and planners a major ambition has been to pursue advanced MIRV development precisely because of the hope that it might enhance U.S. capacity to limit damage to this country by diminishing Soviet offensive capabilities early in any strategic exchange. But from the beginning of the U.S. MIRV effort counterforce implications were muted and relegated to the background. The official rationale for the MIRVing of the Minuteman III and Poseidon missile systems emphasized the need to assure penetration of an expected Soviet ballistic missile defense system. It was the appearance of the first installations of a Soviet ABM network in the mid-sixties which persuaded Secretary McNamara to authorize development of the two MIRV systems proposed by the Air Force and the Navy.

At that time there were powerful arguments—technological, strategic, political, economic—for proceeding. The tremendous lethality of nuclear weapons made it clear to analysts that it might be possible to package several warheads in a single missile payload, permitting a given force either to cover a larger target system or to make redundant (and hence more confident) attacks on a smaller list of targets. The United States had gained great experience in payload packaging through its space program and through vigorous R & D on so-called "penetration aids." It had devised extremely sophisticated and elaborate "penaids"—chaff, decoys, and other devices—to insure that U.S. missiles could retaliate successfully even if the Soviets deployed a heavy ABM defense. As increasing fractions of U.S. payloads were used for "penaids," which were essentially objects to fool an enemy's radar or to require him to use up defensive missiles against phony warheads, there occurred the kind of convergence which so often flows from intensive development programs. Warheads were growing more compact and payloads were growing larger, so that engineers were drawn to the obvious question; Would not the best penetration aids be additional live warheads rather than dummies—"the real McCoy, not a decoy"? Then there would remain no opportunity for a potential defender to conserve his missiles by solving the problem of discriminating between "penaids" and weapons. Every object on his radar screen would have to be treated as a live threat, and he would have to fire a defensive missile against it.

These were the kinds of technological considerations which made MIRV so attractive as a means of saturating almost any conceivable defense, thus

---

anti-ballistic missile program in 1969. In developing that memorandum I drew on work and suggestions by Albert Wohlstetter and David Mcgarvey, Jr., among others. The Senate's executive session took place on July 17, 1969, but was not cleared for publication until November; see the *Congressional Record*, Nov. 21, 1969, pp. E9908–E9909. Also see George R. Pitman, Jr., *Arms Races and Stable Deterrents*, University of California at Los Angeles, Security Studies Project Paper no. 18, 1969.

preserving U.S. certainty of its retaliatory power. They were reinforced by the persistent military interest in maintaining a quantitative lead over the Soviets in numbers of deliverable warheads. It was politically impracticable to seek a substantial increase in the number of U.S. missiles, since the Soviet threat was then growing less rapidly than anticipated in the era of the alleged missile gap and the Secretary of Defense had already reduced the planned buy of Minuteman from over 1,700 to 1,000. With MIRV, however, the approved number of delivery vehicles, on land and at sea, would be able to throw several thousand warheads if need be.

It is noteworthy that the MIRV concept had its genesis early in the Kennedy Administration, when it was by no means clear that the U.S. missile force would assume so large a lead over the Soviet force by mid-decade. In the words of Dr. John Foster, "The MIRV concept was originally generated to increase our targeting capability rather than to penetrate ABM defenses. In 1961–62 planning for targeting the Minutemen force, it was found that the total number of aim points exceeded the number of Minuteman missiles."[3] This was the period when the Ann Arbor doctrine of Secretary McNamara lent a positive impulse to counterforce technologies and the existing Soviet ICBMs were deployed in soft bases rather than hard silos. MIRV seemed a happy reconciliation of the desirable and the possible. It promised to be a cost-effective way of acquiring the equivalent of a larger missile force, which could be effective both in a retaliatory mode and in damage-limiting strikes against at least the soft portions of Soviet strategic forces. But as the views of McNamara and his associates came to give greater weight to the dangers of stimulating a new arms spiral and to the waste of buying excess strategic weaponry, the proffered efficiency and targeting advantages of MIRV failed to convince the Secretary that such a system should actually be developed. The concept remained just that—an idea—until the Soviet Union's movement toward ABM deployment made U.S. officials apprehensive about the stability of deterrence.

The elements of the Russian ABM system, including the long-range missile designated the Galosh, suggested that it would employ large nuclear warheads detonated above the atmosphere and that it might be able to destroy incoming weapons over great distances. Confronted with intelligence on Soviet ABM activity in 1965, U.S. authorities began to infer that this country might need both additional warheads and the capacity to separate them sufficiently during flight so that the Galosh could not wipe out several at a single blow. This requirement was perceived as contingent, but it gave decisive impetus to the MIRV program, which McNamara finally authorized for development in 1965. A year later he revealed that the Soviet Union had

[3] Quoted by Ralph Lapp, *Arms beyond Doubt: The Tyranny of Weapons Technology* (New York: Cowles, 1970), p. 21; see also Ian Smart, *Advanced Strategic Missiles: A Short Guide,* The Institute for Strategic Studies (London), Adelphi Paper no. 63, December 1963.

in fact begun deployment of the Galosh system around Moscow. And by the end of 1967 U.S. officials were acknowledging publicly that a program to develop MIRV in response to the Soviet ABM was under way. Still, the crucial phase of MIRV development, the extended and laborious series of flight tests on both the Minuteman III and the Poseidon boosters, did not begin until the summer of 1968.

These years, 1962 to 1968, represent a tragedy of bad timing in the mismatch between technical and political developments. After the Cuban missile crisis of 1962, political events were trending, however haltingly, toward serious negotiations on strategic arms control. The nuclear test ban treaty, the ban on space-based weapons of mass destruction, and the nonproliferation treaty were modest way stations on the path to the broader strategic discussions dictated by the condition of mutual deterrence. But MIRV technology and ABM technology were threatening to erode that condition more rapidly than political arrangements would stabilize it. If MIRV technology had become a serious prospect a decade later than it did—which might well have been the case but for the remarkable progress of the sixties in miniaturizing electronic components, perfecting missile guidance, improving re-entry vehicles, and devising compact hydrogen warheads—the eventual Strategic Arms Limitation Talks would have faced a substantially simpler arms control problem than they did. Or if the talks had not been unduly delayed by such sad distractions as the Soviet intervention in Czechoslovakia, they might have come to grips with MIRV well before the system was near to deployment. Or if the Soviet Union had taken account of the certainty that its initial ABM deployment would spark compensating changes in U.S. offensive forces, it might not have installed the sixty-seven interceptors outside Moscow which fueled an American MIRV effort scheduled to add thousands of warheads to the forces poised for retaliation against the Soviet heartland. All these if's, but only one reality: in the summer of 1968 Secretary of Defense Clark Clifford, believing that SALT negotiations were imminent and that an ongoing MIRV test series would provide added leverage for those talks, approved the start of Minuteman III and Poseidon flight tests.

Throughout this period the fact of an American MIRV program had registered but slightly in Conress, the significance of the effort not at all. MIRV had reached the flight test stage with an invisibility scarcely imaginable for a program expected to cost upwards of $10 billion. The members cognizant of the Minuteman III and Poseidon programs were those on the Armed Services committees and the Joint Committee on Atomic Energy—men who, it must be said, inclined to skepticism about the possibilities for international arms control and who evaluated MIRV less as a threat to the stability of mutual deterrence than as a hopeful means of protecting U.S. strategic superiority. Outside the still closed circles of the national security cognoscenti, members of Congress were generally ignorant of MIRV, although sizeable sums had already been appropriated for the program in previous defense bills. One finds hardly a mention of MIRV in the lengthy debates on ABM during 1968, despite the fact that MIRV was already closer to deployment than the defensive system and was potentially a comparably destabilizing weapon.[4]

On Capitol Hill probably the first serious and critical discussion of the implications of MIRV took place in the informal staff caucuses spawned by the ABM debate in late 1968. There a small number of Senate staff men began to argue that the heavy focus on ABM was misplaced and that the urgent need was for Congress to examine the MIRV issue. Deployment of ABM would take several years, they contended, during which the Congress would have repeated opportunities to delay it if that seemed wise. MIRV, on the other hand, posed a special problem that required immediate action. Flight tests had now begun, and once they were completed, it would be difficult to monitor any agreement banning deployment, since it would probably be necessary to inspect a missile in the silo to determine whether it had one or several warheads. Thus there was a critical need to seek a mutual agreement not to test such destabilizing weapons, on the theory that untested MIRVs would probably not be deployed and that, if they were, such systems would be too inaccurate to perform effectively in the counterforce mission. This argument was bolstered by the observation that Russian ABM deployment was proceeding at a snail's pace and that a rush toward MIRV deployment as a counter to the expected defenses was, at best, highly premature. Many of these same points had been put to Secretary Clifford, who later was to indicate that had he known the SALT talks would be delayed, he would not have authorized the start of MIRV testing.

In the Hill staff discussions of late 1968 and early 1969, there was spreading awareness that in the short run MIRV might be an even graver problem than ABM. Nevertheless, the general feeling was that the budding coalition against ABM should not change horses in midstream by diverting its energies to MIRV. Most participants felt that the political momentum developing on the ABM issue held the most promise of asserting congressional authority over strategic decisions. Furthermore, it was argued, MIRV was too complicated and could not be successfully articulated as an issue for legislative action.

There was much good sense in this view. Congressmen and senators were already acquainted with many details of the missile defense question; it was not clear that they could be brought to see the strategic problem whole, with the complex interactions of ABM and MIRV. To develop MIRV as a public question for resolution in the open forum of Congress would require a broad

---

[4] A useful review of the evolution of MIRV is found in Lapp, op. cit., pp. 17–35. Also see Herbert F. York, *Race to Oblivion: A Participant's View of the Arms Race* (New York: Simon & Schuster, 1970). The discussions of the staff caucuses rely on my own participation in those meetings.

educational campaign, the resources for which no one could identify. By contrast thousands of citizens were already aroused and mobilized to oppose ABM, grass-roots forces were supplementing Capitol politics, and distinguished authorities were providing competent and thoroughgoing technical critiques of Sentinel/Safeguard.

The latter factor was one of the most important distinctions between ABM and MIRV in the minds of many legislators and their assistants. They commonly believed that a weapon system could not be defeated on strategic grounds. There was an implicit conviction that the strategic challenge to ABM was viable largely because the proposed system could be denounced as technically unworkable. This was not a logical but a political fact. Those engaged in the legislative arena had felt a need for multiple arguments in their attempt to curb a defense program. And, as the technological emphases of the ABM debate revealed, many members felt that their strongest argument was that the system would not work, according to creditable technical opinion. The vital strategic considerations which should have been paramount were thus reduced to a secondary role in the ABM case.

On the other hand there was no technical challenge to MIRV. No responsible or knowledgeable person could assert that the system would not work. That was the exact problem: it was likely to work all too well. And the technology would probably sho1person could assert that the system would not work. That was the serious critique of MIRV would have to rest upon strategic and arms control grounds, considerations even more esoteric than the technological judgments central to the ABM controversy. Under the circumstances, it is as understandable as it is regrettable that there was little chance for marshaling a large number of congressmen to review the question of MIRV testing and deployment.

Given these bleak political prognoses, it is surprising that MIRV became as vivid an issue as it did in subsequent months. That it became a public issue at all owes much to the sustained efforts of a first-term Senator, Edward W. Brooke of Massachusetts, who was appointed to the Armed Services Committee in January 1969. An alert and perceptive man, Senator Brooke had a zest for complex problems and a determination to seek a stronger congressional voice in the shaping of national security policy. While much of his initial interest in serving on the Armed Services Committee sprang from a belief that the committee could be instrumental in freeing resources from the defense budget for use in other priority areas, he also saw the committee assignment as an opportunity to develop a budding concern for arms control and strategic policy. The preceding year's exposure to the ABM question had excited this interest and planted a seed of apprehension that Congress was neglecting comparable and dangerous innovations in offensive weaponry.

By the time Senator Brooke reached the Armed Services Committee, he had tentatively concluded that MIRV was the more sinister development.

Extended staff analyses and discussions with ranking members of the executive branch fed the Senator's doubts that the hazards of MIRV testing and deployment had been carefully explored. They also bred the suspicion that the Minuteman III and Poseidon programs were proceeding at their present pace largely because of the momentum they had acquired on the basis of the original intelligence projections on Soviet ABM capabilities; since those projections had not been fulfilled, Senator Brooke thought it obvious that the entire rationale for MIRV should be re-examined. His soundings "downtown" further convinced him that the implications of MIRV had never received adequate study at White House level in either the previous or the incumbent Administration. The President, he surmised, was likely to be as vague about these matters as most members of Congress.

During his first weeks on the Armed Services Committee, Brooke pressed spokesmen for the Department of Defense, including Secretary Melvin Laird, for clarification of the MIRV program's purpose and status. In these off-the-record, classified sessions he confirmed the impression that the program was advancing toward deployment well ahead of a demonstrated military requirement. There also appeared to be good reason to believe that a suspension of flight tests, which were then a third of the way through the planned two-year development series, held much promise as a means of verifying an agreement to refrain from deploying MIRV. While Department of Defense technical authorities frowned on a test ban proposal, primarily because of a deep philosophical commitment to the tenet that one could not effectively limit research and development, others in and out of government shared the judgment that a joint test suspension by the United States and the Soviet Union was a workable and important objective. It could be especially helpful in facilitating a wide-ranging SALT agreement; alternatively, a steady movement toward completion of MIRV testing would diminish the opportunities for negotiated limitations with Moscow and would virtually guarantee that the Soviet Union, which was not yet conducting MIRV flight tests, would perfect and deploy its own systems of this type. The massive Russian investment in overcoming U.S. strategic superiority left no doubt that a unilateral American advantage in MIRV technology was not in the cards. Persuaded that the United States was conducting an ill-considered weapon program that was quite inimical to the country's interest—and to its stated goal of mutual arms limitation—the Senator concluded that the argument for seeking a mutual suspension of MIRV tests should be put directly to the President.

The time was opportune. Mr. Nixon was already coming to grips with some aspects of the strategic balance in the course of lengthy preparations for the still contemplated SALT negotiations, in which Moscow and Washington had reasserted their interest early in 1969. Moreover, as Senator Brooke reviewed the President's March 14 announcement reorienting the American ABM program toward a less provocative deployment, he found particularly impressive the President's stress on the need to avoid destabilizing weapons which seemed to threaten one or the other side's retaliatory capability. Was this a hint that the President now appreciated the risk and futility of the strategic superiority he had long advocated and the necessity to modify the Ann Arbor doctrine of Secretary McNamara, with its emphasis on counterforce strikes? Perhaps Mr. Nixon's own strategic education was leading him to fresh and balanced perceptions of the profound dilemmas the new technologies were creating.

In mid-April 1969 the Senator requested and received a private conference with the President. Brooke had no illusions about the intense and potent pressures which the bureaucratic politics of the MIRV issue would impose on the President. But the Senator enjoyed a healthy working relationship with Mr. Nixon and was confident of receiving a fair hearing. While the two men were not personally intimate, they had developed a professional rapport in the 1968 campaign, when Senator Brooke had aided the candidate actively in the belief that moderate Republicans could best maintain influence in a Nixon Administration by joining the campaign and arguing their views as vigorously as possible. Brooke had learned that Nixon was a more open-minded and intellectual personality than generally thought (for example, their campaign conversations anticipated Nixon's later overtures toward the People's Republic of China), and Nixon had gained a respect for the Senator which, until their final breach in 1973, was to survive repeated disagreements on major policy issues. From this background the Massachusetts Senator had earned cordial access to the President. MIRV would be the first issue on which he made use of that personal access.

THE INTIMATE POLITICS OF MIRV

The Senator met briefly with the President at the White House on April 16, 1969. He summarized his views on the MIRV problem and hand-delivered a letter setting forth the rationale for a mutual MIRV testing moratorium. The President, who evidently was not familiar with the implications of MIRV or the idea of a flight test ban, listened attentively and sympathetically, promising that he would have the plan staffed and studied fully. Thus began a subtle and prolonged political process which, while falling short of the Senator's goal of a mutual MIRV ban, had a major impact in refining the character and purpose of the U.S. strategic effort.

From this initial encounter onward, Senator Brooke attempted to present his case on MIRV in terms of the President's own logic. His letter of April 16 applauded the Administration's sensitivity to potentially provocative deployments and, noting the President's call for an era of negotiations to replace the era of confrontation between East and West, pointed to the special threat which MIRV posed to the prospective strategic arms control discussion.

The opportunity for successful strategic arms control is perishable, since both the United States and the Soviet Union are pursuing multiple warhead capabilities for their offensive missiles. Should deployment of MIRV systems occur, effective force levels will rapidly increase several-fold. . . . without the kind of large-scale, on-site inspection which appears politically unachievable, it will be virtually impossible to determine whether a missile has one or many warheads. In short, if MIRV is not controlled prior to deployment, it probably will not be controlled.

These are among the considerations which lead me to believe that the most urgent issue now, if we are to preserve the possibility of significant arms limitations, is to arrange for a cessation of operational development (i. e., flight tests) of multiple warhead systems. This is a domain in which the United States has a substantial lead and, weighing the balance of forces, can afford to exercise some restraint. Furthermore, our elaborate optical and electronic intelligence capabilities can provide a reasonable measure of confidence that we will know whether the Soviet Union continues tests of this character.

The Senator's letter went on to describe a variety of mechanisms and proposals to increase confidence that any agreed test suspension would be respected. He pointed out the fact, well appreciated by systems engineers, that an early disruption of flight tests would be a major barrier to progress on MIRV technology, since the lengthy test series required to field such weapons depended on incorporating numerous technical modifications to resolve problems discovered in the initial flights. The letter also emphasized that the plan focused on observable activities, namely, full-scale systems tests, and that limiting MIRV in this fashion would not require monitoring laboratory work or ground tests which would be difficult to verify.

At no time did Brooke advocate either a unilateral or an unverifiable cessation of U.S. work on MIRV, for, even if the international political calculations had been favorable to such a scheme, he recognized that the domestic political context would not support it. To be given a fair chance of consideration in the executive branch and a modicum of support in the Congress, his proposals to curb MIRV must be geared to mutual restraint by the Soviet Union and the United States, and they must offer credible arrangements for adequate verification. These themes he struck in his first presentation to President Nixon, concluding:

> I know you share my conviction that the President and the Congress have no higher responsibility than to choose the risks which this nation will bear. That is, of course, precisely the question before us. I profoundly hope you will share my judgment that the best chance for reducing the long-term risks to national security lies in a prompt effort to establish a MIRV moratorium of this character.
>
> If we fail to seize this option, technology will once more have robbed politics of a precious fleeting opportunity to create a more rational foundation for peace.

It was this sense of alarm which sparked the Senator's energetic effort. He was by no means hostile to technology per se, much less to the men who invested their lives in perfecting it. Indeed, he enjoyed close rapport with the thriving research and development community which formed a major constituency in Massachusetts. But Brooke was becoming convinced that, in the field of national security more than any other, the task of political leadership revolved increasingly around the guidance and control of technology for public purposes. In this view MIRV was a classic instance in which technical programs were outrunning sound policy and threatening to so complicate the strategic equation that the policy-makers would face inordinate problems in forging arms control arrangements. He hoped to enlist the President's commitment to overcoming the political inertia which permitted massive technical programs, once begun, to proceed with little or no policy review.

Although the two men were new to such issues, both could sense the need for firmer and more farsighted leadership on these questions. In their conversation that April afternoon, Nixon revealed that he was quite prepared to consider the Senator's recommendation. Differences in personality and role, however, dictated that the President would approach the MIRV issue with great wariness. Brooke was arguing for a prompt and bold initiative to keep open the broadest possibilities for an eventual strategic arms agreement; Nixon, just beginning what would become a prolonged study, was disinclined to act quickly on any relevant issue until that study was complete.

As the President took the Brooke proposal under advisement, the Senator turned to the job of mobilizing potential allies in the bureaucracy, the Congress, and the country. Staff explorations had already shown that some variant of a MIRV moratorium would be attractive to ranking officials of the State Department and the Arms Control and Disarmament Agency; probable opponents held senior positions at the Defense Department and the National Security Council. The Senator's basic objective was not to arouse the Congress and public opinion against the Administration, but to build independent political support for a satisfactory outcome in the bureaucracy's contest to shape the President's position on strategic policy.[5]

The meeting with Mr. Nixon had contributed to this goal in two ways. First, by bringing the MIRV issue directly to the President's attention, Senator Brooke had been able to place the moratorium idea in a favorable perspective and to assure that the recommendation would not simply die for lack of awareness at the top. Second, by advancing a concrete plan of action, Brooke's initiative would constitute a building block on which those of similar view within the Administration could erect their own proposals for the Chief Executive. The Brooke plan was more than just a trial balloon, but it had some of the same qualities, setting off wide ripples in the bureaucracy and ferreting out allies and adversaries on the issue. With an active legislator seeking to persuade the President, executive proponents of the MIRV test

[5] Of special interest on the Administration's mood at this juncture is John Newhouse, *Cold Dawn* (New York: Holt, 1973), pp. 148–165.

suspension would at least have a chance to put their own best case to the White House. Opponents of the initiative, on the other hand, would be obliged to develop their arguments and present their case in detail, rather than win the decision by default or because of their presumptively superior power within the bureaucracy. In short, from the beginning the Brooke overture on MIRV was designed to sway the bureaucratic balance of power among those offices and individuals contending with the MIRV problem.

Senator Brooke had deliberately avoided a public exposition of his concern and conclusions about MIRV until after he reviewed the matter with the President. But Brooke was too sophisticated to assume that he could merely state a rational argument for a new policy and expect the Administration to act on his recommendation. Even with the President's personal interest aroused, a complicated strategic concept could languish for months in administrative review. And even granted a conscientious attempt by the National Security Council staff to coordinate views from the interested agencies, there was no guarantee that all the possible allies within the Administration—and the Congress, for that matter—would be alerted to the fact that the President was weighing some action on MIRV. The Senator felt that his private approach to the President should now be coupled with some public exposure of the MIRV issue. He chose as his forum a meeting of the American Newspaper Publishers Association in New York on April 24, 1969. His address there, entitled "A Choice of Risks," aroused broad interest in the Congress and elsewhere as the original outline of a limitation of multiple-warhead missiles.

The Senator sought to persuade the publishers, and through them other legislators and citizens, that the controversial ABM deployment, though scarcely a trivial matter, was definitely of subordinate importance to the practically unnoticed MIRV program, "the most disturbing breakthrough in strategic weapons since the advent of intercontinental ballistic missiles." He explained the adverse impact which MIRV, by effectively multiplying offensive force levels, would have on strategic equilibrium, and he underscored the added difficulties such weapons would pose for arms control. With such systems deployed, it would be exceedingly difficult for one side to determine through its own national verification means exactly what size force the other side had fielded. Brooke stated briefly his conclusion that a mutual suspension of MIRV tests should be an urgent objective. He added, however, that a test moratorium would only be a stop-gap measure, intended to buy time for more elaborate agreements to be negotiated. "For example, such a suspension must be conditional upon mutual limitation of ABM deployment and an understanding on the total number and size of strategic launchers." But he contended forcefully that a MIRV moratorium could be a "critical lever" in facilitating more ambitious arms limitations.

The Senator was careful not to formulate his MIRV discussion as a challenge to the President, and he avoided any passionate or ideological overtones. Instead, the speech was a sober assessment of strategic issues in which he spoke quite generously of the President, rejecting the charges of those who had denounced the Safeguard ABM proposal as politically inspired. While remaining skeptical of the ABM deployment, Brooke made clear his own conviction that the country could not ignore the potential vulnerabilities of U.S. strategic forces to which the President was responding. That, in fact, was the principal theme of his statement to the publishers: unless political leaders could head off MIRV deployment, the United States and the Soviet Union could well drift into a condition of heightened strategic vulnerability which would render the balance of terror genuinely precarious.

Brooke's address circulated widely on Capitol Hill. Senator Clifford Case inserted it in the *Congressional Record* together with his own endorsement of a MIRV moratorium. A number of other congressmen, including notably John Anderson of Illinois and Jeffrey Cohelan of California, vigorously advocated the plan. The Brooke letter to the President of April 16 had invited Administration support for a congressional resolution calling for a mutual MIRV test moratorium. In addition to providing a vehicle for legislative involvement in this important policy area, the resolution might serve to minimize any political risks to the President should he agree to the proposal. During April and May, while awaiting the President's response, the Brooke office refined the draft of the resolution and quietly began recruiting cosponsors for it. The Senator was especially interested in attracting the assistance of senators not prominently identified with the ABM fight, since he considered it imperative to broaden the base of concern over strategic issues. Surprisingly, considering the complexity of the subject, a great many senators began to align themselves with the moratorium idea.

Some members were prepared to go beyond the Brooke plan and support a unilateral cessation of MIRV tests by the United States, at least for the short term. Congressman Jonathan Bingham introduced a resolution to this effect in the House in May, and Senator Case prepared a similar plan for the Senate, but conditioned U.S. suspension on continued intelligence information indicating that the Soviets would match our restraint. Precisely described, the Case resolution did not call for a unilateral American halt to flight tests; if the Soviets persisted in testing, the United States would resume its own development program. Thus what was really contemplated was a tacit understanding not to test MIRV, initiated by the declaration by the United States that it would refrain from testing so long as the Soviet Union did so. Nevertheless, the tone of both the Bingham and the Case resolutions and their supporting rhetoric conveyed a certain unilaterist flavor which was to bedevil the broader campaign for a MIRV moratorium. While the Brooke formula gained some strength from the contrast between these resolutions and its explicit emphasis on mutuality, legislative and bureaucratic opponents of a moratorium repeatedly played upon the

Administration's suspicion that the critics of MIRV were "unilateral disarmers." This utterly misleading epithet nonetheless proved a damaging charge against the moderate arms control advocates in Congress.

It is true that Senator Brooke was privately pressing the Administration, in conversations with Henry Kissinger of the National Security Council and in a letter to the President on May 23, to exercise some restraint by slowing the U.S. test series until the current review of the MIRV issue could be completed. But this suggestion of a delay in further tests was not conceived as a public commitment to halt them. Brooke sought vainly to postpone a Poseidon test on May 24, as well as other flights scheduled in the weeks leading up to the preliminary discussions in the Strategic Arms Limitation Talks. An unannounced decision by the President to stretch out the series would give crucial time to test Soviet sentiments on a joint ban and would be fully reversible if Moscow failed to evince a willingness to collaborate on such a plan.

Again Brooke tried to demonstrate to Nixon that the true U. S. interest lay in forestalling the movement toward MIRV, reporting to the President on his detailed investigation of MIRV in the executive sessions of the Armed Services Committee that "we have testimony from DDR & E [Director of Defense Research and Engineering] that the Soviets would require extensive testing to get an accurate MIRV. . . . Hence, if we could get the Soviets to accept a test suspension, the threat of SS-9 to Minuteman could be reduced." Better than to be compelled to respond technologically to a threat, the Senator averred, would be to preclude the threat politically. An agreement banning MIRVs would make it unnecessary for the United States to install a costly and controversial ABM system to defend the Minuteman deterrent. The Senator once more pressed the President not to allow MIRV testing to go so far that it foreclosed the option of stabilizing the strategic balance by mutual agreement at a relatively lower force level. Brooke's communications with the President at this juncture were entirely off the record, but they probably tainted the senator as a "unilateralist" in the minds of some executive officials.

By mid-June the Administration still had not responded in any detail to the Brooke proposal of April 16. At the Department of Defense, many senior officials assumed that the MIRV moratorium proposal would die aborning. In the terse phrase of one DOD executive, "Brooke will never get the Senate to buy that." The odds and the attitudes changed on June 17 when forty other members of the Senate joined Brooke in sponsoring Senate Resolution 211 (S. Res. 211). The resolution called for a mutual suspension of MIRV flight tests by the Soviet Union and the United States and expressed strong support for an early start on comprehensive strategic arms negotiations. If the bureaucratic opponents of a moratorium had hoped to finesse the Brooke plan as the dream of a mere novice, they were now confronted, even in advance of a vote, with vivid evidence that the dream was shared by an impressive fraction of the upper chamber.

The next day the Massachusetts Senator transmitted the resolution and introductory remarks to the President with a concise summary of the main points motivating himself and his associates:

(1) We believe MIRV is incompatible with the sensible strategic doctrine you adopted in your presentation of March 14. It is a serious threat to hardened missiles and to mutual deterrence.

(2) We believe there is no urgent need for the United States to proceed at the present time with MIRV tests, since Poseidon and Minuteman III are intended to penetrate a heavy Soviet ABM system which is not yet materializing.

(3) We believe that the United States has an overriding interest in persuading the Soviets not to perfect the kind of accurate MIRV capability which could threaten the Minuteman force; we cannot hope to persuade them if we insist on proceeding with MIRV technology ourselves.

(4) We believe that each side has a larger interst in persuading the other not to introduce MIRV systems than in deploying MIRV technology of its own.

At the President's news conference on June 19, before he had read the Senator's letter and final text of the resolution, Mr. Nixon described the Brooke proposal as "very constructive" and said he was considering the possibility of a moratorium on tests. He rejected "any unilateral stopping of tests on our part," declaring that only a mutual moratorium would be acceptable. This was, of course, the substance of S. Res. 211, but the President's implication of unilateralism blurred the distinctions among the several suggestions being advanced on Capitol Hill. The forces pushing S. Res. 211 would face a constant problem of distinguishing their call for a mutual MIRV ban from what some officials and commentators thought they were proposing.

In the House of Representatives comparable momentum began to build up in support of the concept. Congressmen Anderson and Cohelan mobilized over 100 representatives to introduce the S. Res. 211 formula, and Congressman Clement Zablocki of Wisconsin convened the first congressional hearings on the several proposals which had been filed. Practically all the witnesses before Zablocki's Subcommittee on National Security Policy and Scientific Developments, including such private experts as Donald Brennan and Herbert Scoville, concurred in the judgment that MIRV deployment was premature, and the majority argued that a test moratorium made sense.[6] While most of those testifying believed that U.S. intelligence could provide adequate verification of Soviet compliance with a test suspension, DOD spokesmen raised doubts about possible clandestine Soviet development of

[6] Hearings before the Subcommittee on National Security Policy and Scientific Developments, Committee on Foreign Affairs, U.S. House of Representatives, *Diplomatic and Strategic Impact of Multiple Warhead Missiles*, 91st Cong., 2d Sess., July and August 1969. The committee's report of Oct. 9, 1969, urged a high priority for a MIRV freeze in SALT.

MIRV. Dr. Foster, the Director of Defense Research and Engineering, and G. Warren Nutter, Assistant Secretary of Defense for International Security Affairs, contended that there were ways in which the Soviet Union could evade a test ban, perhaps by disguising certain space launches or by testing only a single re-entry vehicle from a payload capable of carrying several of them. These were wholly legitimate questions and had to be analyzed in any thorough consideration of a MIRV moratorium. But apart from the fact that there were solid answers to each of them, these charges that a moratorium would be unverifiable diverted attention from the broader strategic context in which the whole problem of MIRV was embedded.

For example, knowledgeable students of MIRV pointed out that an attempt to subvert a ban on multiple-warhead tests by flights of a single warhead from a MIRV payload would probably be detectable. Through careful "signature analysis" of the single re-entry vehicle flown in such a test, U.S. experts should be able to estimate its general shape, size, and weight, permitting a comparison with the capabilities of the rocket which launched it. If intelligence observed launches of a 2,000-pound re-entry vehicle by a rocket booster capable of throwing 20,000 pounds over intercontinental distances, the suspicion would be strong that something devious was under way. Alternatively, close observation of the launch and postlaunch phase of Soviet test missiles would provide good prospects of detecting the small course corrections and maneuvers in which a MIRV-type platform had to engage when launching its individual re-entry vehicles. Admittedly, some analogous experience might be gained through multiple satellite launches directed to a number of "space points," but no such program could provide truly comprehensive development of a reliable MIRV capability. And if the Department of Defense thought something less than a thorough and realistic MIRV test series would be sufficient, why, one wondered, was the United States spending hundreds of millions of dollars, tens of missiles, and more than two years on flight tests explicitly designed to perfect an operational MIRV? In short there were convincing methods for meeting the verification requirements stressed by the Defense Department witnesses.

But beyond the specifics of monitoring the moratorium, one had to assess the proposals against a variety of contingencies. To begin with, the scheme clearly could endure only if other agreements fell into place. If the two countries froze offensive force levels at roughly the current numbers, there would be less than 250 of the giant Soviet SS-9 missiles, the "MIRVable monsters" considered the greatest threat to the American deterrent. The Department of Defense had itself testified that the SS-9, if eventually MIRVed, would be a serious danger to Minuteman only at much higher force levels, in the range of 400. Thus a test moratorium combined with a freeze would mean that even an improbable Soviet success in cheating the test ban would not be decisive, since the Soviets would have too few SS-9s to gain an advantage. Still more important in this connection would be the hoped-for limitation on ABM. Without having to cope with a substantial ABM network, the United States would be able to visit devastation on the Soviet Union even if only a small number of single-warhead missiles survived a surprise attack executed by a Soviet force which had been secretly MIRVed.

The advocates of a MIRV moratorium were pressing for the first of what would have to be an interlocking group of arms controls: a test ban reinforced by a freeze on offensive weapons reinforced by a strict limit on ABM deployment. In this broader and more balanced frame of reference, those who challenged the moratorium's verifiability betrayed a singular lack of vision. Their preoccupation with the problem was undoubtedly genuine, but their perspective seemed badly askew when one realized that the alternative to the modest risks of a first-step moratorium was an easy acceptance of unlimited MIRV testing and deployment, with all that portended for an intensified and hazardous competition in strategic arms.

Despite the cool reaction of the Defense witnesses who testified before the Zablocki subcommittee, informed opinion in the country at large was steadily coming around to endorsing the MIRV proposal. By July 1 editorial support had come from many quarters—*Wall Street Journal, New York Times, Washington Post, Boston Globe, Minneapolis Star,* and *Milwaukee Journal,* among others. In the nation's research and development community, especially on university campuses, concern over MIRV was mounting rapidly. Hoping to facilitate the President's acceptance of the moratorium by highlighting the wide public consensus on the plan, Senator Brooke again wrote to the President on July 30. He contrasted the MIRV proposal with the dispute over ABM and called attention to the fact that the moratorium was backed both by proponents of Safeguard, such as Dr. Freeman Dyson and Dr. Gordon MacDonald, and by critics of the deployment, such as Dr. Jack Ruina and Dr. Herbert York. The same was true in the Congress, where a number of supporters of ABM deployment, including Senators Gale McGee and Robert Packwood, had joined the compaign to pass S. Res. 211.

Brooke was most anxious that the President not misconstrue the legislative approach to the MIRV issue as either a hostile movement toward the Administration or a rerun of the ABM battle. He also wanted to counter the skepticism of some Administration technicians by presenting to the President the independent opinions of respected outside experts who thought the moratorium was a workable and essential plan.

It is very important for those developing the Administration's position in the SALT talks not to fall captive to a sense of inevitability regarding the advance of MIRV technology on either our side or the Soviet's. We can control this technology, if there is a determination to do so and a willingness to make the effort promptly.

Similar letters went to Dr. Kissinger, Secretaries Laird and Rogers, Under Secretary of State Elliot Richardson, and ACDA Director Gerard Smith. All of them were engaged in the Administration's extended examination of MIRV and other aspects of the SALT agenda.

There was now a heightened sense of urgency in the campaign to ward off MIRV deployment, for the Soviets had not agreed to the U.S. suggestion that preliminary SALT discussions should begin before July 31. Every month's delay in the negotiations was a grave matter, as the American MIRV program continued its progress toward a scheduled initial deployment of Minuteman III in mid-1970. Had the SALT talks begun in August 1969, there might have been a maximum opportunity to deal with MIRV, at least so far as the U.S. government's disposition was concerned. The responses to Senator Brooke's July 30 barrage of correspondence revealed that Secretary Richardson and Ambassador Smith, key figures in planning for SALT, shared the hope that a MIRV ban would be a priority target in the negotiations. So did Deputy Defense Secretary David Packard, who thought there were no insurmountable problems to verification. Secretary Rogers told a press conference on August 20 that the Senator's proposal was helpful and reiterated the Administration's willingness to consider a mutual moratorium.

The Department of Defense, replying to the Senator through Dr. Foster on August 30, declared for the first time that it had no "intrinsic objection to a joint moratorium," although the Defense Research and Engineering Director restated his insistence that there be adequate verification arrangements. The Department of Defense letter drew a distinction between the modestly sized U.S. MIRV, designed for ABM penetration, and the potential large-warhead MIRV of the SS-9, for which the Department could find no explanation other than possible use against U.S. missile silos. Dr. Foster acknowledged some uncertainty, however, as to whether the triplet warhead recently tested on the SS-9 was in fact a MIRV, an uncertainty resolved months later with the finding that it was not. These questions notwithstanding, the late summer of 1969 found the U.S. government more open to a MIRV ban than at any previous time.

Sadly, a Russian diplomatic slowdown now caused the SALT process to drag out, steadily diminishing the time with which to deal with MIRV test limitations. Furthermore, when initial SALT exchanges belatedly began at Helsinki late that year, and again when they resumed at Vienna in April 1970, the Soviet delegation appears to have reacted indifferently to the U.S. indication that MIRV could be considered. The United States approach to the issue at SALT was undoubtedly cautious and perhaps even tepid, but it is amazing that the Soviets failed to pick up the matter. Their reticence on MIRV corroded the effort within the U.S. government to pursue a mutual MIRV ban.[7] The crowning argument after December 1969 became "The

---

[7] See Alton Frye, "U.S. Decision-Making for SALT: Executive and Legislative Dimen-

Soviets are not interested," a diplomatic reading whose finality no one could contradict without firmer evidence than Moscow provided. In the Byzantine byplay surrounding SALT preparations in the two governments, one surmises that both delegations were constrained not to appear overeager for prompt action on MIRV—the United States because it felt the advanced U.S. MIRV program afforded important leverage which it should not voluntarily sacrifice without extracting a limit on Soviet ABM deployments; the Soviet Union because it recognized the American technological lead on MIRV and believed it could not initiate hard bargaining from a position of weakness. One Russian diplomat told me at the time that the United States should have pressed the moratorium idea, since we were the ones who had MIRV programs and the Soviet Union could not very well offer to stop something it was not doing. Odd logic, but perhaps the governing one in the Soviet government.

A less sanguine interpretation must also be recorded, particularly in view of the sustained Soviet deployment of SS-9s in subsequent months: Moscow may have concluded that its payload advantage, with large boosters unmatched in the United States inventory, would be a decided asset when it ultimately developed a MIRV, and it may simply have chosen to keep open the option of a sizeable counterforce capability. That it might have elected this option out of an ominous intent to go for a first-strike capability is extremely dubious, given the inherent difficulty of such a goal. But the Russian military planners might well have been convinced that some counterforce damage-limiting capability, as defined by Secretary McNamara, would be useful if war actually occurred through accident or idiocy. They might also have concluded that the U.S. MIRV program had passed a point of no return on a road which would probably lead to a significant counterforce capacity. And some Russian military professionals no doubt held the view in vogue in many American circles that "you can't control technology." Some members of the Soviet SALT delegation voiced precisely those sentiments.

Whatever the basis for their failure to encourage a concerted diplomatic attack on the MIRV issue, the Soviets certainly chilled the atmosphere. This may have been due to nothing more than the difficulties of coordinating a position on MIRV within the Soviet bureaucracy, a task surpassing even the parallel chore in the United States. Nevertheless, the Soviet Union bears a heavy responsibility for avoiding direct negotiations on MIRV at a moment

---

sions," in Mason Willrich and John B. Rhinelander (eds.), *SALT: The Moscow Agreements and Beyond* (New York: Free Press, 1974), pp. 66–101. Of general interest as an initial overview of problems confronting the SALT negotiations is Harold Brown, "Security through Limitations," *Foreign Affairs*, 47, April 1969, pp. 422–432. Dr. Brown, who had been Director of Defense Research and Engineering and Secretary of the Air Force, subsequently became a principal member of the U.S. delegation to SALT.

when the U.S. domestic political setting was uniquely favorable to re-straining such weapons. One suspects it will prove to be a classic instance of strategic shortsightedness.

IV. *Signals for Restraint: The Congressional Impetus for Strategic Arms Control*

Although the Brooke resolution had been launched with powerful support, the proposal came to rest for some months in the Senate Foreign Relations Committee. There were several reasons for this. Some members expected the SALT talks to get under way immediately, in view of the President's announcement that the United States had proposed a July 31 starting date. They were prepared to await the results of the initial discussions, leaving to the executive maximum latitude to decide which issues should take their place on the agenda. Others felt that the MIRV issue had received a sufficient boost in the wave of press and congressional discussion which Senators Brooke and Case and others had engineered that spring and summer. And a decisive body of opinion frankly feared that too much attention to MIRV would dilute efforts to beat the President's ABM proposal. This fear persisted among Brooke's allies no less than others, a few of whom darkly hinted that the Senator may even have been leading an Administration-inspired ploy to save the Safeguard deployment by building a distracting backfire on MIRV. Nothing could have been further from the truth, of course, as demonstrated by Brooke's active role in seeking to curtail the ABM program. No matter: the committee sat on the resolution.

The Massachusetts legislator repeatedly sought to persuade his peers that the Senate should act promptly in advance of SALT to make clear its support of a MIRV limit. Writing to Chairman Fulbright of the Foreign Relations Committee on September 15, Brooke urged immediate consideration of the resolution as ,a means of influencing the Administration's current deliberations over a joint moratorium. He argued that since the Senate would later be called on to advise and consent to any SALT treaty, the course of statesmanship would be for the Senate to tender its counsel on crucial facets of the negotiations. There was little dispute that the affirmative record already built in the House Foreign Affairs Committee, as well as in the Senate body, warranted quick approval of S. Res. 211. Still, the committee deferred action, driving Brooke to a rare state of exasperation which he conveyed in an open letter to Fulbright on October 23. More than four months had passed, wrote the junior Senator, and the delay was a cause of "grave regret." The letter chided the chairman to provide a "clear measure" of his oft-stated commitment to arms control by reporting S. Res. 211. "Let it not be said that Senators dawdled while technologists carried us forward to what might become a disastrous imbalance of terror."

The chairman replied that he had in fact urged that the resolution be reported favorably on October 7, but that other members, including some cosponsors, had felt it should be withheld until an expected meeting with Secretary Rogers, who would visit the committee after conferring with Soviet Foreign Minister Gromyko at the United Nations. Another member of the committee, Albert Gore of Tennessee, caught the gist of his colleagues' sentiments when he responded to Brooke by asking, " . . . now that the conference is set to begin in Helsinki, do you think we should proceed? I doubt it." This mood was dominant in the committee and would not change until a catalytic development in early 1970.

The committee's reluctance to act on the MIRV issue was a keen disappointment to the small group of legislators and staff who had sparked the moratorium proposal. The effort was not wasted motion, however, for it had energized the executive branch review of multiple-warhead systems and had helped to create a fresh sensitivity to the destabilizing potential of such weapons. More importantly, the unexpected awakening of Congress to the implications of qualitative changes in the offensive force structure provided the basis for a little-publicized but vital attempt to clarify some perplexing ambiguities in U.S. policy. Although the prospects for successful diplomacy to cope with MIRV remained cloudy, the lively politics of MIRV elicited an unprecedented presidential decision, explicitly modifying the counterforce emphasis of the McNamara years and confining U.S. MIRV technology to a strictly retaliatory, second-strike mission.

The genesis of this decision lay in President Nixon's own evolution of the doctrine of strategic sufficiency and his emerging appreciation of the requirements of stable deterrence. No less than three times in his March 14, 1969, statement the President ruled out adopting certain strategic options because they might appear to threaten the Soviet Union's confidence in the survivability of its own deterrent forces. Nixon appeared to grasp the hard truth that there could be no agreements to undergird strategic equilibrium unless each side felt secure in its capacity to deter the other by retaliating against any nuclear attack.

Implicit in this rationale was the perception that counterforce capabilities could be inherently dangerous in a relationship grounded—not by choice but by necessity—on mutual deterrence. But implicit understanding is not firm policy, and the Administration had not spelled out detailed guidance for the multipronged technological programs of the defense establishment. Unfortunately, there were serious tensions between the President's inclinations to avoid threatening the Soviet deterrent and the actual direction of the U.S. MIRV program. In the opinion of those committed to S. Res. 211 and its House counterpart, unless MIRV development was firmly aligned with the new presidential doctrine, it would move recklessly toward an actual capability incompatible with a deterrent posture. Whether or not SALT resolved the MIRV problem—and particularly if the talks were not successful—it was absolutely essential that the United States define its technological objectives in terms of the goal of stable deterrence.

As the Senate Armed Services R & D Subcommittee had explored the details of the various MIRV projects, it became evident that very ambitious technologies were on the drawing boards, though not yet emerging in the actual flight test programs. Senator Brooke feared that the President might not have had the opportunity to measure the details of the technology against the general thrust of his revised strategy. For example, on January 16, 1968, a Pentagon press announcement had specifically contradicted a report that MIRV would serve primarily as a "countercity," retaliatory weapon; the Department declared that "each new MIRV missile warhead will be far more accurate than any previous or existing warheads. They will be far better suited for destruction of hardened enemy missiles than any existing warhead."

Months after the Nixon Administration had begun to abandon the goal of strategic superiority, Air Force Chief of Staff General John Ryan was still striking the familiar theme of counterforce. Testifying before the House Appropriations Committee on October 7, 1969, General Ryan declared, "We have a program we are pushing to increase the yield of our warheads and decrease the circular error probable so that we have what we call a hard-target killer which we do not have in the inventory at the present time." This could hardly be reconciled with the President's new commitment to avoid threats to the Soviet strategic capability; if perfected, this kind of advanced MIRV system would reduce the President's policy to mere rhetoric.

With hope fading for timely mutual action in SALT, the Senator shifted his attention to firming up U.S. declaratory policy on the counterforce issue and to conforming the incipient MIRV technology to that policy. On December 5, 1969, a lengthy communication to President Nixon cited General Ryan's recent description of the ambitious goals of the Air Force MIRV development and highlighted the contradiction between those goals and the President's doctrine of strategic sufficiency. Brooke presented estimates of the first-generation MIRV capability against targets of varying hardnesses and reported calculations that improved accuracy, which had already increased tenfold in a decade, could make even small warheads lethal against hard silos.

"I trust I am correct," wrote the Senator, "in understanding your recommendation of Safeguard and your remarks on March 14 as establishing the firm policy that the United States will not seek a capability to disarm the Soviet Union." If so, it was imperative that the United States refrain from pursuing ever more accurate MIRV systems which would be totally superfluous to the established strategic mission of a retaliatory strike. Deploring the provocative trend toward a hard-target MIRV, the Senator appealed to the Chief Executive: "It would be a tragedy beyond words if the essential policy you have set forth were undermined by the unnecessary technology of highly accurate MIRV systems."

By this juncture the Senator's critique of MIRV was recognized by National Security Council and DOD officials as politically potent and intellectually persuasive. Consultations between White House staff and the Defense Department ensued, as they formulated a suitable presidential reply to Brooke's latest letter. Brooke had injected his telling assault on hard-target MIRV at a crucial stage of the executive's decision-making, the latter phases of preparing the budget for fiscal 1971 which the President would submit in January 1970. This timely intervention proved decisive, as revealed in the President's response to the Senator on December 29:

> Your thoughtful letter of December 5 prompts me to reiterate my fundamental position that the purpose of our strategic program is to maintain our deterrent, not to threaten any nation with a first strike. . . .
>
> There is no current U.S. program to develop a so-called "hard-target" MIRV capability. *The particular program to which General Ryan referred did not receive Department of Defense Approval for funding in the forthcoming Defense budget.* [Italics added.][1]

While indicating that the United States would continue advanced research on ballistic missile design to insure its ability to penetrate any defenses, the President had drawn the line against a specifically counterforce MIRV system. Cancellation of the Air Force project to enhance the hard-target capability of Minuteman III was a vital step away from such destabilizing weaponry.

[1] Because of the sensitive nature of some portions of this exchange, including some calculations incorporated in the Senator's letter, only excerpts of this correspondence have been released. On June 4, 1970, Dr. John Foster, Director of Defense Research and Engineering, testified regarding hard-target MIRV that "we had a program of investigation along these lines and last year I cancelled it. My purpose was to make it absolutely clear to the Congress and hopefully to the Soviet Union, that it is not the policy of the United States to deny the Soviet Union their deterrent capability." Subcommittee on Arms Control, International Law and Organization, Committee on Foreign Relations, U.S. Senate, *ABM, MIRV, SALT and the Nuclear Arms Race,* 91st Cong., 2d Sess., p. 509.

This was not the end of the problem, however. There remained disturbing ambiguities in the MIRV effort. In particular, work on certain types of penetration aids might contribute to improved accuracy. Moreoever, with the best intentions in the world the United States would have difficulty convincing the Soviet Union that it was in fact abiding by the restraints established by Mr. Nixon. Moscow's military analysts would likely proceed on the familiar "worst case" assumption that even small American warheads would become so accurate that they would threaten Soviet silos. And once MIRVs were deployed, there would in fact be a gradual tendency for them to become more precise and reliable as they underwent routine testing common to any operational missile system.

But the Brooke exchange with the President had accomplished three valuable purposes. It had evoked a more explicit presidential affirmation of the exclusively retaliatory function of U.S. strategic forces. It had won a valuable precedent in the cancellation of an actual program oriented toward a counterforce capacity, and for the time being it assured that accuracy improvements in U.S. MIRV systems would be incidental, rather than central, to the U.S. development programs, meaning that any refinements in precision would be substantially slowed down. These results created a new context in which defense officials must evaluate future development proposals, and they afforded a touchstone for alert legislators to stand upon in scrutinizing DOD programs which might deviate from the announced policy. Most importantly, by slowing the drift toward superaccurate silo killers, there would be more time for diplomats to wrestle with the intricacies of durable, mutual constraints on MIRV, as well as other strategic systems. A modest achievement, but not one to be scoffed at.

The MIRV issue was relatively dormant in early 1970, until a passing remark by Air Force Secretary Robert Seamans rejuvenated it. A number of senators, including ranking members of the Foreign Relations Committee, had assumed that the onset of the SALT negotiations would induce President Nixon to postpone any major deployment decision on MIRV for a least a short period. There was no basis for the assumption, for the Administration had consistently stated that the United States would not halt any of its planned deployments without commensurate Soviet action. Nevertheless, there was an electric shock in the Senate when Secretary Seamans commented on March 10, 1970, that the first Minuteman III missiles would be fielded by June of that year, as scheduled.[2] Suddenly S. Res. 211 was alive again, as senators sought a means of voicing their dismay over what they considered a rush toward a new plateau in the arms race.

Senator Gore, chairing the Foreign Relations Subcommittee on Arms

[2] Statement of Secretary of the Air Force Robert C. Seamans, Jr., in Committee on Armed Services, U.S. Senate, *Authorization for Military Procurement, Research and Development, Fiscal Year 1971, and Reserve Strength*, 91st Cong., 2d Sess., part 2, p. 907.

Control, International Law and Organization, immediately slated hearings on the resolution for the following Monday, March 16. Senator Brooke was the lead witness, backed by Soviet expert Marshall Shulman of Columbia University. They and a host of succeeding witnesses urged quick enactment of the resolution, both to encourage an immediate effort to arrange a mutual MIRV moratorium in the April session of the SALT talks in Vienna and to promote a comprehensive U.S. proposal in those discussions. On March 17, Secretary Rogers alluded to the Senate deliberations in an interview on the "Today" television show, and mistakenly characterized the moratorium plan as a unilateralist measure. Brooke swiftly corrected him, and Rogers assured the Senator that it was not his intent to misconstrue the contents of the resolution. The true unilateralism, as the Senator phrased it, would be to proceed with MIRV deployment, thereby destroying the opportunity for joint action to control a potentially grave threat to stability: " . . . the *prospect* of MIRV deployment may well encourage diplomacy. The *fact* of MIRV deployment might well defeat it."

After months of procrastination, the Foreign Relations Committee now moved with unwonted speed. On the motion of John Sherman Cooper, the committee broadened the provisions of the original draft. It stressed the urgency of a MIRV moratorium and proposed "an immediate suspension by the United States and by the Union of Soviet Socialist Republics of the further deployment of all offensive and defensive nuclear strategic weapons systems, subject to national verification or such other measures of observation and inspection as may be appropriate." This was more sweeping than even Senator Brooke had anticipated, but he embraced the committee language as reported on March 24, 1970.[3]

There were still obstacles to surmount. Brooke had been forced to lobby intensively to build a committee majority, and since some elements of the Administration were less than keen on having the Senate take any action related to SALT on the eve of the Vienna conference, there was still an uphill battle to win Senate passage. Some members of the Armed Services Committee briefly considered a parliamentary ploy by which the resolution would be referred back to that committee, in view of its overlapping jurisdiction with Foreign Relations. Chairman Stennis dropped that notion, however, when Senator Brooke rose in the chamber on April 7 and announced that Senate Minority Leader Hugh Scott and several others had joined as cosponsors of the resolution, providing a majority of the Senate who publicly declared their support for the measure. Two days later, the Senate passed S. Res. 211 by the overwhelming margin of 72 to 6. Never before had the Congress spoken so urgently for such far-reaching strategic arms limitations.

[3] Subcommittee on Arms Control, International Law and Organization, *ABM, MIRV, SALT and the Nuclear Arms Race;* and Committee on Foreign Relations, U.S. Senate, *Resolution regarding Suspension of Further Deployment of Offensive and Defensive Nuclear Strategic Weapons Systems,* 91st Cong., 2d Sess., Report no. 749, Mar. 24, 1970.

The President now enjoyed the broadest reasonable mandate to pursue a negotiated agreement of maximum scope. In realistic political terms the Senate had done about all it could to spur diplomacy.

HOLDING THE LINE ON TECHNOLOGY: ADDITIONAL BARRICADES

The enactment of S. Res. 211 meant that the diplomats had been given a resounding send-off. But had the technologists gotten the message? If the Soviets picked up the American initiative quickly, it might be possible to forestall further testing and deployment of MIRV. But if the negotiations proceeded at the snail's pace that seemed probable, there would be at least some MIRV deployment. In that case it would be crucial that the U.S. development programs accorded with the criteria outlined by the President.

Until now Senator Brooke had not publicized his exchanges with the President on this subject. The time had come to do so, for a number of reasons. First of all, the Senator hoped the Soviets would be reassured in their approach to the SALT table, if they knew that Mr. Nixon had decreed restraint on MIRV technology. Second, one could not be certain that the policy enunciated privately in the President's December 29 letter had been clearly perceived throughout the farflung DOD research enterprises. Finally, the standard formulated by the President in curbing a hard-target MIRV effort had not been explicitly endorsed by the Congress. By disclosing the President's letter, Brooke hoped to pave the way for follow-on legislative action, confirming the policy and intensifying congressional oversight of defense R & D on advanced missiles. Accordingly, the Massachusetts Senator described the President's "major contribution to strategic restraint" in a statement of April 23, 1970, simultaneously calling on the Soviet Union to undertake similar concrete acts of restraint in the interests of rapid progress in SALT.

Within the Armed Services Committee, Brooke had won considerable standing for his work on strategic questions. Using the President's declared policy as a preface, he was able to enlist committee support for a symbolic but important reduction in the so-called ABRES project, a continuing program which explores advanced ballistic re-entry systems. On Brooke's recommendation the committee cut $5 million from the $105 million requested for fiscal 1971 and adopted report language which seconded the President's turn away from a hard-target orientation.

> This reduction relates to effort in support of any future hard-target kill capacity. Those efforts which are pointed toward a strictly retaliatory objective which can be met with substantially less accuracy and more modest yields than needed for the counterforce mission are to be fully supported.[4]

[4] Committee on Armed Services, U.S. Senate, *Authorizing Appropriations for Fiscal Year*

For the first time, one of the congressional committees responsible for authorizing the Defense Department budget had spoken against counterforce technology. The ABRES fund reduction would hold in the final conference with the House. This would be a significant legislative barrier to the rampant pursuit of MIRV systems specifically aimed at the counterforce objective.

Building on this committee provision, minor in dollars but major in strategic implications, Brooke devised two amendments to the defense procurement bill, intending to trigger another substantial debate on MIRV and, if possible, to invoke the full Senate's authority for stringent limitations on future MIRV improvements. The first proposal concerned the very straightforward problem that would occur in the event of a SALT agreement covering MIRV: Most U.S. submarines were being converted to carry Poseidon missiles, for which only MIRV payloads were available. Once converted, the boats could no longer carry the un-MIRVed Polaris missiles without expensive reconversion. Hence a major impediment to American acceptance of a MIRV ban, should one prove feasible, was the fact that the costly Poseidon system and a number of U.S. submarines would not be permitted; i. e., a MIRV prohibition would in this sense amount to an actual arms reduction, which no one expected either side to agree to in the initial phases of SALT. One cure for this would be to develop a single-warhead system for the Poseidon, which would require some tens of millions of dollars and a development program lasting about eighteen months. There was an added advantage to a single re-entry vehicle (RV) for Poseidon. It could be launched at greater ranges, enabling the subs to operate over wider reaches of the ocean, with a concomitant reduction of their possible vulnerability to antisubmarine warfare.

In order to keep open the option of SALT consideration of the MIRV issue, Senator Brooke offered language which "authorized and directed" the Secretary of Defense to develop a single re-entry vehicle system for Poseidon and Minuteman III. (For a variety of technical reasons, including its possible use of similar re-entry vehicles from the Minuteman II system, the Minuteman III could accommodate a prohibition on MIRVs more easily than Poseidon.) The Department was agreeable to this kind of contingency program, although Secretary Laird objected to being directed to undertake it. After some legislative-executive discussion over a period of weeks, the mandatory language was deleted and a modified version of the amendment was accepted by Chairman Stennis on August 27, 1970. Even this discretionary language failed in the House-Senate conference, largely because of House Chairman Rivers' vehement opposition to "cluttering up his bill with language amendments." Nevertheless, the legislative history provided clear en-

---

1971 for Military Procurement, etc., 91st Cong., 2d Sess., Report no. 91–1016, July 14, 1970, p. 82.

couragement to the Department of Defense to prepare for the possibility of a MIRV ban by beginning work on optional single-warhead systems under its own authority.

Far more complex and controversial was a second MIRV-related provision filed by the Massachusetts Republican. A troublesome feature of the entire discourse on the counterforce issue, including the innumerable debates on a potential hard-target MIRV, was that no one had defined the terms. What was a "hard-target kill capacity"? Without a clear operational standard, it would be meaningless to declare that one favored or opposed such a capability. There were serious intellectual obstacles to reducing such a concept to a firm definition, in part because one could conceive of many degrees of capability against different targets of varying hardness. In the world of the strategic target analyst, there was a good appreciation of the many variables which contributed to determining the kill capability of any particular weapon against any individual target. The calculations were probabilistic, meaning that no one could in fact assert that this weapon would destroy that target; one could only assert that, on the basis of statistical samplings of missile and warhead performance, it was probable that of a hundred such weapons launched against such targets, fifty or seventy or ninety would destroy their targets. To try to write a workable political prescription in such a murky technical realm was to enter *terra incognita*.

Yet there were certain basic physical relationships which governed a weapon's effectiveness against targets of increasing hardness and which might be articulated in understandable form. Mathematically, the kill probability (Pk) of any missile against a given target was a function of the delivery accuracy (stated in terms of CEP, or circular error probable) and warhead yield (stated in kilotons, Kt, or megatons, Mt). In brief the obvious was true: a bigger bomb detonated close to a target had a better chance of destroying it than a smaller bomb exploded at the same proximity. Furthermore, in establishing or defining a hard-target capability, one was concerned not about every level of hardness (measured in pounds per square inch, or psi, of blast overpressure required to destroy a target), but only about the hardness ranges associated with missile silos, i. e., several hundred psi.[5] Silos might actually be getting harder over time, so that if missile yield/accuracy combinations were constrained to the relatively low ranges sufficient for retaliation against cities, land-based missiles could retain a substantial margin of the invulnerability deemed necessary for stable deterrence.

Senator Brooke's second amendment to the fiscal 1971 defense procurement authorization bill addressed the matter of defining hard-target kill capability. The formula he proposed was a refinement of an initial definition

[5] See Samuel Glasstone (ed.), *The Effects of Nuclear Weapons*, revised ed. (Washington: U.S. Atomic Energy Commission, 1962), especially the accompanying "Nuclear Bomb Effects Computer," and Chap. 4, "Air Blast Loading and Target Response," pp. 149–195.

which had been thrashed out in staff negotiations with the office of the Director of Defense Research and Engineering. The very idea of limiting technology provoked fierce opposition from such quarters as those represented by the ultraconservative weekly *Human Events,* but the revised amendment actually accommodated the technical objections raised by DOD. Instead of a fixed ban on capabilities to attack targets harder than 100 psi, as originally conceived, the final language incorporated a threshold concept which gave some concessions to the Department, e. g., in estimating how hard silos actually were and in setting the kill probabilities considered necessary to attack them. Yet it provided a firm and meaningful guideline which Congress could monitor in the future in order to guarantee that U.S. technology was not exceeding the requirements of deterrence.

Members of the Union of Concerned Scientists and other groups, including more than half the faculty of the Massachusetts Institute of Technology, endorsed the plan. They recognized that the United States was several years and many tests away from a truly high-accuracy MIRV capable of counterforce attacks; and explicit legislative enactment of a ban on superfluous accuracies and hard-target capabilities would offer valuable guidance to the more zealous members of the American technical community, who were eager to perfect the means for putting "100 Kt on the other guy's silo roof." It would also be a reassuring signal to the Soviet SALT negotiators that even if the United States continued to deploy MIRV systems, they would be compatible with the requirements of deterrence.

To serve these goals, the Brooke amendment would have forbidden use of any funds to develop, test, or procure a MIRV system in which an individual re-entry vehicle could destroy a hardened target. The provision defined a hard-target capability as "that combination of warhead yield and accuracy required to generate the equivalent of one-third the level of blast overpressures and related effects considered necessary to enable a single warhead to neutralize a hardened missile silo."

This standard fully comported with the established policy of the executive branch, for as Secretary Laird testified before the Senate Armed Services Committee, the President had "made it perfectly clear that we do not intend to develop counterforce capabilities which the Soviets could construe as having a first-strike potential." Unknown to most senators and citizens, the final version of the Brooke proposal has actually won the concurrence of senior DOD technical professionals, who agreed that it in no way impeded an ample retaliatory capability. But in weighing the Department's position, Secretary Laird decided to oppose the amendment on the procedual grounds that the Congress should not establish statutory limits on technological programs. He disliked the precedent.

When Brooke called up the amendment on August 27, a lively debate ensued. Attempts to recruit prior commitments to vote for the amendment had foundered largely because most members and their staffs were frankly intimidated by language which smacked of complicated physics. It seemed unwise to put the issue to a vote, given so uncertain an outcome, for a rejection of the proposal might be wholly counterproductive, should it appear to Soviet observers that its defeat was tantamount to a senatorial endorsement of a U.S. hard-target MIRV program. Nevertheless, the discussion of the proposal could serve a significant function, providing a useful piece of legislative history confirming the executive branch commitment to hold back on MIRV. Senators Jackson, Tower, and Stennis all opposed the amendment but joined the author of the proposal in explicating the U.S. policy of restraint.

Senator Brooke opened the discussion with an unusually sharp criticism of Secretary Laird's objection that the amendment would set "the precedent that Congress will establish the general characteristics of U.S. military systems." Appealing to his fellow legislators' sense of responsibility, Brooke argued that "Congressman Laird would never have agreed with Secretary Laird." He then documented the numerous instances in which Laird, while in Congress, had himself fought to establish congressional criteria for weapons systems, including strategic bombers, ICBMs, and the Polaris fleet, among others. It was by no means unusual for Congress to write even the most detailed prescriptions for systems. Representative Laird, for example, had offered an amendment specifying that, instead of the mach 2.5 TFX aircraft proposed by Secretary McNamara, the Defense Department should build a mach 3 plane. Other parallel cases abounded. Brooke was even able to cite Admiral Hyman Rickover's call for Congress to exercise its prerogative on such complex questions.[6]

The other senators present, however, were reluctant to do so. Jackson felt that "questions of this nature are best handled in the executive branch." Voicing the deep suspicion of the Soviet Union which permeated congressional attitudes, the Washington legislator hinted that one reason he did not wish to preclude MIRV improvements was his belief that the prospect of such weapons might induce the Soviets to be more amenable in the SALT talks. ". . . I would hope that mutual limits on the procurement of weapons capable of destroying hard targets are negotiable. This would be the most helpful limitation." Senator Tower was more adamant, flatly dismissing any notion that passage of the amendment would be a helpful signal to the Soviet Union. "The only thing they understand is toughness."

Time and again, in this debate as in others, members muddied the waters by insisting that the United States should not bind itself to exercise restraint unless the Soviet Union did so. The implication was that if the Soviet Union pursued a hard-target MIRV for the SS-9, as Jackson and Tower speculated they were doing, the United States ought to do so for its own systems. They neglected the fact that this was a recipe for a competition to maximize

[6] *Congressional Record*, Aug. 27, 1970, pp. S14445–S14457.

strategic instability. The contrary thesis was hard to swallow, but it was a rigorous application of strategic logic. Whatever the Soviets did with regard to their own potential counterforce capacity, the U.S. interest lay in avoiding a deployment of hard-target killers. Such a deployment, by instilling a greater fear in the Soviets regarding the survivability of their deterrent, could increase Moscow's propensity to launch its weapons in moments of acute crisis, lest they be caught on the ground. Thus the risk of pre-emptive war would rise. Brooke's argument for a firm barrier against hard-target MIRV was founded in the conviction that even if the Soviets were unwise enough to pursue a counterforce option, the United States objective was to render our own forces invulnerable, not to render the other side's vulnerable. And could anyone really doubt that the American people would be in still graver jeopardy if Moscow, thinking its own forces were insecure, were to choose some kind of hair-trigger, launch-on-warning posture? As Brooke summarized the case, MIRV systems could reinforce strategic stability "only if they are exclusively, explicitly, and credibly designed for the retalitory, second-strike mission."

In spite of their hostility to the Brooke proposal, both Tower and Jackson endorsed the second-strike emphasis of U.S. policy. The resulting record was amorphous and less than satisfactory, but it did constitute a rare legislative exploration of the need to synchronize technology with policy. Moreover, even without Senate adoption of the precise language offered, the debate made clear the kind of guideline which Senator Brooke and other like-minded members would have in mind in scrutinizing future DOD research and development efforts. As the only definition of hard-target capability being advanced, this formula would become a starting point for later examinations of advanced missile development. Thus merely having raised the issues in this fashion helped to shape the context in which defense planners, diplomats, and politicians would assess the MIRV problem. This was one more barrier to an improvident technological endeavor. It undoubtedly contributed to the strong stand later taken by Senator Stennis in resisting proposals from various quarters that Congress should actually press for a counterforce MIRV development.

That such barriers were needed was apparent from another flurry of activity on MIRV during the autumn of 1970. In a September 22 speech Air Force Chief of Staff Ryan continued to portray the Minuteman III system as "our best means of destroying time-urgent targets like the long-range weapons of the enemy." Senator Brooke urged Secretary Laird to clarify the contradiction between Ryan's statement and the Administration's repeated commitment to an avowedly second-strike strategy. Laird reiterated that policy and acknowledged that Ryan's statement could be "misconstrued." He explained the general's remark as referring to possible retaliation by U.S. weapons against "remaining weapons of an aggressor nation which had struck first." For the first time in public, the Secretary noted that "even if used in the context described by General Ryan, the capability of Minuteman III against hardened silos is relatively low." How low was indicated in a DOD press-briefing response to reporter George Wilson of the *Washington Post*. Even if all warheads from a Minuteman III were directed against a single target, it would take more than one such missile to achieve a significant probability of neutralizing a hard silo. This was the most detailed revelation to date of the limitations on the first-generation MIRV systems, and Senator Brooke underscored them: "So long as more than one MIRV missile is required to destroy an adversary's weapon, the destabilizing potential of such multiple warhead missiles will not be realized."

The episode was valuable in highlighting once more the U.S. declaratory policy of a strictly second-strike posture, but it showed how hard it would be to avoid an intolerable ambiguity in American capabilities. It also revealed that an inordinate effort was required to put some defense officials on notice that they must avoid both provocative programs and inflammatory comments. For senators dedicated to promoting strategic stability, the tough lesson was that they not only had to keep an eye on Soviet developments and deployments; they had to watch the words and weapons of the American defense establishment as well.

The obligation persisted. During the 1971 debate on the fiscal 1972 defense authorization, Senator James Buckley of New York undertook specifically to reverse the policy of restraint in regard to highly accurate MIRV technology. He offered an amendment calling for development but not deployment of such a system. This time, however, both the Defense Department and Chairman Stennis of the Armed Services Committee strongly opposed such a provocative move. The Mississippi Democrat flatly declared that the United States did not need such improvements in payload and accuracy, whose only purpose would be "to destroy enemy missiles in their silos before they are launched." An official statement in opposition to the Buckley plan reiterated the U.S. position "not to develop weapons systems whose deployment could reasonably be construed by the Soviets as having a first-strike capability. Such a deployment might provide an incentive for the Soviets to strike first." The amendment went down to overwhelming defeat.[7] A firm consensus seemed to have jelled.

Inexplicably, the apparent consensus received a severe jolt in mid-1972, in the aftermath of the successful Moscow summit agreements on strategic arms. Within days after the President's return to Washington, the Department of Defense obtained permission to seek additional R & D funds from Congress for several technological hedges against the possibility of eventual failure of the SALT understandings. In the $110 million supplemental request was a $20 million item to begin development of a more accurate,

---

[7] Senator Harold Hughes recapitulates the debate on the Buckley amendment in the *Congressional Record,* Aug. 10, 1972.

higher-yield re-entry vehicle for the Minuteman III system. Evidently operating under a vague and general White House approval for some "SALT add-ons," the Department had consulted its wish list of exotic technologies and, disregarding previous policy guidance on the matter, had resurrected the hard-target killer scheme. The House authorized the funds with little attention to their detailed implications, partly no doubt because of the desire to cooperate with a President who had managed to negotiate the historic SALT agreements. Unfortunately, the President and his National Security Council staff did not seem to have grasped the specific significance of the hastily approved supplemental request which the Defense Department had presented to Congress. In late July 1972, confronted by Senate criticism of the MIRV development effort, the White House privately acknowledged its chagrin over the contradiction between the program and stated policy, but for bureaucratic reasons it found it difficult to reverse the Secretary of Defense. Once the problem came to White House attention, the best hope of those closest to the President seemed to be that the Senate would quietly delete the offensive item.

At this point the confusion of signals made the outcome uncertain. Sensitive to the implications of such an initiative, particularly in the wake of the Moscow attempts to undergird a stable strategic relationship, the Senate Armed Services Subcommittee on R & D examined the program closely in executive session. Senator Thomas McIntyre, though perplexed at the executive's conduct on the matter, correctly gauged the situation as one in which the Defense Department had gotten out in front of the relevant strategic policy guidelines. Pressing for a persuasive rationale to reverse the previous declarations against hard-target capabilities, the subcommittee chairman found the Department's case singularly unconvincing and so reported to Chairman Stennis. Senator Brooke had also learned of the plan and conveyed vehement objections to both the President and the Senate Armed Services Committee.

The key Senate leaders concluded that the burden of proof for so drastic a change in policy rested with the Defense Department, and that the departmental spokesmen had failed to meet that burden. Accordingly, they declined to authorize the program, and their views prevailed in the conference committee with the House. It had been a most disturbing example of executive vacillation on a fundamental element of strategic stability, but, thanks largely to the useful precedents at work in the Senate, essential restraints on MIRV had been retained.[8] The Department did not resubmit the scheme in the next year's defense budget, although there would remain the danger of gradual progress toward excessive accuracy and lethality in the first-generation MIRV systems being deployed.

The lengthy history of congressional involvement in the MIRV issue

[8] See Alton Frye, "Of Senators and Silo-Killers," *Washington Post*, Aug. 29, 1972.

contrasts markedly with that in the ABM case. Where the latter issue mobilized virtually the entire Congress to intense concern and activity, legislative intervention on the MIRV problem centered to an unusual degree around one man, Edward Brooke. As we have seen, the campaign to control MIRV proceeded on two tracks, one aimed at stimulating a diplomatic limitation on such systems, a second directed at eliciting a clear affirmation of U.S. commitment to an exclusively second-strike strategy and limiting American MIRV technology to levels compatible with that strategy.

Tested against the maximum goals, the campaign failed. There is not yet a meaningful constraint on MIRV testing or deployment. The United States is slowly installing such systems, and having belatedly begun MIRV tests in 1973, the Soviet Union may be expected to do likewise. But every legislator is condemned to survive on half-measures and partial successes, and the congressional attempt to cope with MIRV produced real and important victories. The overwhelming approval of S. Res. 211 gave impetus to U.S. diplomacy in SALT. The tenacity of interested legislators contributed to a shift in the U.S. negotiating position to include MIRV in the purview of negotiable issues. There is good reason to believe that the United States has been prepared to accept reasonable limitations on MIRV, and it is regrettable that the SALT negotiations were unable to resolve the question in timely fashion. For that the Soviet Union's initial indifference, feigned or real, to stopping MIRV tests and deployment was a decisive factor, and Moscow bears a heavy responsibility for the general sluggishness of the negotiations.

One must reckon, however, with the knowledge that these are among the gravest negotiations in history, and their pace reflects the stupendous caution of both sides. One must also remember that opportunities yet exist to place diplomatic perimeters around the MIRV technology, perhaps by very sharp limits on the number of MIRV-capable boosters in each side's force structure and by circumscribing each country's future test program. Action on those possibilities, as Roman Kolkowicz and others have surmised, probably had to await Soviet achievement of at least a limited MIRV technology, since Moscow's military authorities seem highly reluctant to grant the United States technological leadership in the field.[9]

The dangers of the strategic arms competition have undoubtedly mounted with the introduction of MIRVs, but those dangers must not blind one to the remaining possibilities for building a more secure nuclear balance. In the long term even the hazards of MIRV could be managed if the two powers found it feasible to place increasing emphasis on invulnerable sea-based forces, phasing out land-based ICBMs and bombers—the magnets which might attract counterforce strikes by MIRV. But that kind of blue-water option would require great study of methods to guarantee perpetual invul-

[9] Roman Kolkowicz et al., *The Soviet Union and Arms Control: A Super-Power Dilemma* (Baltimore: Johns Hopkins, 1970).

nerability for submarines—and greater diplomacy to engineer a move toward actual reduction of less secure weapons. It seems fair to say that the American government's disposition to address the whole range of possible limitations on strategic weapons is more affirmative than before, partly because the energetic politics of MIRV has shored up arms control sentiment in the Congress and the country.

Yet the real accomplishments of the congressional interventions on MIRV lay in the refinements of U. S. strategic policy and practice. Senator Brooke's incessant hammering on the dissonance between the President's doctrine of sufficiency and the actual character of planned MIRV technology forced the executive branch to explicate its policy in detail. In the process there emerged a heightened awareness of the necessity to eliminate the lingering ambiguity over the missions and capabilities of American strategic forces. President Nixon's repeated exchanges with Senator Brooke represented the most explicit declaration against counterforce capabilities by any Chief Executive: "We have not developed, and are not seeking to develop a weapon system having, or which could reasonably be construed as having, a first-strike potential." The cancellation of the advanced hard-target MIRV program recommended by the Air Force in 1969 was a concrete measure of the Administration's willingness to enforce such a standard. And the Congress's endorsement of restraint on highly accurate MIRV systems, reflected in the fiscal 1971 budget cut and legislative language governing the ABRES project, was a signal step toward a common view of the issue between the two branches. Indeed the Senate rejection of the hard-target MIRV proposal which followed the SALT agreements found Congress protecting the declared policy of the President against deviant forces in the executive. Without the elaborate previous efforts to engage congressional interest in the issue, no such outcome could have been conceivable.

None of this insured that the Soviet Union would believe the United States was going to observe the restraints it had established for itself, but surely these public attempts to harmonize American intentions and actions were constructive gestures toward Moscow. They not only invited the Soviet Union to exercise comparable restraint in avoiding provocative technologies but molded a more wholesome psychological setting for SALT. Perhaps most importantly, the evolution of a firm declaratory policy against hard-target MIRV provided a benchmark for conscientious officials, in and out the Congress, to use in gauging the tendencies of U.S. technology. Those who felt MIRV technology should proceed without political inhibitions would no longer be able to assume that anything goes. The net result was that the burden of proof had shifted. Proponents of ultraprecise MIRV systems could not take for granted that counterforce capabilities were acceptable objectives or that technology could seek its own level without regard to the political or strategic consequences. There was now a dramatic exception to the idiot rule so widely applied in defense R & D, "If it can be built, it should be built." The presumption was against technology which would be superfluous to the retaliatory mission on which deterrence rested, and the country had inched toward a fuller understanding of the essential premise of national security in the nuclear age: mutual deterrence depends on mutual vulnerability.

The case of MIRV is instructive in what it reveals about the moods and mechanisms of the congressional role in strategic policy-making. As John Sherman Cooper and Philip Hart had gained special standing as the initiators and leaders of the critical review of ABM deployment, so Senator Brooke came to hold a unique position among his colleagues and vis-à-vis the Administration so far as MIRV was concerned. In both instances men who demonstrated careful preparation and exceptional knowledge of strategic issues won the deference of their peers. There was no formal arrangement which prescribed Brooke's role, and indeed other members took a number of initiatives on MIRV. But the pattern became one of voluntary and informal consultation, in which with few exceptions other members of the House and Senate coordinated their efforts with the Senator. His leadership was accepted de facto, and other members avoided precipitate actions bearing on MIRV. For example, several senators and congressmen who favored a direct assault on funding for MIRV in 1969 and 1970 deferred to Brooke's judgment that the most promising avenue for S. Res. 211 would be to retain its emphasis on mutual and agreed arms controls, an emphasis which efforts to legislate unilateral fund cuts would have sacrificed. By sustaining a well-reasoned and responsible criticism of MIRV, the Massachusetts legislator was able to serve as a catalyst for significant policy changes.

The important lesson here is that Congress does not always have to *act as a body* to influence policy in even the most esoteric reaches of executive decision-making. Aggressive and well-prepared *individuals* within either chamber can hope to penetrate closed areas on national security policy and make their views effective. Indeed, given the immense difficulty of mobilizing and educating the full membership of the legislature on all the important questions, there is much to be said for this kind of policy entrepreneurship. If the man's arguments are patently foolish, they will generally be ignored. But if they are persuasive—and if executive officials believe that he might win his case on appeal to the full Congress anyway—they may well have substantial impact. This kind of catalytic role is less overt than an ideal model of democratic politics would dictate. But in a modern government facing issues of the gravest complexity and necessarily operating through a bureaucracy sometimes prone to self-paralysis and anachronistic behavior, a lone legislator can often perform invaluable service. His role may occasionally seem presumptuous, but it is absolutely necessary.

SALT: CROSSCURRENTS FORE AND AFT

Congressional restraint on ABM and MIRV, as well as Senate enactment of S. Res. 211, accurately conveyed the prevailing desire to facilitate success in the Strategic Arms Limitation Talks. But just as "peace at any price" was a phrase alien to the American lexicon, so, too, was "success at any price" a rule scorned by the political leaders of both Congress and the executive. From the beginning of the negotiations in November 1969, President Nixon and those managing SALT diplomacy were especially sensitive to the persistent congressional pressures for a firm U.S. stance in the talks. Not only were these inclinations congenial to those dominant in the executive branch; they came from senior quarters of the House and Senate, from men who had to be reckoned with in any final accounting of the agreements which might result. Mr. Nixon's native caution in dealing with the sober realities of the SALT agenda undoubtedly swelled when, as a student and admirer of Woodrow Wilson, he recalled that a disaffected minority of the Senate had defeated the Treaty of Versailles. Comparably historic undertakings were in the works, and although he displayed his clear commitment to moving beyond the Cold War and to curbing the excesses of the strategic arms competition, the President would not risk them by ignoring the views and preferences of those forces in Congress that held power to frustrate them in the end.

For the most part, however, executive consultation with Congress during the long months of negotiation (November 1969 to May 1972) was routine and pro forma. Ambassador Gerard Smith, chairman of the SALT delegation and director of the Arms Control and Disarmament Agency, appeared tens of times before various committees of the House and Senate to provide status reports of the talks. His efforts were supplemented by innumerable other meetings and testimony involving various officials concerned with SALT. But these encounters were uniformly circumspect and reportorial rather than engaging and consultative. It is fair to say that the leaders of Congress and the relevant committees received less detailed and substantive exchanges on SALT than did the allied governments of the North Atlantic Treaty Organization, which were regularly briefed at length prior to each session of the negotiations.

It would be invidious, but not untrue, to suggest that the diplomats trusted their peers in allied nations more than they did the elected representatives of their own government. This was partially due to a genuine fear of leaks about the ultrasensitive discussions, which the Americans and Soviets had agreed to keep under the closest possible wraps. The Nixon Administration, like its predecessors, tended to hold the notion that Congress was a sieve, although the legislature's record of respecting classified information is far more creditable than the stereotype implies. The leaks which did emerge from SALT, as has generally been true of classified data, came from the bureaucracy and occasionally from Soviet officials.

One must acknowledge, however, that even the responsible committees were willing to keep their distance from the intricate day-to-day diplomacy of strategic arms control. Very few members of Congress tried—and even fewer managed—to insert themselves deeply enough into SALT to be well-informed throughout the process. And given the standoffish attitude of the executive officials directing the negotiations, it took aggressive effort on the part of a congressman or senator to penetrate the labyrinth of SALT planning and discussion. The House Subcommittee on National Security Policy and Scientific Developments, chaired by Clement Zablocki of Wisconsin and ably staffed by Dr. John Sullivan, was virtually the only group in the lower chamber to stay abreast of the SALT process. In the Senate there was somewhat wider but still limited knowledge of the evolving negotiations.

Partly because of the expected Senate role in ratifying any treaties which SALT might produce, a number of senators took relatively active roles in overseeing the talks. Probably the principal senatorial monitors were John Sherman Cooper and Henry Jackson, one a Republican member of the Foreign Relations Committee and the other a Democratic member of Armed Services. In their divergent policy stances toward SALT, these two men epitomized the underlying currents of tension between the two national security committees. Foreign Relations had a long-standing and natural claim to supervising arms control negotiations; its subcommittee on this topic had played a central part in all arms control efforts for many years. In the case of the strategic arms talks, the full committee assumed more of the subcommittee's work, particularly after the defeat of subcommittee chairman Albert Gore in 1970.

Periodically in the past and extensively in this instance, however, the overlapping jurisdictions of the two committees had brought the Armed Services Committee into a somewhat competitive posture in this field. In collaboration with Foreign Relations, Armed Services had held hearings on the military aspects of the nuclear test ban treaty in 1963; on its own it had looked into the military problems posed by the nonproliferation treaty. Among some of its members, including Senator Margaret Chase Smith, there was considerable resentment at the way Foreign Relations had grown increasingly active on defense-related issues and some pressure to defend the Armed Services Committee's jurisdiction against this alleged encroachment. These precedents and pressures contributed to a decision by Chairman Stennis in 1969 to establish a Subcommittee on the Strategic Arms Limitation Talks. The committee leadership correctly claimed that the extraordinary military components of the pending negotiations demanded a special and continuous effort on their part to assess SALT.

As chairman of the new subcommittee, Henry Jackson gained added leverage in a field where his competence and prestige had already given him a unique position. It was inevitable that, having been the first choice of both Richard Nixon and Melvin Laird to be Secretary of Defense, the Washington Senator would have easy access to convey his views to the highest levels of government. And if some of his colleagues suspected him of retaining an unwarranted cold warrior attitude, Jackson nevertheless enjoyed unsurpassed standing as a defense expert among a broad spectrum of congressmen and senators in both parties.

During the several sessions of SALT, alternating between Helsinki and

Vienna, Senator Cooper and others spent some time with the U.S. delegation in the field. Though they had no official connection with the delegation, these senators sought to gain a first-hand impression of the atmosphere and action in the actual negotiations. There and in briefings they solicited in the United States, Cooper and his associates on the Foreign Relations Committee sought to maintain an informed and affirmative presence in the executive councils at the heart of the talks. A former ambassador himself, Senator Cooper well understood the value of sustained political interest in a negotiation to keep it on the tracks.

Several factors combined, however, to diminish the influence of those senators most intent on pushing a SALT agreement. The first was their professed commitment to a strategic freeze, which was read in some executive circles as an eagerness that practically guaranteed their votes for almost any agreement. While the Administration was relatively impervious to guidance and suggestions from any faction of Congress, it paid rather greater heed to those legislators whose more restrained support of SALT left their future votes on ratification in doubt. This is not to say that the clear support which Senator Cooper and his allies lent to SALT was counterproductive; far from it. Their early and consistent endorsements of the process were essential ingredients in molding a political environment in which such vital discussions could move forward. But one must acknowledge that such endorsements carried a certain cost in diminished influence on the actual talks themselves. It was a perverse truth of politics that, to a certain degree, the known friends of SALT could be taken for granted by the Administration.

Another consideration also came into play. The proponents of SALT tended to be the opponents of ABM, a system to which the President committed much personal effort and political capital. In salvaging his Safeguard ABM deployment from congressional defeat, Mr. Nixon accrued heavy debts to Senator Jackson and others who led the fight for the system. To these men their public labor to deploy a defense of Minuteman sites against the growing Soviet ICBM threat was not a cavalier gesture. Jackson in particular became fervently convinced that the responsible course for the United States was to go forward with Safeguard defense of the deterrent. In this perspective the initial arguments for Safeguard as a bargaining chip were transmuted into a conviction that retaining the right to install the first elements of Safeguard should be an objective of the United States in the SALT talks. It was a classic illustration of commitment breeding commitment, and it came to influence both the Nixon team and its legislative collaborators.

The result was a significant complication of the entire bargaining context in which SALT proceeded. The original U.S. sketch of options for an ABM agreement included a total ban, or "zero-level," which would require both sides to disassemble the partial deployments they had in progress, and a single-site defense of Moscow and Washington, the so-called NCA, or National Command Authority, option. Unfortuantely, the talks moved so slowly that both the threatening Soviet installation of SS-9 ICBMs and the countervailing deployment of Safeguard represented expanding commitments by the two countries. During 1970 and 1971, Jackson urged Henry Kissinger and the National Security Council staff to drop the emphasis on zero-level or NCA defense in preference for a full defense of the Minuteman force at four Safeguard sites. Jackson stressed that such a defense of the deterrent could be readily distinguished from the kind of population defense which the Soviets had begun to build; he also took a dark view of the Soviets' intentions, inferring that if they resisted a presumably stabilizing defense of the deterrent, they must be headed toward a counterforce capacity to attack the hardened silos. He stated this position forcefully in a private letter to President Nixon in October 1970, reiterating it frequently in later months.

Largely as a result of these developments, in July 1971 the United States advanced an ABM proposal which would permit a four-site defense of Minuteman in exchange for the one-site area defense installation near Moscow. This constituted a significant hardening of the American position and led to a series of maneuvers by the two delegations which, without strong political commitment to agreement at the top of both governments, might well have disrupted the prospects for agreement. Although the plan was not unreasonable in technical and strategic terms, politically the Soviets were unwilling to consider any arrangement that did not constitute visible equality for the parties. No doubt the Soviets, in refusing to accept the distinction between a stabilizing defense of the deterrent and a destabilizing defense of cities, feared that a continuing U.S. ABM program could well generate superior technology that might later serve to limit the effectiveness of Russia's deterrent. After some posturing on both sides, the terms of the ABM accord gradually came together in a two-site package, one each for NCA defense and for defense of the deterrent.

As the U.S. negotiating position slipped away from his preferred option, Senator Jackson grew more and more critical of the Administration's conduct of the talks. In his opinion more effective and firm-minded diplomacy could have won for the United States a valuable ABM hedge against Soviet capacity to jeopardize the Minuteman silos. In private communications with Kissinger, Ambassador Smith, and other SALT authorities, the Senator was underscoring his anxieties in the months immediately prior to the Moscow summit of May 1972. The apparent haste and disarray of the final activities surrounding the SALT agreements of that month confirmed for him that the President was rushing recklessly toward an understanding in a manner hardly conducive to protecting the American interest.[10] The SALT delegations were

[10] Newhouse, *Cold Dawn*, pp. 201–202.

still drafting language on a last-minute flight from Helsinki to Moscow, and properly collated documents were not ready for the formal signing ceremonies in the Kremlin. Nixon and Brezhnev signed the true forms later in a private session. Jackson was not persuaded by the evident fact that the admittedly hectic hours preceding the signing of the ABM treaty and the interim agreement on offensive weapons were consumed by relatively minor negotiations of issues that had been carefully defined and prepared in the thirty months of work leading up to the summit. Even before the presidential mission left Moscow Senator Jackson was publicly voicing apprehension.

Thus the abundant praise which greeted Mr. Nixon's signal success at the summit was dampened by sharp criticism from the very legislator to whom he had paid greatest deference in SALT. On the plane home from the Soviet Union, the President confided to intimates his anxieties that the SALT agreements would create troublesome domestic repercussions. He worried that Congressman John Ashbrook, an Ohio Republican then challenging the President's renomination in a number of primaries, might gain ten percentage points in the California contest which was then imminent. Lest the ratification effort itself be endangered, Mr. Nixon returned directly to the Capitol to present the results of his summit diplomacy to a joint session of Congress and the American people.

The focal point of the Administration's concern quickly became the position to be adopted by Senator Jackson, whose stern words on the procedures and policies pursued in Moscow had shaken the White House.[11] Judging the remaining ABM options to be worthless, he promptly took the lead in defeating the Defense Department request for authorization to begin preparations for an NCA deployment. Though vocally displeased with the SALT package, Jackson quickly abandoned any thought of flatly opposing either the ABM treaty or the interim ceiling on offensive weapons. Recognizing the overwhelming sympathy for the accords, Jackson chose a different tack; he would position himself and the SALT Subcommittee to hold greater sway on the next and even more far-reaching phase of SALT which would search for permanent controls on offensive forces. To this end Jackson developed an amendment to be offered to the resolution of approval of the interim agreement. It was this amendment which would preoccupy the Senate for weeks in August and September, delaying final approval of the interim agreement until long after the ABM treaty was ratified 88 to 2 on August 3.

The proposal struck many as simple and sensible. It invoked as the stan-

---

[11] A widely circulated statement of the Senator's critique was a syndicated column which he authored for *Newsday;* see Henry M. Jackson, "Weapon Agreements: A Senator Questions U.S. Concessions," *Los Angeles Times,* June 25, 1972, sec. F7. A parallel view was that of Charles J. V. Murphy, "What We Gave Away in the Moscow Arms Agreements," *Fortune,* September 1972, pp. 111–115, 203–208. *Per contra* see Alton Frye, "SALT: The Accord Deserves Our Support, *Washington Sunday Star,* June 18, 1972, pp. B3–B4.

dard for forthcoming negotiations the very principle of equality on which the Soviets had insisted in the ABM pact. It also warned the Soviet Union that, pending a permanent agreement on offensive weapons, the United States would view a Russian deployment endangering the American deterrent as contrary to this country's supreme national interest; the obvious purpose was to warn the Soviets not to perfect a hard-target MIRV system for the giant SS-9 or similar boosters. And finally the amendment called for the maintenance of a vigorous research and development and modernization program in support of a "prudent strategic posture." On its face it was a difficult amendment to oppose, and the Administration, eager to smooth its relations with Jackson and to enlist his support of other projects, expressed its approval.

In an adroit parliamentary maneuver, Jackson enlisted more than a third of the Senate as cosponsors even before debate bagan. There was a touch of political brilliance in the proposal. For senators who harbored some doubts about the first SALT agreements, especially regarding the numerical advantage in delivery vehicles which they accorded Moscow, the Jackson formula offered a perfect hedge. Its supporters could vote for the ABM treaty and interim agreement while venting their concerns through a statement of principles to govern the next round of negotiations.

On the other hand Chairman Fulbright of the Foreign Relations Committee, together with Senator Cooper, perceived serious implications in the Jackson language. They argued that it called into question the United States' own good faith in the bargain concluded in Moscow, inasmuch as the Administration had repeatedly claimed that the nominal disparity in launchers did not damage U.S. security. They suspected that the amendment would cloud the political message of an unqualified ratification. Furthermore they feared that a strict insistence on "equality," as Senator Jackson seemed to define it, would constitute a straitjacket for the later negotiators. In their opinion America's technological advantage dominated the calculations more than the literal numbers of strategic launch vehicles. From their standpoint the Jackson amendment was superfluous and psychologically debilitating, and they pressed the President to clear up the meaning of his support for such language.

The upshot of this infighting was a revision of the amendment in early September. The Administration continued to give its support to the proposal while reserving the right to differ with any interpretations offered by its author. Out of a confused and frequently bitter debate the modified amendment eventually won passage on September 14. It pointed to a powerful and active role for the SALT Subcommittee chairman in the next rounds of SALT. Indeed many observers saw the major reshuffling of the SALT delegation and the drastic downgrading of the Arms Control and Disarmament Agency in 1973 as a direct consequence of the Administration's determination to appease Senator Jackson.

Once it became apparent that the resolution of approval would not be a clean and uncluttered endorsement of the interim agreement, other Senate forces moved to insure that the measure covered other essential concerns as well. Senator Harold Hughes, an Iowa Democrat who had become an active member of the Armed Services Committee, joined with Senator Brooke in raising the need for firm guidelines against both U.S. and Soviet counter-force MIRV systems. They were prompted by the revelation that the Admin-istration had advanced its ill-timed proposal to develop a hard-target MIRV only days after the Moscow agreement. With the help of a timely and diplomatic intervention by Senator John Pastore of Rhode Island, a modified Brooke-Hughes amendment was attached to the resolution, stressing that neither side should seek unilateral advantage by developing a first-strike potential. Another amendment, offered by Senator Mansfield, specifically incorporated portions of the Nixon-Brezhnev Declaration of Basic Principles of Mutual Relations of May 20, 1972. Other language commended the President for concluding the agreements and urged him to seek Strategic Arms Reduction Talks (SART) not only with the Soviet Union but with the People's Republic of China and other nuclear powers.[12] If the Jackson criteria were the most dramatic provisions added in the Senate, these addi-tional sections reflected the continued desire to accelerate the negotiations into their next phase and to refrain from provocative strategic innovations.

There had been quite a wrangle in the Senate over the SALT accords. It reflected varying estimates of the risks and opportunities presented by these unprecedented agreements. And it anticipated closer scrutiny by several fac-tions in Congress of the Administration's conduct of future negotiations. Yet there could be no question that, even with the cautionary note sounded by the Jackson amendment, the Congress of the United States wished the President to move forward, prudently and expeditiously, with the task he had begun. The momentous issues of nuclear weapons had bred a sober demand to move from Cold War hostility to collaboration in a durable structure of peace.

SALT II: A SLIPPERY SLOPE

Events at home and abroad conspired against further progress in arms limita-tion. From the outset of the doomed second Administration of Richard Nixon, the American government performed erratically—and the Soviet government all too habitually. With Nixon under siege for the duration of

[12] Richard Perle of Senator Jackson's staff compiled a most useful record of these proceedings, *Strategic Arms Limitation Talks (SALT): Legislative History of the Jackson Amend-ment, 1972*, including the full record of congressional debate on the ABM treaty and the resolution authorizing approval of the interim agreement on offensive weapons, Aug. 3–Sept. 5, 1972, offset and released through the office of Senator Henry M. Jackson,.

the festering Watergate debacle, the White House was too distracted to provide needed leadership. And the loss of the experienced Gerard Smith left the SALT delegation to languish. During early 1973 Dr. Kissinger paved the way for a joint declaration at the Nixon-Brezhnev summit of that summer, pledging the two governments to reach a permanent agreement on offensive forces before the end of 1974 and emphasizing that it must include qualitative limitations as well as quantitative restraints. But the Middle East war and its aftermath consumed Kissinger's energies throughout the fall and early 1974, leaving arms negotiations on the back burner. His tardy attempts to find a "conceptual breakthrough" for a new agreement in the spring of 1974 and to revive the stagnating discussions at the ensuing Moscow summit conference revealed that the Russians had decided to draw back and await the outcome of America's domestic turbulence before proceeding with new and far-reaching commitments.

The long pause in SALT was costly indeed. As 1973 unfolded, the Soviet Union finally began to test its own MIRV systems, flying not one but four new missiles, including another giant system on the scale of the SS-9. Though occurring years after they were originally expected and in spite of estimates that it would cost the Russians a decade and $30 to $40 billion to retrofit their missile silos with the new designs, these developments left the quest for stability badly shaken. The prospect of an eventual Soviet advantage in counterforce-capable systems provoked the United States to dangerous countermeasures, just as the existence of the first-generation American MIRV systems had guaranteed a matching Soviet effort in such technology. Secretary of Defense James Schlesinger announced a new targeting policy to include some Soviet military installations and called for the development, though not the deployment, of an improved-accuracy and higher-yield MIRV system for the Minuteman III missile force.[13]

The Defense Secretary's rationale was complex, and his distinctions were important. He made clear that existing capabilities were quite ample for a broad range of flexible applications, including selective strikes against some military facilities. In adopting a new targeting doctrine, the stated objective was to increase the options available to the President should a crisis arise in which Soviet forces conducted limited strategic operations not calling for massive retaliation against population centers. Schlesinger also emphasized that tighter control and selectivity in targeting of the present arsenal did not require the improved counterforce capacity which would flow from the

[13] Secretary Schlesinger's views evolved significantly after his initial disclosure of the new targeting policy in remarks before the Overseas Writers Association on Jan. 10, 1974. See particularly his testimony before the Subcommittee on Arms Control, International Law and Organization of the Senate Committee on Foreign Relations, *U.S.–U.S.S.R. Strategic Policies,* Mar. 4, 1974; and *Report of the Secretary of Defense to the Congress on the FY 1975 Defense Budget and FY 1975–1979 Defense Program,* Department of Defense release, Mar. 4, 1974, pp. 1–6, 25–66.

development programs he espoused. Rather the latter initiatives were dictated, in his judgment, by the undesirability of allowing the Soviet Union to acquire—or believe that it could acquire—a preponderant advantage in counterforce weapons, as it might expect to do with its new systems. At the same time the Secretary insisted that the United States would prefer to discourage the evolution of forces on both sides toward a counterforce emphasis. Thus the fundamental purpose of the sharp change in American policy was calculated to create, in familiar bargaining-chip terms, an improved setting for progress in the SALT negotiations.

There was a perverse quality to this line of argument. It asserted that neither side could in fact achieve a "first-strike capability," in the sense that no one could expect to have counterforce systems which were entirely effective against either the United States or the Soviet Union. It granted that under any conceivable plan of attack either country would have ample surviving forces to strike back. Yet, precisely because a successful first strike was impossible, Defense Department spokesmen concluded that counterforce capabilities were "safe" to develop. In only modest caricature, counterforce weapons could not be effective, so it was all right to build them.

This rationale suffered from several grievous flaws. It rested on an exaggerated confidence in the stability of the very balance of terror it challenged. In the Secretary's humane impulse to chart some way out of the awesome strategic stalemate in which the great powers held each other hostage, he hoped to create limited options short of all-out attacks on cities. But he acknowledged that many such options already existed with available weaponry, and he neglected the serious implications for long-term stability which his proposed innovations could have. The probability was not that either Russia or America would actually gain an effective counterforce capability to disarm its adversary, but that each country would fear the other's movement in this direction so greatly that it would take the kind of destabilizing countermeasures that would diminish the chances for agreed limitations in the short run and for a stable strategic relationship in the long run. The superficial logic of the military quest for enhanced counterforce capability could have little appeal when weighed against the political and behavioral effects it was likely to have on the contestants. Even the careful and measured expositions offered by Secretary Schlesinger badly slighted the implications of pursuing this path. If the threat of a vigorous United States counterforce program was intended to cow the Soviet Union into curtailing its troublesome R & D activities, it was a gamble of the highest magnitude.

As with so many events of 1973–1974, one speculates that the Defense Department's request to resume the hard-target MIRV program was partially a product of the creeping paralysis which afflicted other parts of the American government. The newly appointed Defense Secretary took office at a time when presidential attention to such matters had dropped to the vanishing point under the relentless demands of Watergate and when Secretary

Kissinger was giving little heed to the subject. With the weakened condition of the SALT delegation and the new head of the Arms Control and Disarmament Agency, Fred Iklé, an active ally of the Schlesinger program, there were no forces in the executive branch to array the considerations which cast doubt on the wisdom of these initiatives.

Unfortunately, the threatening behavior of the Soviet military establishment, both in its role during the Middle East war of October 1973 and in its astonishing variety of strategic developments, had altered the mood of Congress also. Attacks on détente, not as a bad goal but as a bad deal, were commonplace on the Hill by early 1974. The notorious wheat deal which sent grain to the Soviet Union with a U.S. subsidy and the numerical advantages Moscow enjoyed in the interim agreement on offensive forces had placed many congressmen on their guard, and the demand for "equality" in Soviet-American agreements resonated through the Capitol. There were spreading suspicions that the Soviet government was less interested in winding down the competitive relationship with the United States than in stealing a march on a too-eager American government. Particularly in view of the lack of progress in SALT, many legislators had come to feel that the Soviets must be convinced the United States was prepared to resume the arms race if there were no acceptable alternative. In spite of forceful arguments by Senator McIntyre and others that development of hard-target MIRV was in no way an effective response to the possible threat of Soviet MIRVs to the U.S. Minuteman force—such a program would jeopardize the Soviet deterrent without protecting our own—the House and Senate concluded that Moscow should be confronted with the likelihood of a matching counterforce program unless it agreed to abandon its own movement in that direction.

While reasserting the policy that the United States should avoid "any combination of forces that could be taken as an effort to acquire the ability to execute a first-strike disarming attack against the USSR," the Senate Armed Services Committee authorized $77 million to begin a new accuracy/yield program. It withheld a decision on deployment and underscored the value of such efforts to strengthen the U.S. negotiating posture in the lagging SALT discussions. With Chairman Stennis reversing his previous position against such technology, on June 10, 1974, the Senate defeated a McIntyre-Brooke amendement to delete the funds by a vote of 49 to 37.[14] The initial increment of funds was a trivial fraction of the $1.5 billion it would require to complete development of the new re-entry vehicle and

[14] Report of the Committee on Armed Services, U.S. Senate, *Authorizing Appropriations For Fiscal Year 1975 for Military Procurement, Research and Development, and Active Duty, Selected Reserve and Civilian Personnel Strengths, and for Other Purposes*, Report no. 93–884, May 29, 1974, pp. 20–24, and the individual views of Senators Harold Hughes and Thomas J. McIntyre, pp. 181–190; the relevant debate covers *Congressional Record*, June 10, 1974, pp. S10183–S10204.

warhead, and another $5 to $6 billion would be necessary eventually to install such payloads on the 550 Minuteman III scheduled for deployment. But a crucial corner had been turned, and congressional restraint in this area seemed to have ebbed away. The last opportunity to preclude a dangerous competition in counterforce weaponry now lay with the negotiators.

The opportunity was fleeting. The realization of that fact finally hit Secretary Kissinger with full force at the Moscow summit conference of 1974. Having failed to win the sought-for curb on MIRV deployment, the Secretary expressed unwonted urgency in declaring that the two powers were headed toward an exceedingly dangerous—and evidently useless—proliferation of nuclear warheads. Unlike the narrow military considerations which characterized some of his associates' opinions, Kissinger's perspective gave due weight to the larger political implications of the prospective competition. " . . . it is also the justifications that will have to be used in each country to sustain large armament programs that will, over a period of time, present a major obstacle to the humane or even safe conduct of foreign policy." To ward off such tendencies, the process of negotiation which he had so laboriously erected with his Soviet counterparts must do more than operate; it must produce concrete results.

At long last the shrewd diplomatist seemed to comprehend the anxieties of those in Congress who had sought to engage his and the President's concern on the MIRV issue for five years.

> If we have not reached an agreement well before 1977, then I believe you will see an explosion of technology and an explosion of numbers at the end of which we will be lucky if we have the present stability—in which it will be impossible to describe what strategic superiority means. And one of the questions which we have to ask ourselves as a country is what, in the name of God, is strategic superiority? What is the significance of it, politically, militarily, operationally, at these levels of numbers?
>
> But my prediction would be that if we do not solve this problem well before . . . the expiration of the (interim) agreement, we will be living in a world which opportunities for nuclear warfare exist that were unimaginable 15 years ago at the beginning of the nuclear age. . .[15]

Final agreement on offensive force limitations proved impossible in 1974 but in November of that year President Ford and Secretary Brezhnev met at Vladivostok to reaffirm their governments' determination to achieve a durable accord. They accepted in principle and as the basis of an agreement to be negotiated forthwith a ceiling of 2,400 for total strategic delivery systems and a sub-ceiling of 1,320 for MIRV-capable missiles. While the President stressed the value of these limits as a lid on the arms race, the specter

[15] Department of State news release, press conference by Secretary of State Henry A. Kissinger at the Intourist Hotel, U.S.S.R., Moscow, July 3, 1974, pp. 4, 10–11.

remained: Would such high ceilings contain or confirm the grim trends earlier sketched by Secretary Kissinger? The question grew more acute in January 1975 when the Soviet Union began to deploy its own MIRV systems

V. Defense Budgets and Programs: The Fruits of Congressional Competition

The scene said much. It was the spring of 1970. In the auditorium of the New Senate Office Building, Senator Marlow Cook, a first-term Republican from Kentucky, was addressing a conference on national security issues which he and a number of colleagues had sponsored. Among the participants were a bipartisan panel of dignitaries, including such notable figures as Ambassador Averill Harriman, President James Killian of M.I.T., Arthur Larson, and Hans Morgenthau. Noting that it was a rare event that brought junior legislators into active debate on complex international issues, sophisticated weapons, and other matters normally left to the executive branch, Cook said, "People often ask why we freshmen senators are trying to take on these big questions of defense and national security. And I always answer that if we freshmen don't ask those questions, we are never going to get to be sophomores."

It was an apt comment. By the late nineteen-sixties, the mood of the American Congress had shifted sharply and substantially toward a more aggressive institutional posture vis-à-vis the executive's long-standing dominance in the field of national security policy. This evolution of congressional attitude was both a cause and a consequence of a broader trend in public opinion.

Whatever the prospects for a durable change in the congressional role on strategic matters, the fact of a significant shift in the context of deliberations on national security is reflected in a number of concrete measures. In 1969, for the first time in memory, the Gallup Poll data showed that a majority of respondents considered the defense budget too high. This significant turn in public opinion, though no doubt volatile and subject to sharp reversal in the event of an increase in international tension, was a function of many months

97

of critical press reports and congressional debate over the size and efficiency of the military departments.

In one respect a fine paradox was involved. To a considerable extent the frustrations of Vietnam must surely have influenced this negative shift of public attitides regarding defense spending. Yet in fact the struggle in Southeast Asia had placed less strain on American resources and manpower than even the Korean conflict. The relatively gradual buildup of forces in Vietnam had not boosted the defense budget above 9 percent of the gross national product (compared to 13.5 percent in Korea and over 40 percent in the Second World War).[1] Even the inflation it had sparked was milder than the spurt in prices of the early 1950s. Thus the United States found itself growing more critical of defense spending at the very moment when its economic capacity could most easily accommodate the added strain of a limited war. One is drawn to the conclusion that latent forces of long standing and of larger dimensions than economics alone—or even Vietnam—were shaping new social inclinations on defense issues.

To assess the altered context of legislative-executive relations in this field, two key criteria commend themselves. How has the institutional balance of power shifted between Congress and the President in the field of national security? And what has been the quality of the particular policy outcomes which have occurred in the altered context? In other words, is the perception of a growing congressional assertiveness in these matters valid or chimerical, and what have been the effects of this growing assertiveness on policy-making in this vital area?

One may characterize the recent transformation of the congressional role in national security policy by noting shifts along several continua. Congress has moved—and forced the entire government to move—from a relatively closed to a relatively open process in addressing these issues. Congress has shifted from a relatively prodefense attitude to a relatively negative and skeptical posture; nourished by competing demands for resources, the impulse for thrift has begun to reassert itself after a long period of openhandedness on defense budgets. And Congress has turned from a relatively deferential stance toward executive leadership in national security to a determined effort to get into the act itself, grasping for handles that work effectively in steering executive conduct of defense programs.

Until the late nineteen-sixties, national security was the virtual monopoly of an almost hermetically sealed community in Congress, no less than in the executive. To be sure, there was often quite sophisticated interplay among the small number of players in the closed game of legislating for defense in the key committees. Arnold Kanter has shown that there was frequently

---

[1] See Charles L. Schultze et al., *Setting National Priorities; The 1971 Budget* (Washington: Brookings, 1970), pp. 17–53; see also Department of Defense (Comptroller), *The Economics of Defense Spending: A Look at the Realities,* 1972, especially table 1–1, p. 3, and table 5–1, p. 30.

quite precise guidance developed within those committees, involving significant adjustments of defense budgets and program objectives.[2] But given the fact that these insulated proceedings had little ventilation in other sectors of Congress and the public, it is exceedingly difficult even now to judge how well the Armed Services and Defense Appropriations subcommittees were performing in previous years. Was the executive branch truly responsive to committee direction, as many participants warrant, or did the Defense Department and other presidential associates "snow" the committee on the decisive questions, while encouraging committee members to maintain the illusion of power? For example, in fiscal 1961 the House Appropriations Committee, concerned to enhance the mobility of forces in being, created a new budget item for "airlift modernization." In view of the strong interest in mobility evinced by the Defense Department during this period, one wonders whether the committee's action was basically its own initiative or a result elicited by executive officials who wished to move in that direction anyway. And certainly the dominant congressional instinct to go forward with the B-70 and to retain a larger strategic bomber fleet failed of success. Bitter experience provokes at least the suspicion that executive leaders might have blurred and evaded a fair fraction of the guidance provided by the committees. This tendency would have been facilitated by broad departmental authority to reprogram defense funds and by the general lack of criticism of the committees by their peers in Congress.

Paradoxically, as the spiraling costs of defense programs and the descending gloom of the Vietnam imbroglio bred a loss of confidence in executive decision-making for national security, they made Congress less sensitive to its own lack of confidence in addressing these policy questions. Especially, though not exclusively, in this field, the legislature has had an institutional inferiority complex of long standing. By the Nixon years, however, the country's sense of poor presidential performance in national security persuaded many congressmen that they could hardly do worse. There emerged a growing bloc of legislators of both parties who concluded that the risks of congressional incompetence in these domains were scarcely greater than the realities of executive incompetence. Indeed, the perception finally prevailed in the Capitol that only by accepting the risks of a larger congressional role could there be any sustained hope of diminishing the dangers of executive failures on security issues.

In this evolving view were buried a number of valid insights—insights which should have been habitual to a nation schooled in the doctrines of federalism, checks and balances, and the separation of powers. First of all, the hazards of bureaucratic politics are no less grave than those of legislative politics, and they lack the corrective features of open political deliberations. And those hazards are likely to be more, not less serious in the national

<hr />

[2] Kanter, "Congress and the Defense Budget, 1960–1970."

security field than in other areas where Congress is accustomed to challenging the relatively closed decision-making system of the bureaucracy. In truth, reflection would have suggested that Congress itself, by allowing its treatment of national security questions to fall into the more insulated model of the executive—tightly held information in groups rarely exposed to independent scrutiny by colleagues—had acquired a certain infection which joined the defects of the legislature with those of the executive. Instead of compensating strengths the nation was exposed to reinforcing weaknesses.

Second, the mystique of military technology lost its hold as its inadequacy to provide dependable security became apparent. The old congressional saw that the expert should be on tap but not on top—long honored in the breach by the exaggerated deference Congress paid to defense professionals—came once more to guide the attitudes of many members. A therapeutic revelation spread into many corners of the Capitol, namely, that the central issues of national security policy really were political and strategic, not technical. This perception demanded of conscientious congressmen a more energetic effort to grasp and shape policy in the inhibiting milieu of nuclear strategy, force posture, and weapons procurement.

Related to and confirming Congress's newfound appreciation of the fundamentally political character of national security decisions was a lasting lesson of the prolonged debates over Vietnam and the ABM system and similar disputes. Congress came to see that the so-called "requirements of national security" are enormously elastic. There is a vital role for systematic and technical analysis of the elements of such requirements, but in the end judgments must be rendered, preferences must be expressed, and the dominant values clearly transcend the narrow range of quantifiable factors which bear on national security. As the knowledge of this elasticity of security planning dawned on more members, Congress began to grope for ways to elevate its consideration of defense budgets and programs to a level at which they could be weighed against competitive needs in nondefense areas. By and large, legislative decisions on defense issues would remain compartmentalized, but there was now at least an implicit understanding that the familiar concept of trade-offs within the defense field had much wider application and, indeed, that at some level Congress had the responsibility to assess the claims of security against those of other valid programs.

One of the lingering concerns of some observers was whether Congress could couple its wholesome new perspectives on security policy with a judicious use of the systematic analyses which had come to contribute so much to sound decision-making. There was a danger that once Congress came to construe such issues as essentially political, its members would develop a cavalier disregard for hard data and careful studies to support policy. Generally speaking, the fear seemed overblown, for the most active congressmen were making special attempts to incorporate scrupulous technical analyses in their own political rationales. The fresh skepticism toward resolving national security issues primarily on technical grounds did not constitute an anti-intellectual reaction, but a prudent quest to orchestrate all the elements necessary to rational policy.

JOHN STENNIS: CONSERVATIVE INNOVATOR

In the fluid context of national security policy, there have lately been a number of significant events and innovations in congressional treatment of defense issues. The discussion here will concentrate on the Senate, where new departures have markedly surpassed those of the House, bound as it is to procedures which have given its Armed Services Committee a virtual stranglehold on these issues.[3]

Where in the earlier years of the Cold War the defense budget normally sped through Congress with little fanfare and less scrutiny in committee or on the floor, in 1969 and 1970 review of the defense program consumed many months in committee and many weeks in Senate floor debate. Scarcely any roll-call votes occurred on the defense bills of the early sixties; by the end of the decade numerous amendments calling for reductions or redirections of defense funds became the focal points for intense Senate debate and action. In considering the fiscal 1971 defense procurement authorization, Senators proposed no fewer than forty-seven amendments to the committee bill. While the more far-reaching modifications were rejected, notably restrictions on deployment of the anti-ballistic missile system, an across-the-board budget cut, and a proposed timetable for withdrawal from Vietnam, fully a dozen amendments were approved, including some of major consequence.

It is important to weigh the outcome in the full Senate with an appreciation of the altered stance and intensified labors of the Armed Services Committee itself. The fact that the more drastic floor amendments were defeated is no indication that promilitary sympathies are maintaining an easy sway in the Senate as a whole. It reflects, rather, the enhanced credibility which the committee has begun to establish in recent years. Whatever the accuracy of the rubberstamp image which the committee had previously acquired through regular acceptance of executive recommendations, the rise of John Stennis to the chairmanship in early 1971 and the influx of several new members to the committee coincided with a determined campaign to demonstrate its capacity to fulfill its responsibilities for overseeing the Defense Department. In a brisk exchange with Senator J. William Fulbright during his first year as chairman, Senator Stennis elicited a direct apology from his

[3] Among the crucial factors accounting for the House committee's monopoly position is the sheer difficulty under that chamber's rules of challenging any committee within its proper jurisdiction. With so large a membership, floor action there provides much less opportunity for interested members from other committees to develop substantive issues and amendments.

Foreign Relations Committee counterpart for a comment suggesting that the Armed Services Committee and its senior member had become puppet-like spokesmen for Pentagon interests. Chairman Stennis was acutely sensitive to such aspersions. From his first months as head of the committee he had undertaken a series of steps to make clear his independence and his conscientious performance as an agent of the Senate.

In an unprecedented move to provide more detailed evaluation of the defense procurement proposals, Stennis established a number of subcommittees to deal with separate elements of the budget. The full committee had itself customarily reviewed annual defense bills, but its work has been supplemented by the efforts of subcommittees on Research and Development, on Tactical Air Power, and in related areas. To expedite the flow of business, a number of joint hearings have been held with the Senate Appropriations Committee, including some of the principal explorations of the ABM issue. And a rare instance of bicameral cooperation between separate committees was the Senate-House Subcommittee on CVAN-70, a controversial nuclear aircraft carrier.[4] As noted previously, the committee has staked out a clear claim to jurisdiction in an area which it had previously entered only on occasion by creating a Subcommittee on the Strategic Arms Limitation Talks, charged with a responsibility for monitoring the SALT negotiations between the United States and the Soviet Union.

A quarter century in the Senate had seen John Stennis follow closely in the path marked out by his Georgia colleague, Richard Russell. As Russell's health faded after 1968, Stennis had assumed interim leadership of the committee, although his strict sense of protocol and his special respect for the ailing chairman dissuaded him from undertaking major innovations during those months. Both he and Russell were appalled at the deadly stalemate in Southeast Asia, although even as late as 1968 Stennis seemed particularly inclined to the notion that unleashing the Air Force would produce decisive results there. Despite the high esteem in which his colleagues held him, Stennis' prior committee work did not adequately fortell the distinctive qualities of his subsequent chairmanship.

Stennis had often displayed a flair for probing certain defense questions—strategic force posture, the effectiveness of air power in limited war, the readiness of NATO forces—during his years as chairman of the Preparedness Investigating Subcommittee, a position he retained on elevation to full committee leadership. That subcommittee has grown relatively dormant, although its staff members have been drawn into service of the parent committee. At the same time the committee has added several professional staff assistants, some with many years experience in defense budgeting, and has made full-time use of other personnel on loan from the General Ac-

[4] Hearing before the Joint Senate-House Armed Services Subcommittee, *CVAN-70 Aircraft Carrier*, 91st Cong., 2d Sess., April 1970.

counting Office. The committee has responded to costly overruns on various weapon systems by instigating regular reporting procedures by the Defense Department and the GAO on the cost history, performance, and project cost growth of some thirty selected weapons projects. Closer inspection of defense requests and operations has become the order of the day. While the task far exceeds the committee's capabilities to penetrate such mammoth budgets and programs, it is clear that serious initiatives have been taken to improve the committee's efforts. Still lacking, however, is any substantial committee staff with professional competence in systems analysis or strategic issues. The committee's focus remains primarily on the narrower questions of budget and management, with too little examination of strategic alternatives, or of the comparative desirability of particular weapons for particular strategies. Some members have begun to show stronger interest in these higher-level issues, and it may be expected that executive policies in this field will attract closer attention in coming years.

One can appreciate these changes best perhaps by noting another alteration in committee staffing patterns. Under previous chairmen there had developed a consistent practice of using executive personnel on loan to support the committee's deliberations. These people were usually active-duty military personnel who would return to their uniformed careers after a stint of two or three years on the Hill. Even in an era of maximum confidence between the branches such arrangements represented a transparent subversion of constitutional doctrines; it was an elementary case of the "watchmen watching themselves." John Stennis terminated the procedures and moved to insure that the committee's staff would be strong enough to protect the Senate's independence in any dealings with executive branch personnel.

By 1972 the chairman was also making a cautious start on employing outside staff assistance on a temporary and contractual basis. In particular the committee began a modest program of consulting with senior staff of organizations like the Brookings Institution on specific issues where the committee's own expertise proved limited or the private organizations had special talents. The eventual shape of these relationships was not clear, particularly given the committee's extreme sense of the privileged nature of its business. But it does appear that the chairman and his senior staff have made sensible decisions to draw in additional consultants on well-defined areas of concern. For example, work by Brookings professionals has been quite valuable to the committee in gaining a fuller understanding of a number of manpower questions, including the serious distortions in support costs for a shrinking military establishment. Nor have the consultants been limited to "safe" and noncontroversial questions. They have addressed such crucial problems as the proposed acceleration of the Trident submarine program, helping the committee to identify options which could provide maximum deterrent capability without a premature commitment to construction of a poorly defined and vastly expensive new strategic system. The promise of such embryonic associations with independent analysts is that the committee may develop a greater confidence in its capacity to manage such contractual studies. If so, such arrangements could augment the committee's own resources in a highly potent fashion, bringing to bear in support of the Senate an untapped array of private intellectual capabilities.

The marked changes in committee structure, staffing, and procedure are not mere cosmetics. A great deal of work has devolved upon the subcommittees, and solid results have been accomplished in the last few years, in terms of both the short-run objective of paring fat from the budget and the long-run goal of maintaining consistent legislative control over the DOD. Progress toward the latter goal remains problematic, but its importance has been recognized and the committee seems to have accepted this challenge as vital to its own policy role and to its institutional standing in the Congress.

For the present, while many shared perspectives and close personal ties sustain a common interest between some committee members and senior officials of the defense establishment, the committee's rejuvenation has fostered a healthy degree of tension between the legislators and the executive authorities. The Department of Defense is less prone to take the committee's sympathies for granted and has grown more diligent in preparing its case. While specific results are not easy to identify, it is reasonable to believe that the anticipation of thorough congressional critiques has prompted the Defense Department, together with such other responsible agencies as the Office of Management and Budget, to adopt more stringent management controls and to curtail many of its excesses.

Carl Friedrich's "law of anticipatory response" is very much at work here, and in it may lie the best hope for maximum congressional impact in defense decision-making. When a bureaucracy knows that its plans will undergo close, albeit selective, study by a knowledgeable legislative committee, it has a strong incentive to insure that all its recommendations are justified. This is the process on which Congress must necessarily rely in supervising the complex activities and organization of the federal government. By constant probing of a relatively small number of problem areas, it seeks to induce improved executive performance across the entire spectrum of programs and administration.[5] Such a pattern has been quite visible lately in relations between the Armed Services Committee and the Defense Department. It would be naive to say that all is now well in this regard, but simple fairness obliges one to acknowledge that the system is certainly working better than before.

[5] This was the implicit theory of the original decisions by the Armed Services committees to begin detailed authorizations of procurement and research and development funds. See Raymond H. Dawson, "Congressional Innovation and Intervention in Defense Policy: Legislative Authorization of Weapons Systems," *American Political Science Review,* vol. 56, March 1962, pp. 42–57. I have developed this point more completely in "Gobble'uns' and Foreign Policy: A Review," *Journal of Conflict Resolution,* vol. 8, September 1964, pp. 314–321.

The unwonted vigor of the Armed Services Committee is a product of many influences. Whatever instincts John Stennis may have had to energize the committee, they were undoubtedly reinforced by the fact that he inherited the chair at a moment when the committee, no less than the Pentagon itself, was beleaguered by critics. Until the late nineteen-sixties, potential interlopers in Congress and elsewhere were fended off by the barriers of classified information, technical complexity, and jurisdictional prerogatives. Apart from the Armed Services committees, only the Joint Committee on Atomic Energy and the Appropriations committees of the two houses had gained significant footholds in this field. On occasion the House Committee on Science and Astronautics and the Senate Committee on Aeronautical and Space Sciences had dabbled in questions of military space activities and the potential threat emerging from the Soviet Union's space program. The Government Operations committees of the House and Senate had established subcommittees dealing with some issues of national security, but these bodies' substantial efforts had not generated direct assaults on the defense budget or specific weapon systems.[6]

By the late nineteen-sixties, however, additional voices were being heard. The Joint Economic Committee, bound by its charter to a nonlegislative role but bolstered by a potent reputation, had spawned a Subcommittee on Priorities and Economy in Government, which came to devote many studies to dubious practices, waste, and management problems in military procurement. This group, chaired by Senator William Proxmire, generated much of the public discussion of contract difficulties and cost overruns on such programs as the C-5 aircraft. It also created heightened interest in the broader economic implications of defense procurement, highlighting the diversion of manpower to nonproductive military programs and the adverse effects of a large defense budget on the nation's economic growth.[7] The Joint Economic Committee has been a forceful advocate of spending ceilings for defense, and a sharp critic of Defense Department claims to have brought expenditures under control. The committee has been equally severe on the Council of Economic Advisors for failing to perform more comprehensive analyses of the effects of defense spending on prices, production, and employment.

On the House side, a Foreign Affairs Subcommittee on National Security Policy and Scientific Developments has carved out a position of prominence

---

[6] The fragmentation of congressional treatment of national security compounded the difficulties posed by secrecy and complexity. Of interest is Holbert N. Carroll, "The Congress and National Security Policy," in David B. Truman (ed.), *The Congress and America's Future* (Englewood Cliffs, N.J.: Prentice-Hall, 1965), pp. 150–176.

[7] Typical is the thoughtful assessment in the 1973 Joint Economic Report of the Joint Economic Committee on the January 1973 Economic Report of the President, 93d Cong., 1st, Sess., House Report no. 93–90, Mar. 26, 1973, pp. 65–71. Also see the committee's valuable hearings, *The Economics of Defense Procurement,* 90th Cong., 2d Sess., part 1, November 1968 and January 1969, and part 2, November 1968.

through a series of productive investigations on issues of strategy, arms control, and technology. Under Chairman Clement Zablocki, this group has become a steady source of studious legislative examinations of the political-military issues which previously suffered almost total neglect in the lower house.[8] It has been the principal overseer of the turbulent recent experience of the Arms Control and Disarmament Agency, and has consistently supported retention of a strong and independent role for ACDA in national security planning.

The most influential new presence has been the Senate Foreign Relations Committee. From its extensive background in disarmament and arms control issues, the committee has come to deal regularly with diverse issues of strategic stability, nuclear weapons, and other aspects of national security. At the cost of jurisdictional friction with the Armed Services Committee, former Chairman Fulbright and his colleagues have helped to stimulate fuller congressional study of national security problems. Conducting many hearings of its own on the ABM and other strategic topics, the Foreign Relations Committee has obliged the Armed Services Committee to hold open hearings on issues which were considered only behind closed doors in the past. This has troubled those who feel that the United States was already too prone to discuss sensitive information in public, but it has without a doubt improved the quality and volume of information on which most congressmen and their constituents have relied in forming judgments in this area.

Unquestionably, the general opening up of the closed forums in which national security policy is usually shaped has been a pivotal factor in increasing the Defense Department's responsiveness to congressional pressure. The publication of relevant hearings and reports has made it possible for knowledgeable commentators—former government officials, academic experts, and scientists—to engage in more meaningful public dialogue on a host of questions usually obscured by secrecy. Indeed, one of the most interesting phenomena related to Congress's quest for a greater role is the emergence of a pool of outside experts, men schooled in the defense establishment, who are now prepared to serve as counselors to individual members and committees of Congress. The executive still commands almost overpowering expertise, but congressmen and senators of a critical bent can now enlist creditable professional advice to support their efforts.

For many years defense and foreign policy experts have too often favored the maintenance of special ties to the executive, "where the action is," and have been disinclined to volunteer assistance to Congress. The situation is now radically different, and prominent professionals long affiliated with the executive are tendering their advice quite readily to the Congress. Part of

---

[8] An excellent example is the subcommittee's hearings, *Chemical-Biological Warfare: U. S. Policies and International Effects*, 91st Cong., 1st Sess. The committee report appeared under that title on May 16, 1970.

this trend has the appearance of a government in exile, with members of past Democratic administrations channeling their efforts through a legislature presumably more sympathetic than an Administration of the opposite party. But this is hardly the dominant feature of a tendency which goes far beyond considerations of partisan politics or personal advancement. It seems that this development is part of the larger pattern of rising concern throughout society over issues of national security and the rejuvenation of Congress.

The advisory process is taking many forms and routes, from privately sponsored defense policy seminars for senators, congressmen, and key staff members to informal but influential relationships between expert advisers and individual congressmen. While one must rely on impressions more than any comprehensive data, there appears to be an unprecedented and proliferating network of private advisers who are assisting members of Congress on these questions. There is no reliable measure of their influence, but one is safe in assuming that a senator who might shy away from a complex technical or strategic issue will be more prepared to tackle it if he gains the intellectual confidence which comes from having and comprehending the advice of a former Presidential Science Advisor or a former Director of Defense Research and Engineering. This budding network is of obvious importance and has done much to catalyze the hyperactivity Congress has lately exhibited.

Indeed some "outsiders" have organized themselves for the precise purpose of bringing expert counsel to bear on Congress. The Council for a Livable World, the Federation of American Scientists (FAS), and others have launched what promises to be a continuing program of lobbying *pro bono publico,* bringing together distinguished scientists and members of Congress to exchange views on such questions as the arms race and environmental problems.[9] More narrowly focused, single-issue groups like Business Executives Move for Peace have served as bridges between leading private critics of U.S. policy in Vietnam and many senators. Such groups strengthen their message by enlisting the talents and prestige of senior ex-military officers, diplomats, and scholars. A new Center for Defense Information has come into operation under the direction of a former Navy admiral, Gene LeRocque; it has provided services to a number of congressmen seeking independent critiques of defense proposals. The center's publication, *Defense Monitor,* is frequently employed as fodder for floor debates.

Congress has always known lobbying, but the current invasion of national security expertise is a novel and generally wholesome development. I say this

[9] The monthly newsletter of the Federation of American Scientists, the work of its director, Dr. Jeremy Stone, is a consistent source of authoritative information and advice to legislators seeking new and worthwhile issues in this area. Dr. Stone has rejuvenated the aging FAS and transformed it into a widely respected voice of science in the halls of Congress. It mobilizes witnesses and studies in many fields at the nexus of technology and public policy.

in spite of the suspicion some have voiced that what we are witnessing is an "end run" around the legitimate domain of the executive branch by ex-officials or frustrated executive advisers who are attempting to manipulate the Congress to maintain their sway over policy. Even if this were true, and the idea must be disputed, it is difficult for anyone dedicated to rational public policy to suggest that Congress should be deprived of knowledgeable counsel on which to base its action. It is evident that such counsel increases the tendency of Congress to engage in tough-minded exchanges with executive officials. But the objective is or ought to be sound national policy, and the effort is worthwhile so long as it avoids the self-serving or aimless sniping which sometimes results. And executive prerogatives are scarcely in peril so long as the President and his men retain ample opportunity, not to mention preponderant resources, to explicate their policy and rebut criticisms in Congress and in the media.

One should note another network which has developed within the Congress itself. This is the bipartisan and bicameral group known as Members of Congress for Peace through Law. With more than a hundred members of Congress participating, this organization has taken as one of its continuing interests an evaluation of the defense budget. It has no formal standing in Congress and its direct impact has so far been modest, but MCPL has produced some commendable studies and has provided an embryonic link among many like-minded members of Congress who see a reduced defense budget as a prerequisite to reordering national priorities. The group has built a modest staff and has considerable potential for the future, having already established itself as something of an independent check on the performance of the official authorizing committees. Again, the awareness that MCPL and others are conducting their analyses is an encouragement to the standing committees to do a more thorough job. In 1971, for example, MCPL offered a thorough critique of proposals for a new strategic bomber system which contributed to the subsequent close scrutiny of the B-1 system in the Senate Armed Services Committee.

There is an irony in the fact that present efforts to strengthen the role of Congress in national security matters should involve a multiplication of the actors concerned with these problems, for congressional effectiveness has often been the casualty of decentralization. The proliferation of committees and groups shouldering their way into position to shape legislative initiatives on defense and foreign policy mirrors the fragmentation which was thought to have enervated such efforts. Yet this added fragmentation is in fact a very different phenomenon from that which has prevailed. In the past relatively neat jurisdictions were defined for the major committees, principally Armed Services and Foreign Relations. This was true in spite of the admitted fact that such divided authority largely denied Congress a coherent approach to national security policy, combining as it does elements of diplomacy, strategy, technology, weapons, military forces, and the like. Historically, this serious liability of the committee system has been too easily tolerated, but the new competition for influence on national security policy is forcing a number of committees and individual members to seek the broader, integrated perspectives which these issues require. It will be a difficult task to sustain this constructive pressure through such diverse means, but there seems little chance for modifying the committee system itself, e. g., by establishing a Joint Committee on National Security Policy, however sensible that option might be. Any thought of merging the Foreign Relations and Armed Services committees is too improbable for serious discussion. Reform proposals in the House have lately sought to enhance the powers of the Foreign Affairs Committee, but at the expense of Ways and Means, not of Armed Services.

Several considerations argue that the embryonic pattern of intercommittee rivalry and individual interloping, if it does not succumb to a revived and exaggerated sense of senatorial comity, will produce some distinctive benefits. Since so many groups have now staked out a claim in this area, precedent and the reluctance to abandon a position of power mean that Congress will be conducting multiple probes of security questions from a variety of vantage points. The duplication of effort is in some respects regrettable, especially in the drain on the energies of top-level executives who are called to testify, but the economy of policy-making is far less important than the quality and integrity of policy. Nothing in the concept of checks and balances says that we must content ourselves with double checks; on occasion, triple, quadruple, and quintuple checks may be in order.

Not only does this competitive environment help energize the executive and the committees with primary leverage over defense and foreign policy, it also lays the basis for wider coalitions within the House and Senate as a whole. This manifold process tends to expose lines of tentative agreement among members whose values and purposes may be quite different. The current intense scrutiny of defense budgets and programs flows from many sources—from those who are principally concerned about the enormous expense of modern weaponry, from those whose disillusionment with all things military stems from the war in Vietnam, from those who are preoccupied with the essential quest for arms control and strategic stability, from those who see cuts in military spending as the path to new priorities for domestic development.

These concerns commingle in most senators, with one or another dominating in particular cases. Even though their votes may rarely coincide, a William Proxmire whose work on defense procurement serves his interest in freeing funds for domestic uses has something in common with a John Stennis who muses, "When I first came here, you could get a pretty good submarine for $20 million; now you can't even think of one for less than $200 million." As these overlapping interests begin to surface, the static and predictable divisions of opinion on issues of national security erode, and more fluid alliances arise on individual issues.

These, then, are some of the observable changes in the congressional context of defense policy. Are there also observable changes in the results the system is producing in the policy output? There most decidedly are. While disputes over the ABM have symbolized the new mood in Congress, they have overshadowed substantial achievements in other areas. A number of illustrations may be drawn.

Few people yet realize how wide a swing in defense spending has been engineered. If one takes account of inflation by using 1973 dollars, the budget effectively dropped $34 billion from $112.7 billion in 1969 to $78.3 billion in fiscal 1973, before rising military pay scales wiped out the expected "Vietnam dividend." In current dollars the budget grew to a $92.6 billion request for 1975, but defense consumed less in real terms than in 1973. Defense expenditures in fiscal year 1975 dropped to about 29 percent of the federal budget and little more than 6 percent of the gross national product. As another measure of the sharp reallocation of funds from the national security sector, over a million and a half defense jobs have been eliminated since early 1969, closely paralleling the jump in total unemployment during the first Nixon term. Defense bore the brunt of the anti-inflation expenditure control program in the final phases of disengagement from Vietnam. Large numbers of workers were obliged to shift to different enterprises.

The executive branch accomplished most of these cuts, motivated both by its estimates of desirable spending levels and by its awareness that failure to reduce the budget would invite wholesale congressional attacks on its proposals. In addition the Congress regularly pruned the defense budget still further in 1969 and thereafter, notwithstanding the Department's plaint that its proposals were "bareboned." In the years 1968 to 1973 congressional appropriations for defense totaled some $22 billion less than Administration requests. For fiscal 1973, for instance, Congress reduced projected expenditures by $5.2 billion. This compares with the experience of the preceding decade, when appropriations actually exceeded requests in eight years.

The throttling down of defense appropriations has accompanied sharp shifts in the behavior of the two houses of Congress toward these questions. For most of the years from 1950 to 1968, the Senate, rather than the House, was the prime mover in increasing the level of funding. Under the long term of Chairman Clarence Cannon, the House Appropriations Committee inclined to more stringent controls on the defense budget than did its Senate counterpart. In recent years, however, the upper chamber has been the more reluctant to underwrite these enormous budgets. A major reason has been the general alignment in support of greater economy of both the Armed Services and the Appropriations committees in the Senate, as Senator Stennis has been allied with the successive chairmen of the Appropriations body, Allen Ellender and John McClellan. On the House side, Appropriations Chairman George Mahon has found himself somewhat more closely attuned to the views of Stennis and McClellan than to the continued inclinations of the House Armed Services Committee to be relatively less restrictive on the

Department's desired activities. These trends have been partially obscured by the sheer scale of the mammoth budget, which by 1973 reached the status, even with major reductions, of the largest single appropriations bill in history. Congressman Mahon took note of that fact when he presented the measure to the House on September 13, 1972; he highlighted the substantial changes Congress had wrought in the budget plan and cited "huge blunders in the management of Defense dollars over a long period of years."

It is an impressive fact that reductions of this magnitude began to occur while the United States was still engaged in a hot war. One finds, however, a certain parallel with the latter stages of the Korean war experience, when the legislature also turned down many elements of the Truman and Eisenhower defense programs.[10] Recalling the drastic demobilization after the Second World War, it is hard to discern whether impatience with high defense spending is greater in victory or in stalemate.

One of the most startling indicators of Congress's new disposition to treat the defense budget with the critical eye once reserved for nonsecurity expenditures came in fiscal 1975. Not only was the administration's request for appropriations trimmed $4.5 billion to a level of $82.6 billion, but the committees seemed relatively impervious to department protests. In real terms the budget trend continued downward and Senate Appropriations Chairman John McClellan signaled strongly that Congress would be resistant to attempts to recoup the cuts through the familiar device of supplemental appropriations proposals. The grave economic dislocations afflicting the United States persuaded the Appropriations Committees that, despite their concern over growing Soviet capabilities, it was necessary to keep a tight lid on increases in allocations for defense.

Equally significant is the fact that many of these cuts have reflected concrete decisions regarding specific weapons systems, rather than generalized reductions permitting virtually all Department of Defense programs to go forward but at a reduced rate. During 1969 skeptical congressional reviews of the much-delayed Manned Orbiting Laboratory contributed to that program's cancellation and long-term savings in excess of $1 billion. Similarly, congressional pressures obliged the Air Force to cut back on the proposed buy of C-5A planes and to revise substantially its plans for a large number of F-111 fighter-bombers. In considering the fiscal 1971 budget the Senate committee broke a notorious record of never having rejected a major weapons system; it denied funds for the Cheyenne helicopter system, a technologically promising but expensive program which overlapped the so-called AX tactical support aircraft. Modest funding for completing Cheyenne development was restored in conference, but the production contract

---

[10] For convenient comparison see *Congressional Quarterly Almanac*, vol. 27, 1972, "Defense Budgets and Appropriations, Fiscal Years 1950 to 1973," p. 802. Also of interest is the previously cited Defense Department analysis, *The Economics of Defense Spending*, pp. 190–193.

was canceled and the program soon died. The so-called Sea Control Ships, a pet project of former Chief of Naval Operations Elmo Zumwalt, did not survive congressional adjustments in the 1975 budget. For a time the Stennis committee also ruled out advance funding for a new nuclear aircraft carrier, pending further executive and legislative studies on future fleet requirements for such ships. Eventually and with a reluctance commensurate to the billion-dollar price tag placed on a modern nuclear carrier, the Senate committee did endorse the more extensive rationale for the vessel which the Administration formulated, and the two houses provided funds to start the ship in the fiscal 1973 budget.

Under pressure from other Senate sources, the committee has launched other innovations as well. Closer controls have been approved over so-called "independent research and development" by defense firms, a budget activity which has come to absorb several hundred million dollars annually. The committee has made a modest start on dealing with the severe problem of converting defense research capabilities to nondefense purposes. Chairman Thomas McIntyre of the Research and Development Subcommittee, a moderate of rising stature, easily won Senate agreement to a suggestion that the Budget Bureau seek to add $100 million to the fiscal 1972 National Science Foundation budget in order to support worthwhile research efforts being phased out of the Defense Department's programs. Senate concern about conversion of military R & D capabilities to nondefense uses helped stimulate the recent major expansions of the National Science Foundation budget. McIntyre has also authored important limitations on U.S. chemical warfare programs, including a detailed study of the use and ecological effects of herbicides in Southeast Asia.

The contrast between the House and Senate Armed Services committees was apparent in the two bodies' reactions to a special Administration request to accelerate or undertake certain programs in the aftermath of the strategic arms agreements of 1972. With no serious debate the House body authorized all the requests.

One dissident member of the House committee, Michael Harrington, was so exasperated that he denounced his colleagues' inquiry as "trivial" and scolded them for becoming not a "watchdog" but a "lapdog" of the executive. Not so the Senate committee, in spite of its pronounced desire to lend support to the President at a moment of substantial achievement in arms control. Examining the research and development proposals, Senators Stennis and McIntyre found inadequate justification for a submarine-launched cruise missile and other ventures. The senators persuaded the House conferees to cut the requested $110 million for the "SALT add-ons," i. e, programs added as a consequence of the SALT agreements, to $60 million. More important than the dollar amounts here was the discrimination between stabilizing and destabilizing technologies, a discrimination which the executive had failed to make. By a close vote the Senate committee permitted the speedup of the

Trident submarine program and the B-1 bomber system, the latter of which it had repeatedly cut back, but by 1973 the senators had come to cast a doubtful eye on the pace and management of both efforts. In these cases and in others—the DD-963 destroyer system, the F-14 and the F-15 aircraft, the Main Battle Tank—Senator Stennis and his colleagues led the way in guarding against the military habit of "gold-plating" new weapons, loading all manner of desirable but not essential features on a system with a resultant escalation of cost and decrease in reliability.

The concern over exorbitant cost growth and declining system reliability was, of course, shared by the responsible officials of the executive, but their determination to correct the problem was certainly enhanced by the focus Congress has come to place on the matter. Pursuant to committee requirements, the General Accounting Office spurred these concerns by a series of reports showing that by early 1974 the costs of fifty-five major weapons programs had exceeded their original estimates by 23 percent, or some $26.3 billion. The percentage increases were even higher in cases like the DD-963 destroyer, whose projected costs soared 70 percent. The cost of a single B-1 bomber reached the incredible figure of $76.4 million. And system performance actually dropped in several instances. Inflation severely compounded this problem in later months, with cost projections for a group of key weapons soaring $16 billion in a single quarter of 1974, forcing the Department to curtail its procurement plans for numerous systems. These disturbing figures moved the House, as well as the Senate, to hold hearings on these disastrous trends. With this kind of regular monitoring procedure, there is little reason to expect that the Pentagon's budget behavior will fall back under a shroud of relative neglect on the part of Congress.

Among the several committees involved in overseeing the defense establishment, one observes that each body generates its own favored issues. The House bodies, especially the Appropriations Committee under George Mahon, have paid particular attention to a number of institutional and manpower aspects of the military services. They have resisted "grade creep," the evident increase in the average numbers of officers in the several ranks. While acknowledging that the greater complexity of modern operations might justify some expansion and upgrading of the officer corps, in 1972 the committee imposed fiscal discipline on the services to curb the rampant growth of personnel in the higher grades. It pointed to the Army as a special problem; with 130,000 fewer total personnel than a decade before, the army had 600 more colonels and 2,000 more majors. The Mahon committee also called for more use of civilians in appropriate jobs, emphasizing in its report that uniformed personnel ought to be "out from behind desks and back in aircraft, ships and troop units."

While the Senate committees took some interest in similar matters, a kind of de facto division of labor has evolved, with the Senate giving noticeably greater attention to issues of high policy than to questions of the maintenance and management of the military institution. During Senator Stennis's prolonged absence from the chamber, following the armed assault by hoodlums who almost took his life in early 1973, Senator Stuart Symington took over as acting chairman and led the committee into a number of new inquiries. Investigation of unauthorized bombings in Indochina convinced him and other members of the committee, including the absent chairman, that the executive had consciously misinformed the Congress in order to disguise its activities in Southeast Asia. Discovery of operational misconduct in Cambodia in 1969–1970, surpassing even the unauthorized strikes into North Vietnam which had cost Air Force General John Lavelle his job in 1972, planted a durable suspicion in the committee and dislodged most of the vestiges of the former willingness to grant the executive branch virtual carte blanche in the use of force. Deception is a potent cure for deference.

Similar skepticism flowed from inquiry into the Central Intelligence Agency, concerning which Symington chaired the first open hearings in history. Partly because of anxiety stemming from involvement of the Agency in domestic activities connected with the Watergate affair, the long-dormant joint subcommittee of the Senate Appropriations and Armed Services committees came alive and began to probe what was almost the last sanctuary of the national security establishment. From his hospital room, Chairman Stennis called for new legislation to guarantee that the Agency respected its limited charter; he had in mind both the menace of domestic intelligence activities by the CIA and the dangers of operational involvement in military imbroglios abroad. Much the same process occurred in the lower chamber, where Congressman Lucien Nedzi had become an energetic chairman of the Armed Services Subcommittee on the CIA. The work of Nedzi, together with Congressmen Otis Pike, William Whitehurst, and others who have emerged under the more congenial rein of Chairman F. Edward Hebert, gave promise that the House committee would also assume a more active posture. For the first time in history, the House committee has now begun to invite outside witnesses to testify on the defense program and, though initially pro forma, such procedures may well alter the climate of the opinion within that body. The House committee has already become the base for Congressman Les Aspin, one of the most astute and persistent critics of defense programs and budgets ever to serve in Congress.

To support the efforts of committees and members in both houses, there have been several efforts recently to engage the General Accounting Office in analysis of far-reaching policy issues, including particularly evaluation of weapons systems. Beginning in 1969 Senators Clifford Case and Walter Mondale sought the Office's assistance for analysis of proposed additions to the nuclear-powered carrier fleet; they posed a number of quite specific but extremely complex questions on the need for a new ship and the desirable level of the carrier fleet, on the relative economic and operational advantages of land-based versus sea-based tactical air power, and other factors which properly bear on the determination of the mix of forces projected by the

United States. Similar inquiries concerning the Main Battle Tank program and the so-called AWACS (airborne warning and control system) were made by Senator Thomas Eagleton. On these and comparable occasions the senators were sometimes disappointed at the GAO response, which tended to demur on the larger questions and to address only the cost issues with which the Office is most familiar. Yet the Office was responding within the framework of its own understanding of its mandate and capabilities.

John Stennis himself was among those who dismissed the notion that the GAO could be employed for such wide-ranging policy studies. Speaking on the floor of the Senate on September 3, 1969, he argued:

> All those clauses in the amendments about the General Accounting Office—and I speak with great deference with regard to that Office and its very able Comptroller General and staff—making determinations about the value of alternatives and accurate judgments on the weapons of the future, their cost reliability, are absurd. The General Accounting Office does not have the facilities or personnel to make superior judgments in this field even though they are a very superior organization in their own field.

It is unreasonable to expect GAO, with its history and composition, to enter highly political disputes on intricate matters in which it has no true expertise. Indeed, one suspects that the Comptroller General well appreciated that the surest guarantee of strong opposition to a possible future expansion of the Office's role would be a premature injection of GAO into one or another of the current fracases over weapons systems. GAO could take sides only in the knowledge that today's losers would likely be tomorrow's enemies.

Some movement toward a modernized role for GAO is in fact under way. Senator Abraham Ribicoff has repeatedly offered legislation to strengthen and broaden the Comptroller General's authority and operations. Its thrust is toward enlisting the Office in prestudies of policy and programs, rather than limiting it to post facto audits and critiques. Comptroller General Elmer Staats has welcomed the idea of applying the Office's capabilities to evaluation of programs during their consideration by the legislative committees and in their initial operational phases. While the Ribicoff proposals did not become law in their original form, the Legislative Reorganization Act of 1970 granted substantial authority for independent initiatives by the Comptroller General to examine particular programs and policies. GAO has now moved strongly into program evaluation, with approximately one-third of its increasingly diverse staff engaged in this function.

A notable GAO contribution flowed from the fiscal 1970 Military Authorization Act, which mandated a thoroughgoing review of profits in the defense industry.[11] The GAO analysis of this controversial subject typified

[11] Report to the Congress by the Comptroller General of the United States, *Defense Industry Profit Study*, Mar. 17, 1971, pp. 2, 7–29, 52–55.

the kind of study for which the office is exceptionally well equipped and which can be of great value to legislative deliberations. It found no clear pattern of excessive profits—indeed, rates of return for seventy-four large defense contractors were significantly lower than on comparable commercial work—but the study confirmed that inequities did exist because of inconsistencies in relating profit allowances to the amounts of capital required to perform defense contracts. In general, the government was not taking adequate account of cases in which it supplied factories and equipment for specific projects. The GAO endorsed the thesis of many economic critics of defense contracting that "in determining profit objectives for negotiated Government contracts where effective price competition is lacking, consideration would be given to capital requirements as well as to such other factors as risk, complexity of the work, and other management and performance factors." Acting on this principle, the key committees have acquired added sophistication in appraising contractor performance in the rarefied environment of defense procurement.

The prospects seem reasonably promising for a period of real innovation at GAO. How far and how fast the Office can move is unclear, however, and will depend crucially on the caliber of the analytic staff recruited.

The evolving political moods of Congress resist systematic description, and this overview should be taken for no more than it is, a summary of some recent congressional efforts to gain greater control over national security budgets and policy. How durable or successful these experiments will prove cannot be predicted with confidence. They are certainly modest, first steps toward coping with a perpetual challenge of representative government. In welcoming the effort one must be careful to avoid any naive surmise that Congress has now taken charge and that executive mistakes and excesses will not recur. Congress remains very much the underdog in this realm; the most that can be claimed is that the underdog has begun to sink its teeth into some of the bones long considered the private preserve of the executive overdog. To nourish this semiadversary relationship into a lasting and constructive factor in U.S. national security policy will require sturdy, capable, and persistent leadership by many members of Congress.

John F. Kennedy was fond of the aphorism "When it is not necessary to change, it is necessary not to change." However attractive that notion may sometimes appear, Congress, no less than the great bureaucracies, is a frequent exception to the standard. Few institutions are in greater need of change for the sake of change. The experience of innovation may whet Congress's appetite for more, and a budding sense of achievement may enable growing numbers of congressmen and senators to overcome the reticence and trepidation which have caused them to accept executive dominance in national security policy.

VI. *Science Policy: Congressional Perspectives and Mechanisms*

"Science seeks out ingenious ways to kill
Strong men and keep alive the weak and ill;
That these a sickly progeny may breed,
Too poor to tax, too numerous to deed."

In that gloomy bit of doggerel, René Dubos once captured something of modern science's bitter paradox. The progress of science, and of the technology it both spawns and feeds upon, has proved a mixed blessing. Many of those who once hailed science as mankind's salvation have come to a rueful appreciation that salvation is not inevitable, and that science leads no more certainly to the new Eden than to Armageddon. It has become clear that the beneficence of science is not guaranteed and that governments must make special efforts to see that science is a boon and not a bane.

The increasingly complex relationships between government and science have become the subject of intense interest among students and practitioners of politics, as well as among scientists and engineers. But the burgeoning literature on science policy has so far afforded little insight into one of the most important challenges posed by the enhanced public importance of science. How shall Congress, traditionally and constitutionally the nation's principal representative institution, meet the special political responsibilities of a scientific-technological age?

As used here, "science policy" is a shorthand term for a diffuse topic. It includes both science and technology, research and development, and is intended to suggest two distinct kinds of policies: (1) those governing the use of science and technology as instruments in the service of society and (2) those concerned with the development of science and technology as valued social institutions themselves. One may conveniently identify these different aspects of science policy as the *instrumental* and the *institutional*.[1]

The task of identifying those issues of science policy with which Congress can and should deal ought to rank high among the immediate priorities of American government. While the executive branch of government has gradually been adapting to the requirements of massive federal programs for research and development, the legislature has responded more slowly and spasmodically, treating problems of science policy on a decentralized or ad hoc basis. In recent years, however, Congress has gained a heightened self-consciousness about its performance in this area and about the need for handling science policy more effectively.

The increased legislative concern for this field was decisively stimulated by the crisis atmosphere surrounding the early events of the space age. A review of the initial congressional involvement in shaping an American space program suggests something of the Capitol's disposition toward science policy in general, including the frequent tendency to view support for research and development largely as a function of the nation's security requirements even when conducted by agencies other than the Defense Department. The experience of overseeing so vast an undertaking as the space program sharpened the Congress's sensitivity to the host of technical policy issues related to the nation's educational system, to its physical environment, its economy and competitive position—in short to the many fields in which modern science and public policy are entwined. As these fields come more and more to the center of public concern, one sees more distinctly the turning point in legislative history marked by the immersion of the Eighty-fifth Congress in the conception and creation of a national space program.

THE EIGHTY-FIFTH CONGRESS: A TURNING POINT

When the first session of the Eighty-fifth Congress adjourned on August 30, 1957, the federal legislators were not smugly confident that all was right with the world, but neither were they alarmed by any especially acute crisis, domestic or international. A year previously, the American voters had massively reaffirmed their own peculiar brand of bipartisanship by returning a popular Republican to the White House and a solid Democratic majority to the Capitol. As the first year of the second Eisenhower Administration progressed, matters seemed to be proceeding much as one might have expected, except perhaps for the surprising success of the Administration and the Democratic congressional leadership in coaxing the House and Senate into accepting the Civil Rights Act of 1957.

---

[1] A similar usage of the term "Science Policy" is adopted in Organization for Economic Cooperation and Development, *Science and the Policies of Governments: The Implications of Science and Technology for National and International Affairs* (Paris, 1963), p. 18.

On October 4, 1957, the Union of Soviet Socialist Republics led the nations of the world into outer space by successfully launching Sputnik I, the first earth satellite. Less than a month later a much larger vehicle, Sputnik II, joined its predecessor in orbit. In hardly more than half a decade the atomic age had given way to the thermonuclear age and had now become the space age. And the country which had effected this latest revolutionary advance, with all its strategic and political as well as scientific significance, was not the United States, the accepted world leader in science and technology, but the major antagonist of the Free World, a totalitarian and "primitive" state, Soviet Russia.

No one was more stunned than the government and people of the United States. The astonishing feat had served as a convincing vindication of recent Russian claims of a powerful ballistic missile capability, and initial Western shock at the success of Sputnik soon dissolved into genuine alarm over the military potential of space technology. Clamor for explanation and for action quickly arose: how had the Soviet Union stolen this march on America, and what remedial action could the United States take to recoup, both in terms of prestige and in terms of security?

Even before the second session of the Congress convened, the swelling public concern had prompted action by an important congressional committee. On November 24, 1957, the Preparedness Investigating Subcommittee of the Senate Armed Services Committee began hearings into American satellite and missile programs. The Majority Leader of the Senate, Lyndon Johnson, chaired the proceedings before the subcommittee, preparing himself for a leading role in what was certain to become a major undertaking during the next session, the development of an appropriate American response to the new Russian challenge.[2]

Twelve days after the subcommittee began its inquiry, the anxiously awaited effort to launch an American satellite ended disastrously. The first launch attempt in the Project Vanguard series lasted precisely two seconds, exploding in flames before the eyes of a disheartened America and a disillusioned world. Where was the vaunted scientific and technological superiority of the United States?[3]

It was a nervous but aroused Congress that trooped back into the Capitol on January 7, 1958. The Soviet exploits in space had quickly been generalized in the popular mind (and in some expert opinion as well) into possible

---

[2] The Preparedness Subcommittee investigation produced more than 2,500 pages of hearings by July 1958 and served as an important contribution to the work of the Senate Special Committee on Space and Astronautics. Cf. the special committee's *Final Report*, 86th Cong., 1st Sess., Senate Report no. 100, Mar. 11, 1959 (cited hereafter as *FR*).

[3] In all fairness it should be noted that Project Vanguard was eventually a very successful program which fulfilled its planned goals. As a matter of fact, Vanguard I, which went into orbit on Mar. 17, 1958, was still functioning years later. Unfortunately, the information it was transmitting was redundant, and the extraordinary reliability of the satellite was actually wasting valuable radio frequency space, a final irony for a much-maligned program.

overall scientific superiority. Shortcomings in the American space program had generated doubts about the country's military capability to deter the Soviets. The deficiencies of our educational system, real or alleged, were under increasingly critical scrutiny. No one doubted that the Russians had scored heavily in the contest for influence among the uncommitted nations. The demonstration effect of such an extraordinary success by an authoritarian society could prove highly seductive to countries which had little or no experience of self-government and which lacked a commitment to democratic institutions. All these and other potential ramifications of Sputnik were in the minds of the legislators as, amid creeping despair and even incipient hysteria in some quarters, the second session convened.

Already, on November 7 of the preceding year, the President had used his executive authority to institute certain changes in the government's organization for scientific policy planning. He had named James Killian to the new post of Special Assistant to the President for Science and Technology. At the same time the President had elevated to White House level the Science Advisory Committee, which President Truman had established six years before in the Office of Defense Mobilization. It was not yet clear what additional innovations the Eisenhower Administration was contemplating, but the Congress immediately set to work organizing itself to deal with the problems of the space age and developing its own proposals for reorganization of the executive branch.

On the opening day of the second session, New York's Congressman Kenneth Keating introduced a bill providing for an eighteen-member Joint Committee on Outer Space, comparable to the Joint Committee on Atomic Energy. On January 8, Thomas Lane of Massachusetts submitted a bill to establish a Commission on Outer Space, along the lines of the Atomic Energy Commission, to promote the development and use of rockets, missiles, satellites, and spaceships. Numerous other bills dealing with both congressional and executive branch organization for the space effort poured into the hoppers on both sides of Capitol Hill and were duly referred to one or another committee for consideration.[4]

Meanwhile, Representative Carl Durham, chairman of the Joint Committee on Atomic Energy, was not waiting for action by the full Congress to make needed organizational changes. On January 16 he established a Special Subcommittee on Outer Space Propulsion under Senator Clinton Anderson of New Mexico. A week later, as though picking up the cue, Senator Anderson introduced Senate bill 3117 (S. 3117) to center responsibility for outer space programs in the Atomic Energy Commission, on the assumption that nuclear propulsion would be the critical element in space systems.

That same day, January 23, Chairman Johnson presented to the Senate a

[4] See *Congressional Record*, 85th Cong., 2d. Sess. (cited hereafter as *CR*), Jan. 7, 1958, pp. 31–32; Jan. 8, p. 97; Jan. 13, p. 362. Also see *CR*, Jan. 23, 1958, pp. 700–701.

unanimous report from the Preparedness Subcommittee, which was continuing its investigation of American satellite and missile programs. Among its seventeen recommendations were proposals for an immediate start on development of a rocket producing 1 million pounds thrust, for accelerated and enlarged research and development programs with long-term funding, and for administrative changes either to improve the ability of the Department of Defense to conduct the national space effort or to vest authority for space activities in an independent agency.

While the space program had been the focal point for most congressional activity, some members of the Senate were developing more far-reaching concepts. On January 27, Senators Humphrey of Minnesota, McClellan of Arkansas, and Yarborough of Texas proposed the creation of a Department of Science and Technology, a Cabinet-level agency which would absorb several existing scientific branches of the federal government such as the AEC, the National Science Foundation, and the Bureau of Standards. They also envisaged a broad program of federal support to scientific education by a system of loans and insurance to universities, as well as by the establishment of National Institutes of Scientific Research. As these measures were considered by the Senate Committee on Government Operations, various members advanced amendments to include in the proposed Department the National Advisory Committee for Aeronautics and general responsibility for the national space program. The committee also recommended the creation of standing committees in each house of Congress to oversee these matters.[5]

Thus, the opening weeks of the new session found the Congress a hotbed of policy ideas and activity regarding science and technology. In the next few months dozens of other proposals dealing with various aspects of the country's scientific programs emanated from Capitol Hill. The effort to organize an accelerated space program remained the principal concern, the glamor stock among the many offerings. On February 6, acting on a resolution authored by Lyndon Johnson, the Senate established a Special Committee on Space and Astronautics. Its thirteen members were appointed from several standing committees (Appropriations, Foreign Relations, Armed Services, Commerce, Government Operations, and the Joint Committee on Atomic Energy) with jurisdictions related to space activities, and Senator Johnson became chairman. A month later the lower chamber approved a parallel measure sponsored by Overton Brooks creating a Select Committee on Astronautics and Space under Representative John McCormack of Massa-

[5] *CR*, Jan. 27, 1958, p. 842, and Jan. 28, p. 977. On Mar. 26, the Government Operations Committee released an analysis of S. 3126 (the Humphrey-McClellan-Yarborough bill) which suggests the direction in which committee deliberations over the bill were evolving.

Also see *CR*, Feb. 5, 1958, p. 1471; Feb. 6, pp. 1551–1553, 1632, 1739; Mar. 5, p. 3019. See also *FR*, pp. 2–5, 21–23. *FR* contains a useful chronology of "Legislative Action on Outer Space," pp. 65–76.

chusetts. These committees assumed the major congressional burdens in this field during the year of intense activity which followed.

A number of congressmen had advanced resolutions expressing the interest of the United States in reserving the regions of outer space for "peaceful purposes." From the first, close observers noted an interesting and rather paradoxical contrast between the debate on the space program and the controversy eleven years earlier over the control of atomic energy activities. In spite of the fact that the Russian Sputniks had caused serious concern about American military readiness, few voices were raised in support of a national space program directed largely by the armed services—even though (or perhaps because) Project Vanguard had been a Navy program and the major existing capabilities related to space technology were located in the Department of Defense. Both within Congress and, as it developed, within the Administration, civilian control of the space effort appears to have been preferred, almost to have been taken for granted, from the beginning.

While the government was exploring alternative approaches to these problems, the Administration was taking interim steps, primarily in the Department of Defense. On February 7, 1958, Secretary of Defense Neil McElroy established the Advanced Research Projects Agency (ARPA) within the Department of Defense, and appointed Roy W. Johnson as director. The Congress promptly responded with a Supplemental Appropriations Act containing funds for ARPA. A second act, signed into law on February 12, not only authorized the Secretary of Defense to engage in advanced research on weapons but also included a provision under which, *for one year,* DOD could conduct *nonmilitary* advanced space research which the President might specify.

By early spring, as additional proposals continued to flood the Congress, the Administration had developed its plans for expanding the country's activities in outer space. President Eisenhower, in a message to Congress on April 2, recommended the establishment of an independent civilian agency, the National Aeronautics and Space Agency, to promote space science and aeronautical research. The Agency would absorb the functions of the National Advisory Committee for Aeronautics and the interim space programs which were underway in ARPA. When necessary, it could also perform military research required by the various armed services. The Administration proposal further provided for a National Aeronautics and Space Board, appointed by the President from competent authorities outside the government, which was to assist the President and the director of the Space Agency. The President's recommendations were incorporated in a bill introduced on April 14, by Senator Johnson and Senator Styles Bridges, ranking minority member of the select committee. Identical bills were introduced in the House by Congressman McCormack and several other members. The Congress now had something solid it could sink its teeth into, a detailed Administration plan into which it could weave its own variations and through which a consensus could evolve.

During the next month both the Senate special committee and the House select committee held public hearings on the legislation, and the Senate group received favorable reports from all of the executive agencies to which it referred the measure. The President had been determined to retain the initiative in shaping governmental organization for space, and he had taken pains to insure that bureaucratic competition, especially in the armed services, would not undercut his proposals and invite wholesale congressional reformulation of his plans. From the House investigation there emerged a revised bill which Mr. McCormack introduced on May 20. The name of the proposed National Aeronautics and Space Agency was altered to National Aeronautics and Space Administration, and the position and powers of its director were substantially strengthened. In addition, in its determination to insure coordination of the new agency's work with that of other interested elements of the federal government, the House committee provided for statutory liaison between the proposed NASA and both the Department of Defense and the Atomic Energy Commission. Thus, even while a concurrent resolution declaring this country's desire for joint and peaceful exploration of the space environment by appropriate international means was finding its way through the legislative maze, the select committee was underscoring the need to guarantee the defense establishment adequate information from the civilian space program. Should hopes for peaceful cooperation in space be thwarted, Congress felt that this country could not afford to be ignorant of the implications of the new technology for national security. On June 2, the House adopted by voice vote the revised version of the Space Act reported by the select committee. In the Senate the special committee had become convinced of the necessity for a much stronger Space Policy Board than the Administration had recommended, and the Senate bill provided the Board with a permanent staff to facilitate its task of coordinating related activities throughout the government. Furthermore, the senators had agreed that the proper form of congressional organization would be a joint committee of the two houses, and the upper chamber's bill included specific provision for a Joint Committee on Aeronautics and Space.[6]

When the conferees of the two houses met to reconcile their differences over the space legislation, it became apparent that sentiment in the House had come to favor a separate standing committee of its own, rather than a joint group, to assume jurisdiction in this area. A resolution which Congressman Carl Albert had introduced late in May called for a Standing Committee on Science and Astronautics with broad legislative responsibility in the field of science, including oversight of the proposed space agency. Aware of the

[6] House Report no. 1770 (to accompany H.R. 12575), 85th Cong., 2d Sess., May 24, 1958; *CR,* June 2, 1958, pp. 8892–8918. On the same day the chamber approved House Concurrent Resolution 332 expressing the nation's interest in international cooperation in space. The Senate endorsed the resolution of July 23. See also Senate Report no. 1701 (to accompany S. 3609), 85th Cong., 2d Sess., June 11, *CR;* June 16, 1958, pp. 10229–10246.

growing support for this measure in the lower chamber, Senators Johnson and Bridges submitted a resolution to the Senate establishing a Standing Committee on Aeronautical and Space Sciences, thus abandoning the idea of a joint group. The same day, July 15, the conferees agreed on a compromise version of the space legislation. Within twenty-four hours both the House and Senate had overwhelmingly endorsed the legislation, and on July 29 the President signed into law the National Aeronautics and Space Act of 1958, creating the National Aeronautics and Space Administration.

The act clearly bore the imprint of the dilligent congressional labors. The Administration proposal for an advisory board had grown into a greatly strengthened National Aeronautics and Space Council with a permanent staff and responsibility not only to advise the President on overall space policy, but to help develop a comprehensive program and to aid in allocating responsibility and arbitrating disputes among the various executive agencies involved in space activities. Congressional concern for coordination further revealed itself in statutory provision for a military-civilian liaison committee to insure continuing and effective cooperation between the new Space Administration and the Department of Defense. The act also required regular reports to the Congress and specified the general patent policy which the agency was to follow in the administration of its research and development programs. The congressional belief that "activities in space should be devoted to peaceful purposes for the benefit of all mankind" found expression once more in the act's declaration of policy.

If ambitious ideals had led Congress to create a civilian space agency with primary responsibility for the national space effort, political realism had compelled the lawmakers to hedge against the dangerous possibility that hostile uses of space might someday confront the United States. In a major modification of the President's bill, Congress explicitly reserved to the Department of Defense "activities peculiar to or primarily associated with the development of weapons systems, military operations, or the defense of the United States (including the research and development necessary to make effective provision for the defense of the United States)." This overt declaration that the Congress did not intend to neglect the security of the nation, although laying the basis for some later conflict and duplication between civilian and military efforts in space, had the additional advantage of saving NASA from the political onus of military research, a burden which the Administration bill would have imposed on the agency. As a "pure" civilian organization, NASA would have considerably smoother sailing in its efforts to promote the international cooperation in space which both the White House and the Congress so ardently desired.[7]

[7] A detailed history of changes in the space legislation is found in the conference report on the act. House Report no. 2166 (to accompany H.R. 12575), 85th Cong., 2d Sess., July 15, 1958. Both quotations are from Section 102 of the Space Act (Public Law 85–568). Another measure of major significance to the national scientific effort became law in August. The Department of Defense Reorganization Act of 1958, creating the office of Director of

Whatever the arguments for and against a potent military role in space, the congressional mandate in fact spawned a substantial continuing program in the Department of Defense. International agreements have reinforced the national policy of abstaining from "weaponizing" space, but DOD consistently spent over $1.5 billion a year in its space missions. Not only did DOD keep responsibility for launch support activities at the nation's rocket testing ranges, but more importantly from the standpoint of national security the Department exploited its congressional authority to develop and operate a wide range of observation, communications, and navigation satellites. President Johnson confided to more than one audience his opinion that the information collected through these programs, by removing much of the uncertainty traditionally surrounding the strategic capabilities and deployments of potential adversaries, more than justified the nation's investment in space technology. One may dispute his inference that the returns from earth-orbiting satellites justified the cost of the lunar landing program—an obvious *non sequitur*—but one must acknowledge the enduring importance of the congressional decision to reserve broad latitude for the defense establishment to undertake certain missions in space.

The vigorous congressional participation in the development of the space legislation reflected a heightened realization among the lawmakers of the new importance of science and technology to the nation. Moreover, the standing committees of both houses established before the end of July 1958 testified to their firm intention to play an active and expanded role in future governmental decisions in this field. One of the committees, that in the House, had received jurisdiction of unprecedented scope over scientific policy, and there was reason to hope that it might become the principal legislative center for intelligent oversight and planning in this vital area. Thus 1958 not only marked the birth of the civilian space agency; it also saw important new departures in congressional organization which gave promise of a growing congressional contribution to coherent science policy for the United States.

EVOLVING CONGRESSIONAL PERSPECTIVES ON SCIENCE POLICY

In several respects a healthy transformation of congressional attitudes toward science policy has taken place in the years since the advent of space activities whetted Congress's interest in dealing with such issues. The simple faith that science is good for the nation and therefore deserves the nation's sup-

---

Defense Research and Engineering, constituted an important move toward centralized control of defense research and development (which represents the largest share of federally financed R & D). See also *FR*, pp. 9–10. Alison Griffith contributes a useful and detailed review of the Space Act's legislative history in *The National Aeronautics and Space Act: A Study of the Development of Public Policy* (Washington: Public Affairs Press, 1962).

port—an uncritical belief that long lingered among congressmen as well as citizens—has been gradually eroding. In its place has sprung up a more sophisticated and skeptical disposition toward science and technology. There remains a basically hospitable regard for the benefits of science, but it is tempered by the legislators' growing concern that undesirable side effects of scientific activity should be anticipated and minimized.

This change in congressional attitudes toward science and technology is an understandable result of the educational experience through which many members of Congress have passed in the postwar period. As science policy, in both its instrumental and institutional forms, has become a major responsibility of the federal government, virtually every congressional committee has necessarily been involved in one or another problem in this area. Through hearings, briefings, studies, reports, and innumerable contacts with scientists and engineers, a number of congressmen, particularly those with reasonable continuity of service, have become familiar with various science policy issues.

The congressional experience in this area reflects, of course, the character of federal programs, which means that it has been primarily concerned with technological applications for the specific missions of executive departments and agencies. Moreover, as an examination of postwar federal budgets readily suggests, Congress has been largely preoccupied with military programs and their related technologies. But this experience is relevant to the legislature's responsibilities in nonmilitary fields, and a rising proportion of congressional energies is being directed toward these latter areas.

The changing composition of federal science programs provides a useful index of the shifting interests of both Congress and the executive. Since fiscal year 1960 R & D expenditures in the Department of Defense have grown from $5.6 billion to over $9 billion. But on a percentage basis the growth of nonmilitary R & D is even more striking. For example, the R & D budget of the Department of Health, Education and Welfare more than doubled, from $324 million in 1960 to $1.6 billion in 1967; the National Science Foundation's expenditures rose from $58 million to approximately $516 million. By 1973 NSF spending authority soared to $700 million. The combined expenditures of HEW and NSF had been one-thirtieth those of DOD in 1955; by 1973 they were more than one-fourth. Large but fluctuating increases occurred in the budgets of the National Aeronautics and Space Administration and the Atomic Energy Commission, much of which would be described as nonmilitary.[8]

---

[8] See Report of the Subcommittee on Science, Research, and Development, Committee on Science and Astronautics, U.S. House of Representatives, *Government and Science*, no. 2, *Fiscal Trends in Federal Research and Development* (cited hereafter as *Fiscal Trends*); 88th Cong., 2d Sess., 1964, pp. 13–16; *Budget of the United States: Special Analyses, FY 1973*, 1972, pp. 279–295.

A handful of committees, some with overlapping memberships, have been most deeply engaged in problems of science policy. Perhaps the foremost among these committees, in terms of their involvement in specifically scientific policy matters, has been the Joint Committee on Atomic Energy. Insofar as its stature within Congress and its ability to influence the activities of the executive are concerned, the joint committee has been a decided success. In fact its high standing on both scores has been mutually reinforcing, permitting the committee to maintain an extremely powerful role in a complex field. But the Joint Committee on Atomic Energy has been a unique institution in several respects, enjoying a rare concentration of legislative authority, a surprisingly stable membership for many years, and a staff whose technical competence is unsurpassed on Capitol Hill.[9] These and other factors make the committee atypical of congressional experience in this field, although it has often been cited as a model for congressional operations in science policy.

In both the House and the Senate the Armed Services and the Government Operations committees, usually operating through subcommittees with specialized jurisdictions and skills, have participated vigorously in a variety of science policy problems. The Appropriations committees in the two houses have also had a continuing involvement in a great many such topics, but the responsibility of these committees for all appropriations has reduced their capacity to treat scientific programs in detail.

As foretold by the 1958 debates, some of the most important work on science policy has been carried on by the House Committee on Science and Astronautics and the Senate Committee on Aeronautical and Space Sciences. Since the two committees have worked mainly on the national space program, they are often thought of as the "space committees," but the House body, alone among the standing committees of Congress, has a broad mandate for legislation regarding "scientific research and development." In the Senate the Labor and Public Welfare Committee has developed a central role in supervising the work of the National Science Foundation.

The work of these committees is not as disconnected as might at first appear. One of the few happy consequences of the fact that congressmen are greatly overworked is the extent to which some of their labors are interrelated. A principal instance of this occurs in the committees I have mentioned. Several individuals are members of more than one, and their multiple roles help to create fruitful personal liaisons among the different committees. These interlocking assignments are more common among senators than rep-

[9] On the Joint Committee on Atomic Energy see Clinton P. Anderson and James T. Ramey, "Congress and Research: Experience in Atomic Research and Development," *Annals of the American Academy of Political and Social Science,* vol. 327, January 1960, pp. 85–94; and the excellent study by Harold P. Green and Alan Rosenthal, *Government of the Atom: The Integration of Powers* (New York: Atherton, 1963), especially the concluding chapter.

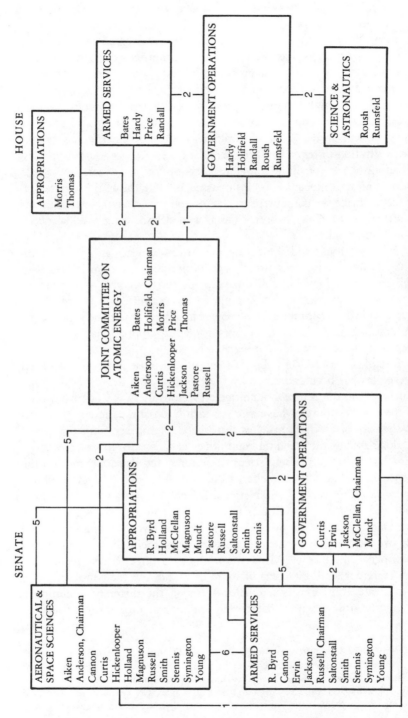

FIGURE 1. PERSONAL NETWORKS AMONG PRINCIPAL COMMITTEES DEALING WITH SCIENCE POLICY (Data are from Congressional Directory, 89th Cong., 1st Sess., March 1965, pp. 289–313.)

resentatives, simply because members of the lower house tend to be limited to a single major committee appointment, while senators have two or more such jobs.

The membership of the Joint Committee on Atomic Energy during one recent Congress illustrated some of the most significant personal links among the committees (see Figure 1). Among the Senate members were Richard Russell, who also served as chairman of the Armed Services Committee and as ranking Democrat on the Space and Appropriations committees; Clinton Anderson, former chairman of the Joint Committee on Atomic Energy who later chaired the Space Committee; Henry Jackson, a very active member of the Armed Services Committee and ranking Democrat on Goverment Operations; Carl Curtis, who also worked on the Space and Government Operations committees; and Bourke Hickenlooper, a member of the Space Committee. House members included Chet Holifield, a leading member of the lower house's Government Operations Committee and chairman of its Military Operations Subcommittee; Melvin Price, who also serves on the House Armed Services Committee; Thomas Morris, formerly a member of the Science Committee and then working on Appropriations; and Albert Thomas, chairman of a major Appropriations Subcommittee.

Many connections like these have developed among the other committees. Thus personal integration of committee roles constitutes one of the central means, imperfect but functional, for coordinating the resources and activities of the congressional subdivisions with responsibility for science policy. Less formal but valuable are the personal relationships among the professional staffs of the different committees. Nevertheless, overlapping memberships and frequent staff contacts afford only a minimum of integration among these committees. Moreover, issues of science policy form only a part of the workload of most of these committees and congressmen.

The widespread impression that congressmen have been antiscience or anti-intellectual is belied by the support Congress has lent to science in the postwar decades. Of special interest is the fact that Congress has been lending a more sympathetic ear to the institutional requirements of science. One reason for this is Congress's recognition that the instrumental policies toward which the legislature has long been favorable depend vitally on the maintenance of the nation's capability for basic research. The billion and a half dollars a year that Congress has regularly appropriated for basic research is convincing testimony to the legislators' willingness to invest in relatively unfettered scientific investigation, partly as a means of nourishing science itself.[10]

[10] Much evidence exists to demonstrate Congress's durable concern for basic research. Budgetary data show that Congress increased appropriations for basic research by 700 percent

A significant change has been taking place in congressional attitudes toward the scientists and engineers who play such a large part in science programs and policies. Many of the congressmen working on these subjects have overcome the exaggerated deference with which laymen often view science and scientists, while retaining a respectful appreciation for the pursuit and exploitation of knowledge. It is now generally understood that scientists advising on government policies, even those with important scientific components, play a political role and that Congress must make a concerted attempt to isolate the political elements of such advice.

There has been a reviving suspicion among congressmen that some scientific spokesmen may be disguising particular and local interests in their appeals for expanded scientific programs as a contribution to the general welfare. And there are signs of impatience in Congress with what some members consider the sanctimonious efforts of some scientists to portray their acceptance of federal research support as more of a sacrifice than a benefit. Although this impatience is moderated by an understanding that precautions must be taken to prevent federal research funds from distorting the academic functions of universities and to insure equitable arrangements regarding such knotty problems as the indirect costs incurred by institutions receiving federal grants, congressmen are inclined to believe that government support of research is advantageous to the recipients of federal money.

By and large these tendencies in congressional attitudes are to be welcomed, for they may help Congress define the political dimensions of science policy for which it is properly responsible. It has become more difficult for scientists to exploit, intentionally or accidentally, their scientific authority for political purposes. Scientists themselves have grown more aware of this possibility and more conscientious in their attempts to distinguish between the scientific and political elements of their testimony or advice to Congress. Careful distinctions of this sort improve Congress's ability to put scientific components of policy in a sensible perspective and to balance them against other considerations which influence policy.

This essential restraint has not meant a withdrawal of the scientific community from the political arena. Far from it. Under the leadership of a rejuvenated Federation of American Scientists, led by the astute Dr. Jeremy Stone, an active political body has emerged among scientists of many disciplines to become a strong and effective voice on Capitol Hill. The growing prominence of FAS—and its significant reach into many corners of Con-

---

from 1956 to 1964; one may cite also quite a number of studies on institutional science policy conducted or initiated by Congress. See, for example, *Basic Research and National Goals*, a report to the Committee on Science and Astronautics, U.S. House of Representatives by the National Academy of Sciences, Washington, 1965; and Report of the Select Committee on Government Research, U.S. House of Representatives, *National Goals and Policies*, House Report no. 1941, 88th Cong., 2d Sess., Dec. 29, 1964, pp. 11–15, 25–35, 49–59; *Fiscal Trends*, pp. 7–10.

gress—demonstrates the value of an institution separate from traditional scientific organizations as the principal political exponent of the technical community. In controversial issues like the Alaskan pipeline, seabed mining, the "Cannikin" nuclear tests in the Aleutian Islands, and the rising crises of world food and energy requirements, the federation has marshaled impressive contributions by knowledgeable spokesmen from within its ranks. Its newsletter and special releases have made the federation a respected presence in political discourse.

As Congress has developed a surer political grasp of science policy, it has come to appreciate the political opportunities it contains. Members of the House and Senate are not oblivious to the potential utility of science policies and programs as vehicles for their own political advancement. The temptation to capitalize on science policy as a fertile field in which to build a political reputation has been especially strong since Sputnik. With the quadrupling of the federal R & D budget since that time, science policy promises to remain one of the major specializations within a legislature whose allocations of power give substantial weight to the dollars for which members and committees are responsible.

The effects of this trend are already visible. Congressmen Holifield, Price, Miller, Teague, and Daddario, to mention but a few, gained notable stature within the House and the nation on the basis of their work on science policy. The same has been true in the Senate, where Lyndon Johnson earned national recognition for his labors on the space program, where Clinton Anderson's work on nuclear energy and space policies was widely acclaimed, and where Henry Jackson's contributions to improved organization and management of science programs in the executive branch won general esteem. Most recently Edward Kennedy has assumed a major role by virtue of his responsibilities for the National Science Foundation and, in Congress itself, his leadership of the Board of Technology Assessment.

At a more elementary level many other congressmen have learned the economic significance of federal science programs to their states and regions. In the nineteen-sixties it became a common occurrence for congressmen to campaign for R & D contracts, grants, and facilities, stressing the virtues of their districts for location of this new federal installation or the capacity of their constituents to undertake some research project. Congressmen, like other observers, have noted that production contracts often follow research awards, and the socioeconomic levels may soar dramatically in communities which acquire a research orientation. With $16 billion of scientific seed money available each year, it was only natural that they should be anxious for their regions to share in the immediate prosperity and the long-range stimulation of R & D programs.

Recent inflation has, one should note, sharply eroded the real level of effort supported by federal R & D funding. The severe contractions of aerospace and related electronics R & D after 1969 have caused acute economic dislocations in some areas, notably Massachusetts and California, and congressional enthusiasm for such endeavors has been tempered to a degree. But congressmen are shrewd enough to recognize that the main reason for the economic downturn was production cutbacks in these areas as the Vietnam war came to consume less American manpower and material. A sizeable fraction of the members of Congress have pressed to retain active R & D efforts in their states in order to build toward an anticipated revival of general economic health. A favorite and well-grounded theme has been the prospective value of converting military- and space-related R & D facilities to other domestic applications. Attempts in this direction have been made with regard to the Edgewood Arsenal in Maryland, as well as the former NASA Electronics Research Center in Cambridge, Massachusetts. Partly because of energetic congressional intervention, the Maryland facility has been shifted from germ warfare research to civilian medical programs and the Cambridge center, now surplus to the requirements and resources of a shrunken NASA, has turned to work on transportation and environmental problems. Without strong representation from concerned legislators, the valuable capabilities at both locations might have been lost to the nation.

Some commentators have disparaged the "pork barrel" pressures which have come to bear on R & D funds, and indeed there are regrettable aspects to this development. Yet there are persuasive arguments of justice and economics in congressional demands for change in the established practice of concentrating research money in a few areas with outstanding scientific and engineering capabilities.[11] There is much to be said for creating additional research complexes as a means of promoting the educational, economic, and social development of less prosperous regions. Partly because of congressional concern on this point, the National Science Foundation launched a program of science development grants to assist promising universities in various regions in their efforts to become major research centers. Although efficiency in R & D investments remains the fundamental criterion among executive agencies, there appears to be a growing sensitivity to the merits of wider geographic distribution of research funds. With the federal government's commitment to alleviating economic distress in impoverished sections of the country, it seems reasonable to expect that more attention will be given to this factor.

The congressmen who have urged greater consideration of this issue have

[11] See Report of the Subcommittee of Science, Research, and Development, Committee on Science and Astronautics, U.S. House of Representatives, *Government and Science*, no. 4, *Geographic Distribution of Federal Research and Development Funds*, 88th Cong., 2d Sess., 1964, pp. 25–55; and Report of the Select Committee on Government Research, U.S. House of Representatives, *Impact of Federal Research and Development Programs*, 88th Cong. 2d Sess., House Report no. 1938, Dec. 28, 1964, pp. 3–30, 89–118. Both reports urged additional attention to the need to broaden the nation's scientific base geographically, as well as substantively.

been expressing not only parochial desires but a very real national interest, even though they have frequently focused on competition for specific contracts and facilities—the TFX aircraft award, the Public Health Service's Environmental Health Center, the NASA Electronics Research Center, and the contract for the abortive Project Mohole deep-sea drilling equipment are examples from the last decade. The increasingly public nature of congressional interest in decisions regarding where federal research and development will be done may serve as an effective antidote to more dangerous, private attempts to manipulate such decisions. One result of publicizing political competition in these matters can be to enhance the bargaining power and freedom of maneuver of the executive, since it becomes obvious to all parties that none has an exclusive claim to the favor of the decision-makers.

A related problem has also attracted congressional attention, one similar to that experienced by Great Britain and other countries in recent years. The British, among others, were alarmed at their so-called "brain drain," by which they mean the net loss of scientific personnel as graduates of British universities migrated to the United States, thus sapping Great Britain's strength in the sciences. More recently, of course, the flow of foreign scientists to the United States has diminished and even reversed, as the national rate of growth in R & D has slackened markedly since the mid-sixties. Within the United States there have been analogous dislocations of trained manpower as scientists educated in some regions take up careers in others. The Midwest in particular has suffered from such movements. A survey by the National Academy of Sciences, covering 10,000 scientists who received their doctorates between 1935 and 1960, threw a good deal of light on this internal brain drain. While the Midwest had trained 40.4 percent of the group, in 1965 it employed only 25 percent. The West and the South, by contrast, had trained only 12.1 percent and 12.2 percent respectively, but they now employed 18.3 percent and 24.1 percent. Figures for New England and the Middle Atlantic States were more nearly balanced; New England had educated 13.1 percent and employed 7.3 percent, while the Middle Atlantic area awarded 22.2 percent of the degrees and employed 19.7 percent of the recipients.[12] With the severe dislocations in scientific manpower which grew out of funding cutbacks in the years after 1969 there have been other complications in the situation, featuring overproduction of scientists in some fields and significant unemployment in a number of disciplines.

While the nation at large has enjoyed the benefits of this kind of mobility, congressmen have correctly perceived that such trends have adverse implications for given regions. Representatives and senators from the Midwest have become especially and understandably vocal about this trend. They have stressed that the region's capacity to produce qualified scientific personnel

[12] A summary of these data appears in the *New York Times,* Jan. 9, 1966, p. E11. Of the individuals involved, 5.6 percent were working abroad in 1965.

demonstrates its competence to conduct a greater proportion of federal R & D than it has received heretofore and justifies stronger measures to maintain the region's scientific capability by directing more research contracts, grants, and facilities to the area. Members of the scientific community have also recognized the importance of dealing with this critical imbalance in distribution of research funds. In the words of Philip H. Abelson, editor of *Science,* "The present allocation of funds for research is not in the long-term national interest. One can only be amazed that congressmen from the underprivileged states have been so remiss in safeguarding the interests of the nation and of their constituents." The prospect is for intensified congressional pressure to rectify the prevailing geographic distortions in R & D activity.

INNOVATIONS AND EXPERIMENTS
IN CONGRESSIONAL MECHANISMS

Because research and development expenditures are dispersed through the budgets of many agencies and are reviewed by different committees of the Congress, the aggregate volume and impact of federal science funds were long neglected by the legislature. But the extraordinary expansion of the space program after 1961 and the spreading realization that total federal expenses for R & D were absorbing more than 7 percent of the national budget generated demands in Congress for a closer examination of the overall magnitude and significance of science programs. These demands triggered a series of efforts to improve congressional performance in this area. The most important innovations have been those directed toward correcting or compensating for the excessive decentralization of congressional activity on these matters and toward providing Congress with more comprehensive and systematic evaluation of science programs.

There has been much jostling for legislative jurisdiction among several committees and individual members during the last few years. In the Eighty-eighth Congress (1963–1964) several committees began to stake out new claims to authority over various areas of science policy. Subcommittees on research and development were established by the House committees on Armed Services, Government Operations, and Science and Astronautics, and by the Joint Committee on Atomic Energy. The rash of subcommittees erupted partly because of fears that the House Select Committee on Government Research, established on September 11, 1963, might be the forerunner of a standing committee with permanent, general authority in the field.[13]

---

[13] A concise appraisal of the origin and activities of the select committee is given by D. S. Greenberg, "News and Comment: Elliott Committee—Final Reports Issued as 15-Month Investigation of Federal Research Comes to End," *Science,* vol. 147, no. 3654, Jan. 8, 1965, pp. 109–113. The committee produced ten studies and three volumes of hearings on various topics. Its publications are a storehouse of relevant data and opinion.

The select committee itself was a particularly interesting indication of the new importance of science policy as a political vehicle. A major factor in its establishment was the Democratic leadership's desire to assist the fortunes of Congressman Carl Elliott of Alabama, whose re-election prospects had greatly darkened, by affording him a glamorous assignment. That point should not be recorded, however, without adding that Elliott's committee did genuinely useful work before its mandate expired in early 1965. But, even had Elliott been re-elected, it is doubtful the committee would have been continued, for other committees with permanent authority had also become more active during that period.

Especially notable have been the continuing efforts of the Science Committee's Subcommittee on Science, Research, and Development. Chaired until 1971 by Congressman Emilio Q. Daddario of Connecticut, this subcommittee emerged as a principal congressional agency in the study and evaluation of general issues of science policy. With Daddario's retirement from Congress, Georgia's John W. Davis assumed the chair, with Alphonzo Bell of California as ranking minority member. The subcommittee carried to fruition the effort which Daddario launched in 1967 to create the Office of Technology Assessment. It has also been the key congressional agent in enlarging the role of the National Science Foundation.[14]

The House Subcommittee on Technical Operations, set up by the Government Operations Committee on the recommendation of the now-defunct Elliott committee, also became an important group with broad competance in the field. There has been no sign that Elliott's most radical proposal, a Joint Committee on Research Policy, will ever come into existence. The proposed joint committee was conceived along the lines of the Joint Economic Committee, a body which has no legislative power but which has served Congress well by providing study and analysis on many aspects of economic policy.

The Elliott committee offered a persuasive case for the usefulness of such a body as a supplement to the present committees concerned with science policy. The joint committee would give Congress "the opportunity for continuous review of . . . research and development programs and policies," and could devote more attention to the broad issues of science policy than those committees whose primary duties relate to programs of individual executive agencies. Although this seems a desirable innovation from many standpoints, the opposition of other committee chairmen proved fatal to the

---

[14] Beginning in 1963 the Subcommittee on Science, Research, and Development issued a series of reports and studies under the general title *Government and Science,* two of which are cited above. It also conducted extensive hearings on that subject and began an extended review of the National Science Foundation. Former Chairman Daddario and several of his associates and staff brought to their tasks extensive background in the Science Committee's work on the space program.

scheme. Congressman George Miller, then chairman of the Science Committee and a member of the select committee, took sharp objection to creation
of a joint body and stressed that the Science Committee was already exercising jurisdiction in this area through the subcommittee under Comgressman
Daddario, the most noted legislator in the field. With Elliott no longer in
office to work for the joint group, its prospects quickly faded.

While there now seems little chance that Congress will concentrate broad
authority for institutional science policy in a single committee or in parallel
committees in the two houses, Congress has evolved several other mechanisms by which it might obtain a more comprehensive understanding of this
subject. For some years the House Science Committee has had a Panel on
Science and Technology, made up of distinguished scientists and educators
who meet with the committee from time to time in order to exchange ideas
about political and technical problems. The panel functions not merely as a
device for continuing mutual education about science policy, but as a source
of specific suggestions for possible congressional action. For example, the
panel's concern about security restrictions in a geodetic satellite program
stimulated the committee to press for transfer of the project from military to
civilian auspices. The committee publishes the records of its formal meetings with the panel. Although it is doubtful that other congressmen derive
much benefit from these activities, the panel provides at least one channel
through which broad questions of science policy can be discussed.

The House Science Committee has also taken the initiative in expanding
the use of outside advisers. The R & D Subcommittee has occasionally
looked to the National Academy of Sciences and the National Academy of
Engineering as a means of tapping scientific opinion on various topics,
although it recognizes that the academies and other professional scientific
organizations can be of only limited assistance. Academy study groups and
surveys of scientific opinion are no substitute for continuous, day-to-day
staff work in support of congressional deliberations.

For this reason the Science Committee, the Senate Space Committee, and
other groups have attempted to improve their staff capabilities, mainly by
adding more personnel with adequate technical backgrounds to the lawyers
and nontechnical aides who have made up most of the staffs. Some progress
has been made in enlarging committee staffs, although it has been practically impossible to find qualified scientists and engineers willing to work in the
highly political atmosphere that pervades all congressional committees.
Moreover, the dozen or so technical personnel who have joined various
committee staffs in the last few years are working largely on the instrumental policies and programs of individual agencies and contribute little to an
intergrated understanding of the country's R & D program. Coordination of
the efforts of these staffs remains informal and incomplete.

The increased congressional concern for the overall magnitude and direction of the national scientific effort has produced several abortive develop-

ments and a few concrete results. Congress has moved in two different but complementary directions, seeking first to specify a high-level executive office to which both the President and the Congress could look for comprehensive evaluations of science policy and second to create a central staff to assist the legislature in forming its own perspectives.

It will be recalled that in the aftermath of Sputnik substantial sentiment built up in Congress in favor of a Department of Science, a concept that meant different things to different people. The proposals usually implied a new agency with operational responsibility for a portion of governmental scientific programs and staff responsibility for evaluation and advice on all such activities. Advocated strongly in the late fifties by Senator Hubert Humphrey, then chairman of a Government Operations Subcommittee, the projected department retained the support of other members of that committee, particularly Chairman John McClellan. In 1962 the Senate actually approved legislation to establish a Commission on Science and Technology whose purpose would be to determine the desirability of a Department of Science and Technology. The House, however, failed to act, and although Senator McClellan reintroduced the bill in subsequent Congresses, the scheme has been superseded by other developments.

From the viewpoint of Congress, an important purpose of such a Department would have been to enable the legislature, which continues to rely on the executive for most of its advice on science policy, to look toward one office for a general review of federal R & D. It was clear that the National Science Foundation's statutory authority to conduct such reviews and to help minimize undesirable duplication in the scientific programs of different agencies had become a dead letter, mainly because NSF's governmental position was inferior to that of most departments and agencies whose programs it was supposed to review. Furthermore, although the President was able to obtain some assistance of this nature from the science advisory staff that gradually grew up in the White House, Congress was not always privy to this advice and, because of the privileged relationship between the Chief Executive and his personal advisers, could not hold the President's Science Advisor accountable for this advice.

Anxious to correct this deficiency but not sympathetic to proposals for a Department of Science, the Kennedy Administration adopted an alternative plan sponsored by Senator Henry Jackson. By Reorganization Plan No. 2 of 1962, President Kennedy established the Office of Science and Technology in the executive office of the President.[15] The director of the new Office

[15] Subcommittee on National Policy Machinery, Committee on Government Operations, U.S. Senate, *Organizing for National Security,* 1961, vol. 3, pp. 73–86. See also House Report no. 1635 (approving Reorganization Plan no. 2 of 1962), 87th Cong., 2d Sess., Apr. 19, 1962. See also Hubert H. Humphrey, "The Need for a Department of Science," *The Annals,* vol. 327, January 1960, pp. 27–35; and Carl Stover, *The Government of Science,* a report to the Center for the Study of Democratic Institutions, Santa Barbara, Calif., 1962.

was to be the President's Science Advisor, but in his capacity as head of OST he and his staff were also to be available to testify before Congress and otherwise to provide the legislature with technical counsel on the total U.S. scientific effort. Although, generally speaking, OST did not function in the latter capacity, it proved a valuable instrument for executive decision-making.

In 1973, however, a variety of political and administrative factors led the Nixon Administration to abolish both the Office of Science and Technology and the President's Science Advisory Committee, which had been an important presence at the White House since the nineteen-fifties. Anxious to compress the size of the White House staff and demonstrably less receptive to the products of the science advisory mechanisms he had inherited, Mr. Nixon reverted to the older pattern of concentrating authority for comprehensive science policy planning and coordination in the National Science Foundation, whose soaring budget in the Nixon years had given it a far greater claim to leadership in the field. Nevertheless, close observers interpreted the reorganization as a clear downgrading of the vaunted position which science had enjoyed in American government throughout the postwar period.

Formally speaking, the change did not cripple congressional access to executive procedures in the field, since the director of NSF was subject to legislative interrogation. It remained to be seen whether NSF would actually attain the eminence promised it, especially since the Administration's habit of heavy reliance on the Office of Management and Budget suggested that a great deal of the crucial decision-making might devolve upon the inaccessible processes of the OMB. What was certain was that, with its heightened sensitivity to the importance of science policy and to the hazards of closed decision-making in the OBM, Congress would keep a weather eye out for any tendency to bury from public view vital issues in this field.

After some months of experience with the new arrangements, the National Academy of Sciences created an ad hoc committee under James R. Killian, Jr., to examine the altered status of science at the presidential level. It found a bleak situation and called for a prompt restoration of suitable mechanisms for scientific and technical policy counsel at the White House.[16] As the Nixon Administration's hostilities toward scientist critics gave way to the more accessible White House of Gerald Ford, prospects improved for implementation of some of the committee's recommendations, which had won widespread press endorsements.

Congress has been less than successful in satisfying its need for a central staff of its own, principally because congressmen are not agreed on the requirement for such a staff or, if the need is admitted, on how it should be organized and operated.

[16] National Academy of Science, *Science and Technology in Presidential Policymaking: A Proposal,* Washington, June 1974.

However, there have been some significant steps forward. Prodded by Chairman Daddario's Subcommittee on Science, Research, and Development, the Library of Congress has set up a Science Policy Research Division (SPRD). The division's staff, planned to total more than twenty professionals, assists individual members and committees, preparing special studies, helping with hearings, and attempting to aid Congress in formulating a suitable framework for science policy decisions. Its first director, Dr. Edward Wenk, Jr., brought to his job wide experience in both executive and legislative staff work on science policy, as did his successor, Dr. Charles Sheldon. The Congressional Research Service has also created an Environmental Policy Research Division, paralleling the expansion of government activities in this complex technical area.

Congress has always been extremely conservative with regard to its own staffing, and some legislators appear downright hostile to any scheme that smacks of an enlarged bureaucracy on Capitol Hill, fearing that the experts might swamp the legislators and corrupt the representative process. Despite the recognized need to bolster Congress's various staffs, leaders in both the House and Senate have adopted a go-slow attitude, preferring to beef up committee staffs, open up the channels for external advice (e. g., the National Academy of Sciences), and make slight changes in the auxiliary services of the Congressional Research Service. This has also been the course favored by a number of academic authorities. Among others, Don K. Price has expressed apprehension that a large science staff for Congress might gain excessive influence without the discipline of operational responsibility.[17]

This reluctance to resort to strong central staffing in Congress is understandable, but there are important limitations to the staff and advisory techniques that Congress has traditionally employed.

Historically, committees and the Congressional Research Service, formerly the Legislative Reference Service, have had considerable difficulty recruiting competent scientific and engineering personnel to assist Congress. It took LRS over a year to find a senior specialist in science and technology, after that post had been authorized in 1958. The first incumbent departed in 1961 and it was again more than a year before the Service could replace him. Professionals in the technological and scientific disciplines have rarely found the political climate surrounding work in Congress a congenial one, and congressmen themselves have often felt more comfortable relying on lawyers and social scientists for staff services, even in regard to science policy. Many scientists and engineers view such work with condescension, an attitude justified in part by the often menial and trivial burdens which congressmen have placed on the Library of Congress and committee staffs. These long-standing attitudes have begun to change noticeably in recent years, and

[17] Don K. Price, *The Scientific Estate* (Cambridge, Mass.: Harvard, 1965), p. 262. Clinton P. Anderson offers a congressional viewpoint in "Scientific Advice for Congress," *Science*, vol. 144, no. 3614, Apr. 3, 1964, pp. 29–32.

one discerns greater interest among technical professionals in working for Congress, provided suitable institutional arrangements can be devised.

The recruitment difficulties are complicated by a second problem in the congressional staff situation, the rather harsh subordination—one might even say subservience—that characterizes relationships between congressional staffs and members of Congress. The point was exemplified by the congressman who, when rebuked for treating his staff with utter contempt, replied, "Why, anybody who would work for me couldn't be much good." A peculiar kind of self-contempt infects some member-staff relationships.

When Congress has cried for independent technical advice, it has meant advice independent of the *executive* branch; it has not perceived the potential virtues of a staff that also enjoys some independence vis-à-vis the legislature also. Individually and collectively, congressmen generate political tension that can be the source of exhilaration and anxiety among their staff assistants. A healthier atmosphere for staff workers would be one which maintained the former but suppressed the latter, and indeed there have been some efforts toward this goal. With varying degrees of success, Congress has sought to improve the situation by moving toward nonpartisan staffs with status and job security comparable to those found in civil service.

The concern here is not for the personal discomforts of congressional staffs, but for the effects their status has on their role. It is no insult to the many gifted professionals in CRS and on committee staffs to note that they frequently tend to operate on a leash too short to permit them significant initiative in evaluating or developing policy alternatives. One might stimulate more creative staff work by loosening the reins somewhat and by providing a bit of insulation between staff aides and the legislators they support. This is probably not practical for the existing staffs which function in a well-worn mold of custom and precedent, but a new central staff might be able to achieve greater independence, particularly if that were an explicit purpose in designing its mission and standing. To be sure, there have been half-steps in this direction previously. The General Accounting Office has long enjoyed a wide latitude in fixing its own work schedule and in choosing which executive activities to subject to detailed audit; the Congressional Research Service has also had authority to initiate studies of its own, but it has exercised the authority delicately, laboring under excessive demands on the time of a limited staff. CRS was deluged with over 200,000 congressional queries in 1973 alone. The Legislative Reorganization Act of 1970 pushed both agencies toward a more expansive and aggressive stance in their study efforts, and they have both made some notable innovations, but their very histories and the scope of their responsibilities make it doubtful that either institution can assume the principal role in policy analysis. Congress could use both the kind of close support staff it now has and a less tightly controlled staff to carry on research and analysis.

The degree of staff independence has a vital bearing on a third deficiency in present staff devices. Just as Congress has no committee which provides a continuing review of the government's total R & D effort or of programs that cut across the missions of several agencies, there is also no congressional staff to develop an integrated, comprehensive perspective on these subjects. As in the area of fiscal policy, the decentralization of the congressional committee system ignores the necessity for relating specific scientific programs and policies to a broader outline of national needs and goals. That Congress believes such coordination to be necessary is evident from its insistence that the executive branch attempt to oversee all federal R & D and to eliminate wasteful duplication. Yet, as indicated by much of the discussion attending proposals for increased congressional efforts in science policy, there are nagging worries that Congress has been abdicating its own responsibility by failing to take a more active part in comprehensive oversight of federal research.

Congressional uneasiness on this point reflects an implicit understanding that the instrumental science policies with which Congress is preoccupied cannot be drafted wisely without sound institutional policies. Analysis of the macroscopic features of the federal R & D effort and comparison of its many components with respect to aggregate data and to each other are elementary requirements for a rational approach to science policy at either the instrumental or the institutional level. It is this kind of comprehensive evaluation which congressmen demand when they call for a set of national priorities in R & D. They are, of course, already setting priorities piecemeal when they consider such fragments of the country's scientific programs as fall within the scope of one or another committee. But even Congress's most loyal devotees lament its failure to make provision for systematic evaluation of the overall R & D effort.

The founding of the Science Policy Research Division suggested that congressional staff arrangements may be more flexible than the committee system, but even if one did not share Ralph Lapp's opinion that the SPRD is mere "window dressing," one could not expect the division to prove adequate to Congress's needs. Operating within the Library of Congress, the division has had to struggle to avoid being tied too closely to specific inquiries from individual congressmen or committees and bogged down in the quicksand of constituent service, speech-writing, or other distractions from its major mission. The division's chiefs have tried commendably to provide a satisfactory environment for the staff and to encourage staff members to continue research and publishing in their respective fields, but it is still exceedingly difficult to attract and retain the personnel required for the division's work.

The Science Policy Research Division itself was among the first to recognize the constraints under which it labors and to suggest improved mechanisms for congressional involvement in science policy. In supporting the Daddario subcommittee's continuing inquiry into techniques for "technology assessment" to bolster legislative decision-making, SPRD developed a powerful argument for some kind of "service" to provide "an early warning system" for congressional action on technical policy issues with significant social, political, and economic implications.[18]

Beginning in 1967 Congressman Daddario and later his successor, Congressman John Davis, spearheaded an effort to create an Office of Technology Assessment (OTA) for the Congress. Joined in the Ninety-second Congress by Senators Edward Kennedy and Gordon Allott, the effort was finally successful in winning passage of the Technology Assessment Act of 1972. The act created the first new independent information source for Congress in half a century—but what that source would become was not clear from the legislative history. Authorized to expend $5 million in its first two years, OTA was designed to function under a Board of Technology Assessment which was essentially a joint congressional committee. Not only did it face hard questions as to which issues it would address in its early phases, but its entire structure and operating pattern would evolve largely from experience, as it decided whether to concentrate its resources on contract studies in other institutions or to focus on building a substantial staff of its own.

In addition to the sophisticated leadership of former Congressman Daddario, its first director, the OTA was blessed with a distinguished board and held high promise of filling the large void in Congress's capacity to grapple with questions of this nature. Among other interesting aspects of its early development was the tendency of much of the community associated with the now-defunct President's Science Advisory Committee to look toward an active relationship with OTA, a tendency which promises to open up to wider discussion a number of issues customarily treated in the more closed circuits of the executive branch. Certainly OTA enjoys a remarkable mandate to analyze the broadest possible range of technologies and their implications for society.[19] Besides conducting individual assessments, it is to provide an annual report broadly canvassing issues and problems in this field.

Apart from congressional reticence about staffing, some forces in the executive and the scientific community view this development with alarm. A number of scientists and administrators feel that Congress with minimum staff represents quite a formidable obstacle to progress—as they conceive it—in science policy. They fear that Congress with more effective staff

[18] See *Technical Information for Congress,* report to the Subcommittee on Science, Research and Development, U.S. House of Representatives, 91st Cong., 1st Sess., Apr. 25, 1969, pp. 516–521. See also the same subcommittee's *Technology Assessment Seminar,* 90th Cong., 1st Sess., Sept. 21 and 22, 1967; and its hearing on *Technology Assessment,* 91st Cong., 1st Sess.

[19] See Public Law 92–484, Oct. 13, 1972; and Committee on Rules and Administration, U.S. Senate, *Office of Technology Assessment for the Congress,* 92d Cong., 2d Sess., Mar. 2, 1972. Also see "Technology Assessment: A New Tool for Congress," *Congressional Quarterly,* Apr. 7, 1973, pp. 772–775.

assistance might become impossibly obstreperous. Many observers are concerned that such staff arrangements would encourage Congress to intrude excessively in areas that are the proper responsibility of the executive. Some cite the Joint Committee on Atomic Energy as a case in which Congress has violated the separation of powers, partly because of the committee's able and influential staff. There are also those who discount Congress's need for technical staff on the grounds that the real policy issues seldom depend very much on technological considerations.[20]

There is some justification to these concerns, although they tend to minimize the extent to which policy issues are often embedded in deep technological contexts. For example, the technical decision regarding the method by which the United States would attempt to place a man on the moon, i. e., the choice of the so-called Lunar Orbit Rendezvous (LOR) mode over the Earth Orbit Rendezvous (EOR) mode, incorporated a number of major policy questions. Although the decision was made by the executive in the light of prior legislative endorsement of a lunar landing in this decade, some congressmen later regretted that they did not have an opportunity to participate more actively in the lively debate over LOR versus EOR. This regret stemmed not from a presumption that Congress could have made a better technical choice, but from a recognition that the legislators might have been able to help balance the political-technical trade-offs involved. The timetable for the lunar landing, like most political guidelines, was not immutable, and the legislature might have been willing to modify it if the EOR promised lower costs, less drastic reallocations of technical manpower, greater future benefits, or other advantages. The specific technical features of the alternative modes had great bearing on any net political judgment concerning their respective merits.

Similar political elements are often submerged in technical analyses of competing military systems, a fact which many congressmen find highly disturbing. When it comes to defense programs, there has long been a pronounced tendency among members of the legislature to prefer the more effective system to the less expensive, even if the latter promises to perform a mission adequately. This may be an undesirable propensity, but one of the costs of the democratic process is that legislatures are entitled to their biases. If the executive possesses a higher wisdom on such matters, it is obligated to convince the legislature. Congressman Chet Holifield, for instance, expressed a view common among his colleagues when he challenged rigid adherence to cost-effectiveness criteria in selecting weapon systems. Such criteria, he insisted, "do not place proper emphasis on military effective-

---

[20] Don K. Price tends to hold this view, although he admits that "the need of Congress for scientific advice is roughly the same as that of the President." Price, op. cit., p. 262. This is not to say that only scientists and engineers are competent to make science policy, but that their participation in the process is extremely important.

ness."[21] Much the same attitude marked the reaction of senators who reviewed Secretary McNamara's decision on the TFX aircraft contract. Several of them felt that the Secretary weighted cost considerations too heavily and performance factors too slightly in choosing between competing designs. Only gradually has this disposition been moderated on the Hill, as Senator Stennis and others have begun to highlight the hazards of costly "gold-plating" in military systems.

Whether or not the Secretary's decision in any given case was right or wrong is irrelevant to the point being discussed here, for the correctness of the decision is obviously a function of the criteria applied. As Congress is coming to realize, the choice and weighting of criteria for technical evaluations may frequently amount to important political decisions. If Congress were prepared to underwrite larger costs in order to have a more effective military system or to forgo a particular technical advantage in order to reduce system costs, it would seem reasonable for the executive to take this disposition into account. A competent technical staff, sharing the legislature's special perspective and not dependent on largesse funneled through the executive branch, could help Congress identify and isolate this type of technical-political issue. One hopes the OTA and other legislative instruments can forge such capabilities.

In addition to the substantive value of such a staff, it could help alleviate some of the psychological impediments to legislative-executive relations. As the Presidency has gained ascendancy in American government, Congress has often shown signs of an enervating inferiority complex. The executive's superior command of the intellectual resources essential to modern public policy has become a source of serious tension in its relations with Congress. While these resources have enabled the Chief Executive to overwhelm the legislature and to win acceptance of his political preference, the inequalities between the two branches have also invited blind counterattacks by a frequently frustrated and occasionally petulant legislature. Staff arrangements which give Congress greater confidence in its ability to work with the executive on more equal terms could lead to a more cooperative relationship, rather than to a more obstructive legislature.

Much time and wasted effort are now devoted to skirmishes on inconsequential issues between the two branches, on science policy as on other problems. A stronger staff could help Congress specify valid disputes on policy and programs and avoid petty frictions, thus reducing the malaise in legislative-executive relations.

[21] Quoted by John W. Finney, "McNamara Scored on Nuclear Navy," *New York Times,* Jan. 18, 1966, p. 16. See also the opening statements of Senator John L. McClellan in *TFX Contract Investigation,* Hearings before the Permanent Subcommittee on Investigations, Committee on Government Operations, U.S. Senate, 88th Cong., 1st Sess., part 1, Feb. 20, 1963, pp. 3–5.

An independent and respected staff agency could also relieve one of the more insidious aspects of Congress's present dependence on executive branch expertise. One commentator has written that "the threat of technocracy is more likely to come through an alliance between particular congressional committees and the professional interests within a particular agency or department" than through domination of the Presidency by "a combination of secret bureaucracy and technology."[22] One must admit that this danger is real. Congressional committees and technical groups in the executive branch sometimes circumvent the President's authority and use their close ties as a basis for increased leverage on executive decision-makers. If permitted to develop unchecked, this pattern of relationship might eventually subvert executive authority and simultaneously jeopardize Congress's independence, subjecting both branches of government to manipulation by a politico-technical elite. This menace remains potential rather than present, but it is important enough to justify precautions.

A potent central staff for Congress could help counteract such tendencies by articulating issues and views of interest to Congress as a whole. It should be able to confront particularistic opinions from technical spokesmen in the executive with judgments reflecting a broad congressional standpoint. In the process it may also be able to free particular committees from unwarranted dependence on would-be technocrats. None of these successes is assured, but that is no argument against trying to attain them.

Obviously there would be risks in any scheme to equip Congress with the kind of central staff considered here, but the real questions are whether the risks are greater than the likely benefits and how they compare with the risks and benefits of the alternatives. Congress is right to want to maintain multiple sources of advice on science policy, and no staff should be allowed exclusive rights in this field. But as one element in a complex network of advice to Congress, an independent central staff could become a unique asset.

James Webb, the former NASA Administrator, often stressed the adversary nature of congressional-executive relationships and praised it as a healthy ingredient in American politics. If that adversary relationship is not to deteriorate into mutual paralysis, the parties must be capable of cooperation. A Congress confident not only of its own independent power but of its capacity to exercise that power intelligently—the kind of Congress to which a qualified central staff could contribute—could be a more constructive and cooperative partner in the tasks of government.

[22] Price, op. cit., p. 277.

VII.   *Foreign Policy: The Prisoner as Liberator*

Since at least the time of De Tocqueville, the friends and enemies of representative government have been meditating on the special difficulties of conducting foreign policy in an open political system. Joseph Goebbels glorified those difficulties, counting them a weakness to be exploited and saying that "it will always remain the best joke made by the democratic system that it provided its deadly enemies with the means of destroying it." Thoughtful democrats have worried over the dilemmas of reconciling the values of popular government with the requirements for competent and sustained action in a hostile international environment. To Robert Dahl foreign policy is an area in which the separation of powers has "misfired."[1]

In the United States discussion of this issue has generally turned on the ways in which domestic politics inhibit effective international politics. Of particular concern has been the manner in which Congress, as the principal instrument for diverse political expression, has allegedly impeded the design and pursuit of a sound foreign policy by the executive. For the past generation, preoccupation with the hazards of the nuclear age has amplified this concern. A larger legislative role in foreign policy seemed impractical at best and downright dangerous at worst. This skepticism toward Congress was often accompanied by an exaggerated faith in the rationality of executive decision-making. Recently, however, the arduous experience in Southeast Asia and other developments have generated deep anxiety over the imbalance of power between the President and Congress, especially as regards

---

[1] Robert Dahl, *Congress and Foreign Policy* (New York: Norton, 1964), p. 168. A recent essay in the field is Francis O. Wilcox, *Congress, the Executive and Foreign Policy* (New York: Harper, 1971).

foreign affairs. This anxiety has provoked new demands in and out of Congress for a reassertion of legislative control over the foreign activities of the nation's executive agents.

The congressional impact on policy is more often indirect than direct, informal than formal, marginal than fundamental. Nevertheless, on complex issues of foreign policy the margins are frequently the vital edges, and Congress's ability to help shape them is a real and promising power. The task for Congress, it may be argued, is to learn how best to use these relatively nebulous powers. The ablest members of the House and Senate aspire to be more than simply critics of presidential policy; they seek outlets for independent initiatives, straining to mold policy in a consensus of their own making within Congress and between the branches.

The following analysis rests on the assumption that even if one were convinced that the constitutional provisions separating and restraining the institutions of American government needed drastic revision, the realities of present-day politics preclude such revision in the forseeable future. While there is wide latitude and some prospect for progressive innovations *within* the separate institutional structures, there is much less opportunity for serious adjustment of the basic relationship between Congress and the Presidency.[2] That relationship is likely to retain its mixed quality, at once competitive and cooperative, antagonistic and cordial, with each institution jealous of its own prerogatives yet solicitous of the welfare of the other as an essential element of the American system.

The central question of American government, as it has always been, is whether we can extract from this complex and difficult relationship the fruits it was designed to produce. Can Congress be both ally and adversary of the executive, its partner in devising enlightened national policy and its policeman in guaranteeing efficient administration of the nation's business? Or have events outpaced the capacity of Congress to carry out these classical tasks?

There is widespread distress among congressmen that the federal legislature has suffered a general decline in political effectiveness and public esteem. This is partly due to the tendency to measure congressional

---

[2] This is not to say that institutional changes themselves may not alter the character of legislative-executive relations. Adoption of a four-year term for members of the House of Representatives, concurrent with the presidential term, would have multiple effects, increasing simultaneously the potential independence of representatives from constituent pressure and the potential influence of the President among those congressmen whose election seemed to depend on friendly relations with the Chief Executive. Partly because of the complex and somewhat unpredictable effects of this proposal, its chances remain in doubt. Presidents Eisenhower and Johnson have both endorsed the plan, but Mr. Eisenhower believed it would be necessary to call a constitutional convention to consider this and other major reforms affecting the conditions and terms for service in Congress. See Dwight D. Eisenhower, *Waging Peace* (Garden City, N.Y.: Doubleday, 1965). pp. 638–646.

performance in terms of the President's legislative program. Journalists and scholars alike have encouraged this trend by their frequent reliance on "legislative box scores" showing the status of various bills, usually those identified as important by the President, in their evaluations of the Congress. While these scorecards are convenient means to summarize certain aspects of the political scene, they create a distorted perspective on the work of Congress.

During the 1960s surveys by Louis Harris, for example, showed that overall public appraisals of Congress seem to be tied closely to the proportion of presidential programs it passes.[3] In January 1964 as the bulk of the Kennedy program languished on Capitol Hill, Harris found only a 35 percent approval of congressional performance, while 65 percent of those questioned expressed negative attitudes. As President Johnson began to enjoy numerous successes in his legislative recommendations, positive evaluations of Congress rose to 64 percent in January 1965 and to 71 percent in January 1966. These are astronomical figures by comparison with the incredibly low approval ratings (21 to 25 percent) which both branches were receiving in Harris surveys of 1973, as a despairing nation witnessed the erosion and collapse of the Nixon Presidency.

A simple and plausible explanation for these shifts is that when the public generally approves of the President's program, it resents congressional opposition to it. Yet one is left with nagging doubts as to whether these correlations relate primarily to public attitudes on the merits of various proposals or mainly to expectations created by press coverage of congressional actions in terms of the presidential program. The latter expectations unquestionably obscure some of the distinctive responsibilities of the Congress, and to the extent that they dominate public discussion of the relative performance of the legislative and executive institutions, they make it harder for the electorate to reach a sound assessment of the Congress. One cannot be satisfied with the contention that these correlations merely reflect the fact that only the President enjoys a national mandate and that therefore his proposals incorporate the true national consensus. As many students have observed, the President's mandate is indeed general—so general that it is hardly more than a vote of confidence that tells little about public attitudes on specific issues. Congress continues to claim a superior capacity to articulate representative preferences on a broad range of these more detailed questions.[4] Moreover, by the 1970s popular disillusionment with the President

---

[3] Some of these data are discussed in a useful study by Sanford Jerome Ungar, "Every Day is Open Season: A Critical Analysis of Daily Newspaper Coverage of the United States Congress," senior honors thesis, Harvard University, April 1966, p. 143. See also Wilcox, op. cit., pp. 96–122.

[4] A systematic statement on this point is Dahl, op. cit. The distinctive features of Congress as a representative body are replete with paradox. Thus it is quite possible—even probable—that every citizen is relatively content with the performance of his own representative or senator and yet dissatisfied with Congress as a whole. Such contrasting evaluations are

approached the depths long inhabited by the Congress. In such circumstances it became apparent to many observers that only more vigorous exercise of Congress's powers could revive confidence in the capacity of both branches to pursue a constructive international program.

For many years it was common in discussions of American government for Congress to assume the role of villain in a tragicomic portrayal of the executive as the principal source of enlightened leadership. Especially in international affairs there was disposition on the part of many commentators and citizens to conclude that congressional interference has seriously hampered the President in his efforts to provide creative direction. Congress was seen as the great inhibitor, a view that comprehends but a fraction of the institution's responsibilities and, by ignoring the rest, caricatures the whole.[5] In a popular conception the Congress bears the onus for shortsighted foreign aid programs, for the rigid anticommunism which hindered U.S. foreign policy in the Cold War, for indiscriminate demands that force be used to protect American interests abroad. This image credits the Congress with too much and too little. It attributes to the legislature major responsibility for the general failures of American foreign policy while neglecting some of the distinctive contributions made by the Congress.

One can sketch a more affirmative view than is customary of the legislature's actual and potential participation in issues of foreign policy. The exercise is founded not on naiveté, but on the conviction that the time has come for some corrective to the unrelieved disparagement Congress has suffered. The popular press and the professional literature alike have long bemoaned the legislature's obstreperousness, its shortsightedness, its narrow approach in addressing these issues.

Many of the complaints are justified, but they need not be rehearsed here. Rather, the purpose of this essay is to move beyond the familiar lamentations over the fact that our most pluralistic institution has the vices of its virtues. We need also to discover the virtues of the system's vices, and to exploit them as systematically as possible.

This requires that members of Congress and their staffs acquire some fresh perceptions of the ways in which Congress influences U.S. foreign policy and of techniques by which legislative influence can be applied more rationally and potently. What is needed is a stronger *institutional* perspective, a greater self-consciousness among senators and congressmen regarding their

---

rooted in the fact that constituents may judge individual members of Congress mainly in light of local or regional preferences, while they measure Congress as a whole in a much broader framework of national political concerns.

[5] James MacGregor Burns, *The Deadlock of Democracy* (Englewood Cliffs, N.J.: Prentice-Hall, 1962) is a principal spokesman for this view. See also his *Presidential Government: The Crucible of Leadership* (Boston: Houghton Mifflin, 1966). A contrasting perspective, dealing only with the lower house, is Neil MacNeil, *Forge of Democracy* (New York: McKay, 1963).

collective opportunities to serve the country's international interests. This does not mean merely that Congress should be more jealous of its prerogatives or more aggressive in the legislature-executive struggle to shape policy. Certainly Congress should be concerned to protect the balance of power between the branches and should be wary of sacrificing this long-term interest to short-term arrangements which concede excessive latitude to the President or his associates.

But the "self-consciousness" envisaged here is a more subtle quality. It consists of a sensitive appreciation of the informal no less than the formal means of legislative impact on foreign policy. A retrospect of the last fifteen years suggests some of the constructive opportunities open to the Congress. Here I will discuss four aspects of Congress's foreign policy role: Congress as "constrainer," "communicator," "liberator," and "initiator."[6] The implications of these labels will become apparent as the discussion proceeds.

CONGRESS AS CONSTRAINER

The legendary sign on President Truman's desk read "The buck stops here." In fact, of course, the President has wide latitude for diluting his responsibility for unpopular policies, most importantly by emphasizing the shared responsibility of Congress for many undertakings. It is commonplace to deplore this aspect of the U.S. political system as one of its gravest defects, a feature which makes it extraordinarily hard to fix responsibility within the system. Neglected by this customary criticism, however, are the ways in which a system of shared responsibility can work to the nation's advantage in international politics. Buck-passing has its virtues.

The American political system is properly conceived as one of mutual or interlocking constraints. Each group, each institution, is in a sense the captive of others. If Congress is thought to imprison the President, so too the Chief Executive is able to hold the legislature in thrall. The latter point is illustrated with particular force in foreign affairs, where Congress has been notably deferential to executive management of crises. Within this system of mutual constraints there remain various opportunities for political initiatives by both Congress and the executive. Those who have focused on the inhibitory aspects of legislative-executive relations have not always distinguished between *functional constraints* and *dysfunctional constraints,* nor have they explored fully the kinds of initiatives that characterize the system (and which may also be functional or dysfunctional).[7] In order to attain a net evaluation

---

[6] A brief treatment of some of these concepts is Alton Frye, "Congress: The Virtues of its Vices," *Foreign Policy,* no. 3, Summer 1971, pp. 108–125.

[7] Here the terms "functional" and "dysfunctional" refer to the system's performance as a unit in international politics, not merely to the individual functions of Congress and the Presidency as separate institutions within the system. Thus the basic criterion adopted here is

of the system's overall performance in international affairs, it is necessary to analyze both types of constraints and initiatives. Such analysis reveals that there is—or can be—a deeper rationality to the American political process. Explicitly recognized and skillfully applied, as it sometimes has been, this rationality becomes a valuable asset to the government's conduct of foreign relations.

The system of constraints to which I have referred is an integral part of the bargaining processes that shape America's domestic and international politics. These constraints not only limit power, in fact, they provide some of the essential ingredients in the psychological context enveloping the entire political process. Paradoxically, what is a constraint in one respect can become a powerful lever in another.

Thus the President can often exert greater pressure on Congress by appealing to other, extracongressional constraints under which he labors; for example, he may emphasize the desires of foreign allies or the threats of foreign adversaries, the alleged requirements of public opinion, even his obligation to maintain the prerogatives of the presidential office. Members of Congress, in turn, can raise constraints of their own to bolster their bargaining position. On one occasion they may seek to maintain the sympathy of constituents disaffected by the members' support for a particular foreign policy by stressing the need to back the President at a time of international crisis. On another they may justify their defection from the ranks of presidential supporters by citing the pressure of constituent opinions or interests, which the members may claim vary sharply from those of other districts or states. In one or another connection the legislators may also appeal to partisan or institutional constraints, invoking the need to support their party hierarchy, the chairman of the committee on which they serve, or the representatives of their house in a bicameral conference committee. These are the kinds of constraints, real or presumed, which exert such a large influence in the domestic political setting.

Similar elements exist in bargaining at the international level. The government operates under a variety of political constraints, and it can sometimes improve its bargaining stance vis-à-vis other governments by calling attention to the pressures and limitations under which it labors. It can argue that a course of action is prohibited by commitments to allies or other international obligations. But most convincing of all, as is true for any government, is the appeal to domestic constraints, the claim that a particular policy is demanded or forbidden by the requirements of domestic politics. In such an appeal the President may invoke public opinion at home or his responsibilities as a party leader, but nothing will be more relevant than his

---

the total system's effectiveness in international politics. The logical primacy of this criterion rests on the fact that the system can sustain its internal values only if it enjoys at least minimal effectiveness in the international arena, i. e., survives as a state.

estimate of the constraints posed by Congress. As the institution best placed to thwart his political objectives or to take immediate reprisals against an unwary President, Congress represents the most potent and credible constraint which the executive can cite in its dealings with foreign powers.[8]

In the relations of states with highly centralized or authoritarian structures, there is usually little doubt about the capacity of the government, i. e., the executive, to determine and administer the nation's foreign policies. If the concentration of policy-making authority confers certain advantages in international politics, it carries its liabilities as well. There is little opportunity for such a government to escape the international onus for unpopular or unsuccessful foreign policies. When friction occurs in its relations with other states, it cannot normally be mitigated by claiming that the government was compelled to act in a particular fashion by other domestic political institutions.

Democratic states, and especially the United States, present a more variegated facade to the world at large. The executive is indeed the country's agent in international relations, but it is a limited agent whose mandate may be curtailed in any number of ways by Congress. Important political negotiations with foreign states invariably find members of the U.S. Administration asking themselves "how much Congress will buy." This fact is not lost on foreign negotiators, who may regret it but who cannot ignore it in devising their own bargaining positions. They come to recognize that "possible repercussions on the Hill" operate as a vague but continuous and general limitation on the U.S. government.

The ubiquity of this factor presumably tends to reduce the country's flexibility in foreign relations, but as students of bargaining have pointed out, there are many circumstances in which this very lack of flexibility can be a negotiating asset. When one participant in a bargaining discussion knows that there are limits beyond which another participant cannot go, he may be more likely to tailor his own demands to fit within the perceived boundaries of potential agreement. The limits asserted by the second participant appear most credible when they are beyond his power to control. This is often the situation in U.S. foreign relations, when both U.S. and foreign negotiators realize that any agreement they reach will have to be sold to Congress.

[8] This discussion is stimulated by the insights of Thomas Schelling, *The Strategy of Conflict* (Cambridge, Mass.: Harvard, 1963), especially pp. 21–52. Senator Fulbright once made a similar point on "Meet the Press": "It isn't profitable for me or any other Senator or Congressman to be forever advocating foreign aid. . . . So, it is the President that must take the lead, . . . and I think he makes a mistake in not taking a stronger stand in this field, giving all Congressmen and Senators, we will say, an 'excuse' to go along with it." Quoted in James A. Robinson, *Congress and Foreign Policy-Making* (Homewood, Ill.: Dorsey, 1962), p. 213. Likewise, Congress often gives the President an "excuse" to move in one direction or another.

The history of the nuclear test ban illustrates some of the ways in which Congress's capacity to set boundaries for agreements may enhance executive bargaining power. Following the Soviet Union's resumption of testing in 1961 and the intensification of the perpetual Berlin crisis, sentiment in Congress shifted toward a harder line on relations with Moscow. The Russians' abrupt abrogation of the moratorium on nuclear tests generated a mood of deep distrust, and influential members of Congress made it clear that they would oppose any future suspension of tests unless it was accompanied by adequate arrangements for verifying compliance. Tests in the atmosphere, in outer space, and underwater could be monitored from outside a nation's territory, but it was generally believed that controls over underground tests would have to include local inspection of suspected test sites.

When serious discussions of the test ban issue resumed in late 1962, Soviet Premier Khrushchev seems to have appreciated that if a comprehensive treaty was to be concluded, it would be necessary to include some on-site inspections. Although he insisted that such a provision was really unnecessary, the Soviet leader told Norman Cousins that he realized "Congress has convinced itself that on-site inspection is necessary and the President cannot get a treaty through the Senate without it. Very well, then, let us accommodate the President."[9] On December 19, 1962, in his most dramatic concession of the lengthy negotiations, Khrushchev wrote President Kennedy that the Soviet Union would permit two or three annnual inspections, a number the Soviet government believed the United States was prepared to accept. The Kennedy Administration, however, having previously reduced its demands, felt it could not agree to fewer than seven such inspections, and a comprehensive treaty remained out of reach. Nevertheless, Khrushchev's testimony makes clear that the concession was a response to the constraints he believed Congress to have imposed on the President.

Perhaps the most vital congressional contribution to the eventual limited agreement was removal of what many had considered an insurmountable obstacle to a test ban, the apparent congressional insistence that any treaty must be both comprehensive and verified. Disillusioned with the experience of the 1958–1961 moratorium, many congressmen had denounced the idea of any agreement that did not provide for inspection inside the Soviet Union. On this issue negotiations deadlocked, only to be broken by a historic Senate initiative.

[9] Khrushchev made these remarks to Norman Cousins of *Saturday Review;* quoted in Arthur Schlesinger, Jr., *A Thousand Days* (Boston: Houghton Mifflin, 1965), p. 895. The Soviet Premier claimed to have great difficulty himself in convincing the Council of Ministers to accept the notion of inspection. His subsequent removal from office reminds one that Soviet leaders also act under important internal constraints, though less formal ones than those affecting the American President.

Both Presidents Eisenhower and Kennedy noted Khrushchev's close attention to various aspects of U.S. domestic politics. See especially Theodore Sorensen, *Kennedy* (New York: Harper & Row, 1965), p. 544.

One of the most vocal critics of the test ban discussion had been Senator Thomas J. Dodd, a Connecticut Democrat. Skeptical of Soviet intentions, Dodd had found his worst fears confirmed by Russia's secret test preparations during the earlier, unpoliced moratorium. A compromise agreement with anything less than foolproof inspection seemed anathema to him, as, for some time, did anything less than a comprehensive agreement. But, in the spring of 1963, a series of private exchanges between Dodd and the U.S. Arms Control and Disarmament Agency persuaded the Senator that it was indeed possible to determine unilaterally whether another country was conducting tests in any environment except underground. This led Dodd to join Senator Hubert Humphrey and thirty-two cosponsors in submitting a Senate resolution that called for a limited test ban, covering only tests in the atmosphere, underwater, and in outer space. The resolution sidestepped the inspection issue and helped to revive the dying negotiations. Success came barely two months later when U.S., Soviet, and British representatives initialed a treaty prohibiting nuclear tests in all environments other than underground. By adjusting the constraints on this issue, the Senate had played a critical role in inducing the Soviet Union to accept the compromise text.

There are other ways in which Congress can adjust policy constraints which may have become outmoded or futile. As a forum for the exploration of diverse views and issues, Congress is a natural arena for the floating of trial balloons on delicate matters, by congressmen acting on their own or seeking to test reactions to ideas in which the Administration has an interest. The subject of birth control assistance to nations receiving U.S. foreign aid, taboo in the Eisenhower years and broached rather gingerly by members of the Kennedy Administration, had long been considered an impossibly hot potato for American politicians. Surprisingly, Congress not only reacted favorably to the tentative ideas advanced by Presidents Kennedy and Johnson, but some members pressed for more vigorous efforts in this direction. Through hearings and speeches Senator Ernest Gruening became a leading advocate of larger and more systematic assistance to deal with the population problem.[10] Although the subject remains one from which many members shy away, Congress has helped to make birth control assistance a matter for open and honest discussion.

Beyond attempting to eradicate the unwritten constraints presumably imposed by public opinion, Congress may at times correct more explicit and rigid limitations it has established on the scope and direction of American foreign policy. Of particular interest in this connection is the history of U.S. policy toward Communist China. Through the nineteen-fifties a series of congressional resolutions and other expressions left no doubt that Congress favored every effort to isolate the Peking regime from international affairs. The legislature repeatedly called on the President to oppose seating Red China in the United Nations and to refrain from extending diplomatic

---

[10] Gruening's endeavors are summarized in *Congress and the Nation*, vol. II, pp. 683–685.

recognition to the mainland government unless and until it had demonstrated its willingness and capacity to become a law-abiding member of the world community. For years the doctrine of containment found ready agreement in the executive branch of government and the nation at large. By the nineteen-sixties, however, it was evident that American policy toward China was frozen in a mold that promised little profit to the U.S. national interest or to international stability. Premier Khrushchev mocked the policy of nonrecognition by remarking to President Kennedy that the United States seemed well on the way to surpassing the performance of Czarist Russia, which had taken twenty-six years to recognize the government established by the American Revolution.

While both the Kennedy and Johnson administrations stood firm on the essentials of past policy, in Congress demands began to be heard for new departures in regard to China. During 1965 and 1966 Senator Robert Kennedy of New York called for the inclusion of Red China in arms control conferences. Other senators, including Jacob Javits, urged that the Peking regime be brought into the United Nations without expelling the Nationalist government on Formosa. A dramatic highlight of the evolving congressional stand on China was the nationally televised hearings conducted by the Senate Foreign Relations Committee during March 1966.[11] Chairman Fulbright employed the hearings to educate the American public in the new realities and hard issues of the situation in the Far East.

The hearings, widely acclaimed for having focused attention on a preeminent problem of American foreign policy, did not produce immediate and overwhelming support for specific innovations in the U.S. position, but they clearly marked the end of the previous consensus favoring rigid isolation of Red China. The President could no longer invoke congressional unanimity as a basis for standing pat on the old policy. Indeed the erosion of the former, apparently absolute congressional constraints in this area served as a powerful prod for the Administration to seek alternatives. Progress toward improved relations with Communist China promised to be a slow and arduous process, especially in light of the war in Vietnam, but the demonstrated shifts in congressional attitudes on this issue aroused hope that the process might at least be under way. Tokens of the changing climate were the quiet relaxation of U.S. restrictions on travel to China by Americans and the Johnson Administration's new theme of "containment but not isolation" in regard to Peking. Though slowed in the late sixties, the gradual movement toward contact with China continued with President Nixon's resumption of the suspended ambassadorial talks with Peking and his Administration's modified formula regarding Chinese membership in the United Nations. The evolving congressional posture on China policy not

[11] See Hearings before the Committee on Foreign Relations, U.S. Senate, *U.S. Policy with Respect to Mainland China*, 89th Cong., 2d Sess., Mar. 8, 10, 16, 18, 21, 28, and 30, 1966.

only encouraged the executive to pursue overtures toward the Communist government; presumably it eased the President's difficulties with the Nationalist Chinese, who well understood that the initiatives were being urged on the Chief Executive by influential senators and congressmen.

As it happened, the shifting congressional attitudes toward China paralleled those of Richard Nixon, who found them an opportunity to adapt U.S. policy to the altered circumstances of Red China's position in the international community. It is testimony not only to the President's shrewdness but to the surprising changes in the Congress that Mr. Nixon's decision to visit China and his Administration's abandonment of all-out opposition to Peking's admission to the United Nations brought not outrage but endorsements from most congressmen. Without the newfound realism on Capitol Hill, the White House would have found it exceedingly risky politics to entertain the daring departures undertaken in 1971 and 1972. In these and other cases one gains some insight into ways in which legislative establishment and adjustment of constraints on the executive can affect U.S. performance in international politics.

One cannot blink the fact that Congress has had a share of responsibility for many mistakes, mishaps, and failures of American foreign policy. This responsibility, albeit diluted by that of other individuals, groups, and institutions, extends far beyond the relatively trivial issues of whether this or that country should receive more or less U.S. foreign aid in a given year, or whether the United States should adopt one or another policy for its international information programs. Congress also bears heavy responsibility for the rigid isolationism which contributed to the conditions which brought about the Second World War. A decade later the congressional stance may also have tempted the North Koreans and their Soviet allies to calculate that there would be no U.S. response to an invasion of South Korea. One can build a credible case that in a number of cases congressional constraints on executive action were decidedly counterproductive, both in terms of overall U.S. policy and of the particular interests of Congress as an institution.

This is partly because Congress has not always been sensitive to the fact that in debating international issues and in endorsing or rejecting foreign policies, it is engaged in a complicated signaling process that has important effects far beyond national boundaries. Congressional discussion and decisions, taken by many foreign observers as the true measure of the balance of political forces in the United States, can have far-reaching influence in shaping the expectations others hold concerning the basic trends in U.S. foreign policy. This can either reinforce or undermine the posture presented by the executive in its relations with other governments.

The historical handicap of democratic regimes operating in international politics has been their difficulty in sustaining unified action against some more authoritarian antagonist. The potential for disunity in a republic is always a temptation to its adversaries, who may assume that internal political divisions will paralyze the democratic system. There is reason to believe that more than one aggressor state has counted on congressional constraints to impede any effective action the President might be tempted to take.

The calculations of the German government prior to the Second World War illustrate this tendency. The Nazi leaders, including Hitler personally, were convinced that isolationist strength in Congress would make it impossible for President Roosevelt to intervene in any European war should he be tempted to do so.[12] They based this assessment not only on a general sense of public opinion in the United States but also on a number of congressional actions that indicated determined opposition to any American involvement in a future European conflict. Earliest of these actions, of course, was the Senate rejection of the League of Nations Covenant and the repudiation of President Wilson. Even more specific and conclusive to the Nazi regime were the various neutrality laws passed by Congress in the nineteen-thirties. The records of the German government leave little doubt that these actions by Congress contributed significantly to the conviction in Berlin that the Third Reich could plan aggression in Europe without concern for possible U.S. interference. Indeed the critical documents on German war planning prior to 1939 seldom mention the United States at all except to stress the improbability of American intervention. Even after the fall of France in 1940 and the shift in American opinion toward support for Great Britain "short of war," the Third Reich looked to the isolationist bloc in Congress to frustrate Roosevelt's alleged interventionist instincts. Especially noteworthy as a basis for the German view was the narrow margin by which Congress extended the draft law in 1941; the switch of a single vote in the House would have left the United States with virtually no ready forces by the end of that year.

There is, of course, no certainty that had Congress acted differently on all or any of these issues, the United States would have deterred Hitler from launching the attack on Poland. Quite apart from his personal belief that the United States would be politically paralyzed, the Fuehrer considered the Americans militarily inept. But it is at least arguable that the congressional isolationism of the period, admittedly a reflection of widespread popular sentiment, robbed the United States of whatever deterrent potential it might have exerted in Europe.

The role of Congress in the events preceding the Korean war also merits examination. It is inaccurate to view the outbreak of hostilities in Korea as a failure of deterrence; the withdrawal of U.S. forces from Korea before the summer of 1950, together with public statements by Secretary of State Acheson and other U.S. spokesmen, seemed to have removed Korea from the

[12] See Alton Frye, *Nazi Germany and the American Hemisphere, 1933–1941* (New Haven, Conn.: Yale, 1967). See also Donald W. Drummond, *The Passing of American Neutrality, 1937–1941* (Ann Arbor: The University of Michigan Press, 1955).

American defense zone. But President Truman, among others, has contended that the Soviet bloc would have displayed greater caution in Korea and elsewhere had it not been for the low estate of U.S. military preparedness. The rapid demobilization which had followed the Second World War must be charged, at least in part, to congressional insistence that American boys be brought home. Although the onset of the Cold War had induced some attempts to bring U.S. military capabilities into line with the country's international commitments, Congress had resisted a number of the Administration's efforts to strengthen U.S. forces.

In after years Mr. Truman was moved to speculate that had Congress enacted the proposals for universal military training which he first submitted in 1945, it "would have caused the Soviets to hesitate and perhaps not bring on the Berlin crisis or the Korean aggression."[13] This hypothesis is unprovable, and it is true that by 1949 Congress was somewhat more inclined than Truman to expand defense spending, but it is reasonable to believe that the demonstrated reluctance of Congress over a period of years to support the military recommendations of the executive helped convince the Soviet leaders and their associates that the United States lacked the will and capacity to respond to the invasion of South Korea.

If one recognizes the dysfunctional efforts in which Congress has sometimes engaged, one should also note that legislative-executive collaboration in this field has produced and exploited a number of techniques whose actual and potential contributions have been insufficiently understood.

Those commentators who despise Congress as a modern "Babel-on" overlook the utility of an institution that speaks with many voices and that permits the expression of many points of view regarding foreign policy. Some important advantages grow from Congress's function as an independent source of international communication.

CONGRESS AS COMMUNICATOR

Foreign states are frequently alert to congressional attitudes on foreign policy and to congressional influence on the President's capacity to act in international affairs. Both allies and adversaries have their "Congress-watchers" stationed in Washington. Through these and other channels of international communication the substance of congressional hearings, debates, and votes is broadcast. They form part of the data from which other states derive their ideas of likely U.S. behavior in world affairs. Congress can be a potent force

---

[13] Harry S. Truman, *Memoirs* (New York: Signet, 1965), vol. II, p. 73; also see Samuel P. Huntington, *The Common Defense* (New York, 1961), pp. 33–46. Acheson vigorously disputes the inference that his famous speech regarding the U.S. defense perimeter gave the North Koreans a green light to attack; see Dean Acheson, *Present at the Creation* (New York: Norton, 1969), pp. 691, 763–765.

in shaping the expectations of foreign elites concerning U.S. policy, and, as an independent communicator, Congress can accomplish some distinctive ends in American foreign policy.

One of the most difficult things in delicate political relations between states is to be able to levy sanctions or convey threats without offending other parties. In order to maintain good relations on all issues, diplomats may find it hard to exert pressure on any one issue.

In the U.S. system Congress can to some degree relieve the executive of this restriction. In cases of friction with some foreign power, when the executive may feel obliged to remain silent or to couch a reproach in the softest of terms, Congress may voice its demands or displeasure in more emphatic fashion, reminding the foreign state that the President may be compelled by the legislature to take sterner action than he himself might wish. This pattern has become a regular feature of contemporary American foreign policy; it recurs frequently, for example, in congressional action on foreign aid where restrictions and reductions are often designed to apply pressure on points of contention unrelated to the aid program as such.

The higher logic of foreign assistance efforts stresses the U.S. interest in promoting the development of economically viable, politically stable, and independent societies abroad. In this view the aid program should not be transformed into a vehicle for retaliation against regimes with whose policies the United States disagrees. This rationale is persuasive so far as it goes, but there are instances in which the policies in question tend to frustrate the very purposes of U.S. economic or military aid. It can scarcely be claimed that Congress has always discriminated between this class of policies and others, but one can defend a number of congressional aid reprisals in these terms. Good examples are the restrictions Congress placed on aid to the United Arab Republic and Indonesia during the mid-sixties.

Both these countries had negated much of the value of U.S. assistance by the diversion of substantial resources to military programs. In the view of many, U.A.R.'s policy of implacable hostility to Israel was not only undermining its own development efforts but contributing to perpetual political instability throughout the Middle East. Similarly, Indonesian President Sukarno had followed his campaign against the Dutch position in West Irian by the confrontation with Malaysia. The extravagant costs of his international policies, combined with continued neglect of domestic economic problems, made it doubtful that U.S. assistance to the island nation would serve any worthwhile purpose. It might only help prolong Sukarno's misguided priorities and delay the start of serious efforts to develop the Indonesian economy. Thus, on the plane of grand strategy for the aid program, there was a case for the congressional ban on assistance to Indonesia and, with the U.A.R. in mind, on aid to any country which the President determined to be taking or preparing military action against another nation receiving U.S. aid (i. e., Israel).

In these and most other cases, however, the legislation leaves the President flexibility to determine whether and how to apply the provisions. Thus Congress can communicate a threat, probably more explicit and direct than the executive would be able to use, leaving to the President the final decision as to its execution. If the threat is ignored and the sanction is administered, the President can divert a major portion of the foreign state's resentment by stressing that Congress and not the executive had dictated the action.

It is difficult to tell just what effect such congressional messages have on foreign parties. One must usually infer what result, if any, is achieved. For example, did it make any difference for U.S.–Panamanian relations that, following incidents in the Panama Canal and a break in diplomatic relations between the two countries, Congress passed legislation authorizing a study of a new sea-level canal in Central America? The first Senate action on the bill came on March 30, 1964, only four days before Panama and the United States agreed to re-establish diplomatic ties and to seek a new agreement concerning the canal. The congressional activity could hardly have escaped the notice of Panamanian officials. Assuming that Panama would not welcome a second and more modern canal as a competitor, the congressional expression of interest in an alternate route may have materially strengthened the U.S. bargaining position.

In addition to statutory actions, Congress can often convey signals through its debates and proceedings that might be inappropriate or impolitic for the executive to express in comparable fashion. One example is the vocal and widespread congressional support for reducing the number of U.S. troops in Europe, especially since the NATO allies have generally failed to meet their own designated force levels for defense of the continent. One may complain that such congressional expressions weaken the credibility of the American commitment to Europe, but the United States must also be concerned that its commitments not be taken so much for granted that it loses leverage on its allies. If a threat to cut American deployments is necessary to induce allies to meet their own commitments, there is much to be said for having it communicated indirectly through congressional debate. This procedure manages to make the point without running the risk that allies will lose confidence immediately in the intentions of an incumbent U.S. Administration, a danger that must be avoided if the pressure is to have the desired effect of increasing the cohesiveness and effectiveness of the alliance.

It is evident that the crescendo of congressional attacks on the retention of large U.S. forces in Europe has had major influence in NATO councils. After years of moderate pressure for withdrawal of some U.S. troops, Senate Majority Leader Mike Mansfield pressed the question to a vote in May 1971. Although defeated overwhelmingly, the Mansfield amendment provoked a fierce debate which demonstrated the depth of American feeling that, a quarter century after the Second World War, Europe should assume a greater share of the burdens of self-defense. Clearly, the issue would remain a live one in American politics, and that fact did not pass unnoticed across the Atlantic. By December the NATO allies in Europe had formulated plans to increase their contribution to the alliance, as the Nixon Administration had already been urging, by some $1 billion a year. The relationship of this development to the commotion over Mansfield's plan was scarcely coincidental.[14] The House Appropriations Committee has taken other concrete measures to elicit allied funding of NATO infrastructure projects. In the fiscal 1973 appropriations report, the committee denied moneys for selected construction projects in Germany, a device calculated to induce and enable the Pentagon to solicit greater allied contributions. And the following year the Jackson-Nunn amendment created a continuing standard to relate U.S. troop strength in Europe to allied assistance in reducing the balance-of-payments costs of maintaining the forces overseas. It was a useful compromise to direct cuts in the troop ceiling and provided a specific mechanism for the alliance to handle the perennial dispute.

In the nature of this power to communicate independently and to manipulate constraints on the President there is danger of unwise strangulation of sensible executive policies. The delicacy of using this double-edged power is illustrated by the intense maneuvering over an amendment offered for several years after 1972 by Senator Henry Jackson to condition the grant of most-favored-nation treatment to the Soviet Union on a relaxation of Soviet emigration policies. In essence Senator Jackson and the numerous cosponsors of his measure—a majority of both the House and Senate—sought to force Moscow to permit Soviet Jews to leave for Israel without paying exorbitant exit fees which the Soviet Union had imposed. The issue became a focal point of contention between Congress and the Nixon Administration, which favored diplomatic efforts to persuade Moscow to relent but which opposed atempts to link these pressures with attempts to expand trade. It was the central topic of a dramatic meeting between congressional leaders and Chairman Leonid Brezhnev during the latter's visit to Washington in June 1973.

Russian authorities made clear their resentment of this blatant interference in their domestic affairs, and, despite widespread compassion for the plight of Russian Jews, many Americans felt the point was valid, noting that the United States would not tolerate any foreign attempt to make improved trade ties dependent on changes, for example, in American civil rights laws. Yet, it was undoubtedly true that the threat of the Jackson amendment was a factor in the Soviet commitment to suspend enforcement of its schedule of exit fees. The question soon became whether, having generated therapeutic

---

[14] See especially the concluding debates on the Mansfield plan, *Congressional Record*, May 19, 1971, pp. S7363–S7439; the NATO allies' response is described in John Goshko, "10 European Allies in NATO to Boost Military Spending," *Washington Post*, Dec. 8, 1971, p. 1.

tensions in the diplomatic process, Congress would be wise to make Soviet-American trade hostage to explicit statutory arrangements concerning Russian emigration practices. There was a profound need to balance the humane impulse and objective of the Jackson proposal against the great political goal of ameliorating East-West relations.

The attempt to strike such a balance came in the startling announcement—made by Senator Jackson in the White House press room on October 20, 1974—that, in return for unprecedented commitments by Soviet officials to relax their harassment of would-be emigrés, the proponents of the Jackson amendment would provide discretionary authority for the President to waive the provision. These remarkable understandings emerged from the most intense and prolonged negotiations in which the Secretary of State, working feverishly to prevent disruption of détente through the excesses of either side, became the virtual mediator between the Congress and the Soviet government. The potency of the Jackson maneuver was evident, but it was regrettable that public clamor over it came to jeopardize the Soviet-American trade agreement of 1972, as Moscow resisted what it termed discriminatory conditions on the arrangement.

Congress's functions as an international communicator are not limited to applying pressure on foreign states or to expressing American dissatisfaction with another country's policy. One of the most vital functions derives from the diversity of signals which members of Congress generate. On almost any policy pursued by an executive, there will be a dissenter in Congress. There are times when this can encourage foreign antagonists to believe that an Administration, under fire by critics on the home front, will not be able to carry out the policy it has begun. There is little question that this kind of calculation had an important impact on North Vietnamese estimates of U.S. capacity to sustain the war effort in Southeast Asia. Hanoi's propaganda alleged that President Johnson might be impeached or overthrown by congressional dissidents in this country; Communist units in the field bombarded American troops with excerpts from antiwar speeches by former Senators Morse and Gruening and others, coupled with appeals to lay down their arms.

But congressional dissent from an Administration's policy does not work only to bolster the morale of foreign adversaries. As a principal means for self-criticism of U.S. foreign policy, the process of dissent saves the country from the hazards of presenting a monolithic image to the world. Foreign states at odds with policies or actions of the executive can frequently identify members of Congress whom they consider more friendly. Their attitude toward the United States as a whole takes on a more complex aspect, a factor that reduces the likelihood of permanent and general antagonism between this country and others. Just as Congress sometimes incurs the enmity of foreign powers by constraining the executive, international reaction to controversial U.S. actions will often focus on the Administration, while individuals in Congress maintain cordial personal relations with leaders of the foreign states concerned. These relations can become a valuable national asset, a reservoir of good will which can lay the foundation for subsequent improvement in relations between the countries.

A striking example of this process centered on Senator Fulbright's sharp criticism of U.S. intervention in the Dominican Republic during 1965. President Johnson's dispatch of troops to the Caribbean island aroused considerable alarm among other Latin American countries. But with so prominent a figure as Fulbright sharing their concern over the President's action, Latin Americans were less prone to infer that Yankee imperialism was blossoming throughout the United States. They were able to detect, through the public statements of the Arkansas Senator and others of like mind, that there was no American consensus in favor of abandoning the Good Neighbor Policy and the principle of nonintervention. This was reassuring to many of our Latin neighbors and tended to moderate their apprehensions about the future course of American policy in the Western Hemisphere.

Another case in point is the high regard in which Senator Mike Mansfield is held by Prince Sihanouk of Cambodia. Tension between that country and the United States did not destroy the Senator's standing in Southeast Asia. As a matter of fact, Mansfield became an important channel for a variety of diplomatic exchanges with the flamboyant Prince in the years prior to his overthrow. In the midst of a serious diplomatic breach with the Johnson Administration, Cambodia nevertheless honored the Montana Democrat by dedicating a street to him. This seemingly insignificant incident suggests the way in which Congress, by providing a multifaceted image of official America, can help prevent friction between the executive and other governments from degenerating into blanket and perpetual hostility. The Senator's special rapport with the exiled Prince became an important asset once more in 1973, when the Nixon Administration, failing in its diplomatic overtures to Sihanouk, enlisted Mansfield's aid as an active intermediary in efforts to terminate the simmering civil war in Cambodia as a necessary step toward final extrication from Indochina's multiple horrors.

Thus, as an important source of signals to foreign leaders and publics, Congress helps to color and to complicate their vision of America. If congressional actions sometimes communicate an impression of domestic dessension, there are certain advantages inherent in the very multiplicity of images they transmit. In the most irritating episodes between the United States and other governments, it is usually possible for the foreign state to identify with one or more sympathetic members of Congress and to retain some degree of warmth for this country. This is but one of the compensating virtues in a system with an unmatched propensity to criticize whatever action the executive takes.

CONGRESS AS LIBERATOR

Most of the functions to which we have alluded have been exploited on an ad hoc and unsystematic basis. Only in a limited sense and in comparatively few cases have they been applied as part of a rational plan to increase U.S. effectiveness in world politics. The simplest and most conspicuous such cases have involved the use of congressional resolutions to emphasize popular support for a particular policy or to provide greater freedom of maneuver for the President to handle some foreign crisis.

There have been a number of such resolutions designed to "unleash" the President, to make clear to foreign parties that the Chief Executive enjoys the confidence of the legislature in determing U.S. action abroad. They have often served to reduce the chance that an adversary might assume that domestic politics would prevent the President from responding to an international provocation. Thus, in the summer of 1940, when Nazi victories in Europe aroused concern that Germany might claim the conquered nations' overseas colonies, including those in the New World, Congress signaled its opposition to the transfer of territory in the Western Hemisphere from one non-American power to another. A joint resolution of June 18, 1940, stated support for measures to forestall such transfers, should they appear likely, and paved the way for the dramatic action taken the following month at the Havana conference of the American republics. At that meeting the American foreign ministers adopted a declaration and convention providing for action by their countries, collectively or individually, to take over any colonial possession in this hemisphere that the Axis powers might seek to control.[15] The congressional resolution and the inter-American actions undoubtedly bolstered the hemisphere's deterrent posture and reinforced the explicit warnings delivered in Berlin by the U.S. embassy.

Similar "liberating resolutions" have been employed in several instances during the Cold War, usually on the initiative of the President. Partly because of heightened sensitivity to the danger that foreign antagonists might misconstrue American intentions, as the North Koreans and Chinese were thought to have done in 1950, a succession of chief executives have sought congressional resolutions to provide public and emphatic evidence that the United States would respond to international challenge. In January 1955, fearing action by the Chinese Communists against the Nationalist regime on Formosa, President Eisenhower asked and received an overwhelming legislative endorsement of his authority to take such "measures as he judges to be required or appropriate in assuring the defense of Formosa and the Pescadores."[16] Although the President was confident of his own authori-

[15] S. F. Bemis, *A Diplomatic History of the United States* (New York: Holt, 1955), p. 774f.
[16] Dwight D. Eisenhower, *Mandate for Change, 1953 to 1956,* (Garden City, N.Y.: Doubleday, 1963), pp. 459–483 and appendix N, p. 608.

ty to aid in the defense of Formosa and associated territories, he considered the resolution valuable as a sign of national unity on the issue. Comparable rationales supported the passage of resolutions on the Middle East in 1957 (the so-called Eisenhower doctrine), Cuba in 1962, and Southeast Asia in 1964.

The debate over the Formosa resolution, while ending in unequivocal votes of 410 to 3 in the House and 83 to 3 in the Senate, revealed congressional awareness of some basic difficulties of this mechanism for involving Congress in the process of international communication. Several members of the Senate were apprehensive about granting such blanket authority to the President. Senator Wayne Morse of Oregon, dissenting from this resolution as he was to do from subsequent ones, termed the measure a "predatory authorization" to wage war and questioned whether Congress should accept such a de facto abridgment of its power to declare war. Other senators, including Hubert Humphrey of Minnesota and Herbert Lehman of New York, were anxious to limit the resolution explicitly to Formosa and the Pescadores. They would have excluded the offshore island groups of Quemoy and Matsu, but the Administration argued forcefully that the resolution would be most helpful in deterring the Chinese if the text retained a degree of ambiguity on this point.

As in later cases, efforts to revise the original resolution were unavailing, and for an understandable reason. Such resolutions, ordinarily requested by the President in the context of a developing crisis or with a view to precluding some hostile action by an adversary, are the nearest thing in American politics to a test of legislative confidence in the executive branch of government. In general, congressional respect for presidential primacy in foreign affairs has been high. Members of Congress recognize that the President's prestige is an essential element in his effectiveness as the nation's principal agent in international politics. That prestige becomes a vital asset to the country. As Karl Deutsch once phrased it rather elegantly, "Prestige is to power as credit is to cash." Members are extremely reluctant to cast what would appear as a vote of no confidence in the President's authority to meet a foreign crisis. In most instances they have hesitated to delay or modify resolutions of this type, calculating that tardy passage or addition of constraints on presidential action would tend only to weaken the psychological impact of the vote and hence to frustrate the purposes of the resolution.

Especially if an air of crisis surrounds consideration of the measure, these factors have led to prompt and positive action on such resolutions. President Eisenhower's message on the Formosa doctrine went to Congress on January 24, 1955; the House vote came on the following day and the Senate vote only three days later. When the presumed foreign threat seems less imminent or well-defined, the procedure may take longer but Congress is not likely to reject the Chief Executive's request outright. Desultory consideration of the so-called Eisenhower doctrine, as formulated in a resolution declaring Congress's support of the Administration's plans for economic and military assistance to countries in the Middle East, occupied the two houses for two months in early 1957. Close observers perceived that many members had little taste for the proposal, but the outcome was never in doubt. As Representative James Roosevelt predicted, there was rarely a bill "which had so few friends that will get so many votes."[17] In the Senate John Kennedy and others supported the resolution in order to avoid "political embarrassment" to the President and Secretary of State.

By the very act of requesting such a resolution, the President makes it extremely difficult for Congress to defeat it. In such cases the Chief Executive amplifies his power by political pre-emption. Confronted with a clear issue of support for a presidential policy regarding some foreign imbroglio, the legislature is unlikely to repudiate the nation's designated agent in this field. Indeed, Congress is usually maneuvered into a position where it must accept with little or no modification the Administration's definition of desirable policy and where its opportunities to contribute to policy are severely restricted. Legislative exploration of the merits of the Administration case or of other alternatives is impeded.

The effects of this procedure, though hard to specify with confidence, seem to have been advantageous to U.S. foreign policy on several occasions. The 1955 Formosa resolution probably enhanced the credibility of the country's deterrent posture in the Formosa straits. Under the 1957 Middle East resolution President Eisenhower supplied assistance to Jordan and Lebanon, helping to maintain the independence of those countries and to preserve the precarious political balance in that region. An important element in the Kennedy Administration's policy during the Cuban missile crisis of 1962 was the joint resolution passed only weeks before; by votes of 86 to 1 in the Senate and 384 to 7 in the House, Congress had declared U.S. determination to prevent Cuban subversion and any development in Cuba of an externally supported military capability endangering U.S. security.[18] There could hardly have been a clearer mandate for the President's decisive action to force removal of Soviet ballistic missiles from the island.

Nevertheless, many congressmen and political leaders had long been apprehensive about the broad grants of authority implied by such resolutions. Adlai Stevenson and others opposed the Middle East resolution as a blank check. But neither this resolution nor other measures had actually led to the dire consequences foreseen by their critics. Not so with the resolution dealing with the Tonkin Gulf incident and Southeast Asia which Congress

[17] Quoted in *Congress and the Nation,* vol. I, p. 120; final votes were 350 to 60 in the House and 72 to 19 in the Senate.
[18] Ibid., pp. 132 ff.

passed in August, 1964 by the virtually unanimous margins of 88 to 2 in the Senate and 414 to 0 in the House.[19] In language quite similar to that of the 1955 resolution, Congress declared support for the President's determination "to take all necessary measures to repel any armed attack against the forces of the United States and *to prevent further aggression*" (italics supplied.). That resolution became a prime justification of the Johnson Administration's subsequent expansion of U.S. military activities in Vietnam, much to the chagrin of its supporters.

So bitter has been the disillusionment with the Gulf of Tonkin provision that the Ninety-first Congress moved to clean the record by repealing it, although it took no final action on other such measures whose duration had been left uncertain. The Senate, instead, undertook a sweeping re-examination of the entire catalogue of emergency powers which had accrued to the President in hundreds of statutes which lingered on the books. There is now tremendous reticence in Congress to enact similar resolutions. It is certainly a healthy thing for the legislature to be wary of such proposals, to scrutinize them with greater care, and to draft them more precisely in the future.

Before relegating this useful technique to the category of political taboos, however, one ought to take a thorough look at the peculiar circumstances surrounding the Tonkin measure. Mark Twain once sagely observed that "it is important not to get out of an experience more than there is in it. A cat that sits on a hot stove won't sit on a hot stove again. But he won't sit on a cold one either." One may argue that some wrong lessons have been emphasized about the Tonkin resolution.

It seems probable that the deterrent value of the Tonkin resolution was utterly dissipated by the contradictory signals Hanoi received during the 1964 presidential campaign. Lyndon Johnson's portrayal of Barry Goldwater as "Super-Hawk" contrasted with his own dovish themes on Vietnam. And the contrast must have obscured the warning intended by the August resolution.[20] To the North Vietnamese it may well have seemed that a few stiff attacks, as at Pleiku in early 1965, would persuade President Johnson to depart forthwith. It is only reasonable to believe that if such resolutions are to be helpful, they must be part and parcel of a more consistent set of messages than those emanating from the United States in late 1964. The sad truth seems to be that in 1964 the President himself undercut the force of

---

[19] Former President Johnson's perspective on the Southeast Asia resolution appears in his book entitled *The Vantage Point*, pp. 117–119; to glimpse a revised Senate opinion of the circumstances and facts surrounding the resolution's enactment and the events which precipitated it, cf. Hearing before the Committee on Foreign Relations, U.S. Senate, *The Gulf of Tonkin: The 1964 Incidents*, Feb. 20, 1968, pp. 54f.

[20] See Theodore H. White, *The Making of the President, 1964* (New York: Atheneum, 1965), pp. 322 ff. The campaign contrasts between the candidates prompted an apocryphal voter's bittersweet humor some years after Johnson's election: "They said if I voted for Goldwater there would be half a million U.S. troops in Vietnam. Sure enough, I voted for Goldwater and there were a half million troops in Vietnam."

the message conveyed by the resolution. One guesses that, at that stage, he could not believe the U.S. threats would be disregarded by Hanoi, even if those threats were muted by contradictory allusions to the need for "Asian boys" to fight their own wars.

Those who consider this mechanism an example of unwarranted congressional submission to executive power neglect the substantial factors operating to encourage presidential restraint in seeking or exploiting such resolutions. Whether or not one agrees with the contention that President Johnson abused the 1964 resolution, one should observe that congressional advocates of such a thesis were able to impose heavy penalties on the presumed offender. Apart from the serious costs involved in the public condemnation of the Administration by prominent senators, the President's programs suffered gravely in other areas, especially foreign aid. Every Chief Executive must be sensitive to reprisals and must recognize that impolitic resort to this procedure may bring severe retaliation in fields quite remote from the subject of a liberating resolution. Virtually the entire legislative program of an Administration is hostage to a President's good faith and discretion in exercising his powers under a liberating resolution.

Congressional leaders can and should make this clear to any President in whom their confidence is actually less than suggested by the uniformly high consensus displayed on a resolution. Informal constraints of this nature, applied with more forethought than in the past, are probably the most feasible means to insure that this technique remains a valuable instrument of U.S. foreign policy and does not become a mere pro forma method by which the executive pre-empts congressional participation in the gravest decisions concerning international affairs.

There are signs that Congress is sensitive to the inherent difficulties in simply forswearing this mechanism once and for all. While there has been broad Senate interest in wiping the slate clean of all such "open-ended" resolutions which seemed to grant the President unwarranted discretion, Congress has continued to approach each resolution on a case-by-case basis. Thus, on the verge of repealing the Formosa resolution, the Senate sensibly drew back from doing so when the United Nations expelled Nationalist China in the fall of 1971. Although the Foreign Relations Committee had urged repeal, the Senate perceived that the fluid situation surrounding the China issue might make it risky to take a step which could be misconstrued in Peking as an abandonment by the United States of its defense commitment to Taiwan. Such would not have been the case, obviously, since this country would have retained its treaty obligation to the Nationalist Chinese. Nevertheless, the fact that the Senate acted cautiously in delaying repeal of the 1955 measure suggests that it will continue to treat such issues in concrete terms, weighing the merits of sustaining or withdrawing broad endorsements of presidential action in light of the particular facts of the situation.

The old judicial maxim "Hard cases make bad law" may be relevant. In time the disillusioning experience with the Southeast Asia resolution of 1964 may be seen as a poor precedent in more ways than one. If it does not provide a model for deliberate congressional involvement in a crisis, neither should it create a binding myth which damns each and every attempt to engage congressional authority in support of presidential action in dangerous circumstances. It should become, rather, an admonition for scrupulous and independent judgment by Congress of whether the Chief Executive has wisely gauged the national interest in a given situation and whether the country is willing to bear the likely costs of pursuing that interest.

CONGRESS AS INITIATOR

The familiar slogan "The President proposes, Congress disposes," reveals little of the intricate process of give and take, consultation, and mutual adjustment that goes on continuously between the legislative and executive branches. Even in foreign affairs, Congress has its opportunities to initiate significant political efforts and to shape the environment in which executive policies are undertaken. Its performance as an initiator of proposals and procedures has been uneven, but Congress is responsible for some of the major innovations in recent American foreign policy. In two fields where the role of Congress has been much criticized, arms control and foreign aid, the record is by no means devoid of accomplishment. If Congress is to be damned for not having done more in these and other areas, it must also be given credit for what it has done.

Sensitive as it has been to the requirements of national security, Congress has nevertheless helped to create and maintain a political climate basically sympathetic to the control and reduction of armaments. From the early years of the atomic age prominent members of Congress were among the most vocal supporters of international control of atomic energy. After the Cold War doomed the original American proposals for this purpose, Congress remained a forum which reflected the country's basically hospitable disposition toward efforts in this field. It was significant that a member of the House, W. Sterling Cole of New York, became the first Director General of the International Atomic Energy Agency, the organization established to implement President Eisenhower's "Atoms for Peace" plan. During the nineteen-fifties, a period of waning hopes for arms control, the Disarmament Subcommittee of the Senate Foreign Relations Committee was one of the most active exponents of continued attempts to end the arms race. Under the vigorous leadership of Hubert Humphrey, the subcommittee performed a rare service in the serious study of arms control issues and in educating the public to the dangers of a spiraling arms competition with the Soviet Union. The same has been true in later years, with Albert Gore and Edmund Muskie successively in the chair. The subcommittee did much to congeal the ideas and sentiments that led to establishment of the Arms Control and Disarmament Agency (ACDA) and, indeed, to the ratification of the nuclear test ban treaty of 1963. It has played a central role in later Senate deliberations on SALT, ABM, and MIRV.

The long history of pro-arms control efforts on Capitol Hill was punctuated by a number of congressional resolutions and other actions expressing concern over the failure to reach workable arms restrictions.[21] Senate resolutions in 1953, adopted by voice vote, called for "enforceable limitation of armament." On July 28, 1955, Senate Resolution 71 requested President Eisenhower to submit to the United Nations a proposal to study controls over military spending as a possible means of improving world living standards. With the dawn of the space age, Congress in its prestige to the campaign to keep weapons from being deployed in space. House Majority Leader John McCormack and other congressmen publicly favored internationalization of space activities as a step toward this goal. In 1961 Congress again expressed its hopes for progress toward international arms agreements, overwhelmingly endorsing ACDA by voice vote in the Senate and by a 253 to 50 margin in the House.

As a previous chapter has discussed, a historic legislative initiative on arms control occurred in 1970 when the Senate urged the President to seek a comprehensive limitation on further deployments of strategic offensive and defensive weapons. Passage of Senate Resolution 211 marked a penultimate attempt to induce the executive to offer the Soviet Union the broadest possible arms control package rather than the more modest undertakings then favored in the Administration. President Nixon acknowledged that the decisive Senate action on this resolution weighed heavily in his decisions on the several options advanced by the United States in the Strategic Arms Limitation Talks.

Apart from its direct encouragement to the Chief Executive, this resolution had other important effects. It conveyed to the Soviets, who were quietly voicing skepticism over whether the Nixon Administration genuinely wanted a SALT agreement, an unequivocal indication that the United States was serious in the negotiations. S. Res. 211 also weakened some of the impediments to SALT within the U.S. bureaucracy; no longer could the opponents of a large-scale strategic understanding contend that Congress would never accept such an agreement. By establishing an ambitious position in advance of final executive preparations for SALT, the Senate demonstrated a welcome maturity and a rare sense of timing. It scarcely insured success in the negotiations, but it contributed to keeping a number of momentous issues—especially deployment of MIRV and ABM—open for diplomacy.

Moreover, it established a pattern for legislative attempts to set broad

[21] See "Negotiations for Arms Control and Disarmament," *Congress and the Nation,* vol. I, pp. 142–159.

guidance for such negotiations. A similar initiative occurred in early 1974 when Senators Charles Mathias, Mike Mansfield, Edward Kennedy, and Jacob Javits were joined by two dozen colleagues in an effort to spur the lagging discussions of SALT II. Their resolution, S. Res. 283, sought to induce mutual restraint in nuclear programs and to facilitate early agreement on a permanent limitation of offensive forces by urging the U.S. and Soviet governments to seek stability through actual reductions in existing strategic inventories. The move was partly calculated to temper the strong advice which Senator Jackson was credited with giving the Administration and to make clear to the President and Secretary Kissinger that there remained solid support in Congress for a bold address to the crucial problems encountered in SALT.

The foreign aid program affords more frequent and complex tests of congressional performance on international issues than almost any other area of legislative activity. As in many cases, consistent focus on the program's ardent and noisy foes has obscured the overall quality of congressional work on foreign aid. The obstreperous maneuvers of Congressman Otto Passman, the Louisiana Democrat whose Appropriations Subcommittee once regularly sliced great chunks from the aid budget, were widely noted, while more constructive labors by other members have been generally ignored.

The Senate has been a particularly fertile source of progressive ideas concerning foreign aid. It was Senator A. S. Mike Monroney of Oklahoma who conceived and campaigned successfully for creation of the International Development Association, now an adjunct of the World Bank which provides long-term loans to underdeveloped nations on terms and rates less stringent than the Bank itself can offer. Senator Fulbright, even before he took the chair of the Foreign Relations Committee, had conducted an important study that laid the foundation for the Development Loan Fund as a major component of the U.S. aid programs. As early as 1955 Senator George Smathers of Florida was pressing for more development assistance to Latin America as a region deserving priority in U.S. plans. These senators, along with other members of Congress, were instrumental in bringing the principle of "development assistance" to its present primacy in American aid efforts. When President Kennedy presented his major aid proposals in 1961, calling for multiyear authorizations and a separation of military and economic assistance, he was largely arguing a case first made by Senator Fulbright in 1959.[22] President Nixon advanced similar recommendations a decade later.

Indeed, Senator Fulbright's deep commitment to these and other progressive innovations in the aid program accounts for the apparently paradoxical episodes beginning in 1966, when he and other senators turned against the

[22] Regarding Monroney's role, see James A. Robinson, *The Monroney Resolution: Congressional Initiative in Foreign Policy-Making* (New York: Holt, 1959); see also his excellent study *Congress and Foreign Policy-Making*, pp. 61–62, 70–92.

Administration's aid proposals and attacked them with unprecedented ferocity. Fulbright's assault related to his long-standing conviction that development assistance could best be administered through international organizations, rather than through bilateral programs, and that such assistance should not be mingled with military aid. His insistence on this view had been heightened by the remark by Secretary of State Rusk implying that past congressional authorization of bilateral assistance to South Vietnam had provided an important justification of the American involvement in the war in that country.[23] To the Arkansas Senator this doctrine was intolerable and dangerous; in spite of the Secretary's subsequent retraction of the statement, Fulbright apparently concluded that the time had come to impose stricter congressional controls over bilateral assistance and to demand that development funds be channeled through multilateral agencies.

As the Senate's sharp cuts in the aid budget for recent years have revealed—and as the Senate's temporary repudiation of the aid program in 1971 confirmed—many members are willing to see the program drastically curtailed unless a larger fraction of U.S. assistance is internationalized. Supporters of the aid program have regretted such tactics, but the critics' fundamental argument for multilateral mechanisms accorded with the views of most advocates and analysts of development assistance. As a long-term approach to the economic problems of the developing nations, as well as a means of avoiding some of the principal defects of past American aid programs, the efforts of Fulbright, Church, and others have represented a constructive initiative.

There is, one must acknowledge, a rather tragic aspect of these legislative attempts to promote a rational and stable reordering of U.S. assistance programs. They have been frustrated in part by a confusion of politics that is difficult to fathom from a distance. In the latter phases of the Johnson Administration and the early years of President Nixon's tenure, congressional reform efforts have sometimes seemed to be a kind of vendetta against the executive branch—even when the presumed adversaries have been largely in agreement on the substance of reforms. At the same time, one surmises that some members who are basically opposed to U.S. aid programs have chosen to cloak their opposition in arguments for shifting funds toward multilateral assistance; once having curtailed bilateral assistance, they may well display similar opposition to funding international development institutions.

This accounts in part for the shifting coalitions which created extreme difficulty for efforts in 1973–1974 to extend U.S. participation in the International Development Association. The general displeasure with foreign aid programs of any sort mingled with hostility to those developing nations that

---

[23] See the exchange between Secretary Rusk and Senator Fulbright in Hearings before the Committee on Foreign Relations, U.S. Senate, *Supplemental Foreign Assistance, Fiscal Year 1966: Vietnam*, Feb. 18, 1966, pp. 581–582.

had exploited U.S. difficulties during the oil embargo which followed the Middle East war of 1973. Under such circumstances many members who basically favored multilateral aid mechanisms allied themselves with those opposed to assistance programs of any sort. The result was to place in jeopardy for some time the American contribution to one of the most vital instruments of world economic management.

On another point, some House leaders have felt impelled to resist senatorial and executive branch proposals to segregate military aid from economic assistance on grounds that the House, with its preoccupation with national security issues, would not support a development aid program which did not "piggyback" on military assistance. And there has been the significant, if somewhat imponderable, institutional consideration that the House Foreign Affairs Committee might find its role diminished under various schemes to reorder the U.S. aid programs which have vaulted the committee into a position of unwonted influence in national policy. The harsh infighting on these issues has contributed to the shrinkage of U.S. assistance programs in recent years. The paralyzing politics of foreign aid is taking years to work out, reflecting as it does the nation's intense and conflicting sentiments on the future American role in the world. Yet one may reasonably expect that the eventual structure and content of U.S. assistance programs will incorporate many of the initiatives of the "sympathetic critics" who have dominated recent aid debates in the Congress.

Congress has also served as a useful prod in other realms of international economic policy. After years of constraining East-West trade through a variety of statutes, the legislature found itself pushing the other direction in enacting, over a mixture of Administration ambivalence and opposition, a major new trade bill in 1969. Many members of Congress, especially in the House, were reluctant to move toward expanded trade with the Soviet bloc, and at that time some Administration officials felt such trade should be expanded only as a *quid pro quo* for Soviet accommodation on other issues. The dominant opinion in Congress, however, had come to be that the export control statutes were counterproductive and self-defeating, since U.S. allies were regularly expanding trade with the East. Skillful parliamentary moves over many months by Senators Mondale, Muskie, and Brooke focused the new congressional attitude and produced the Export Administration Act of 1969, a measure which conferred more flexible (albeit unrequested) authority on the President to seek new opportunities for trade in nonstrategic goods. Within a very short period this newfound flexibility proved valuable, as the Nixon Administration actively pursued economic détente with Moscow, dispatching its Secretary of Commerce to explore possibilities with his Soviet counterpart. By making such overtures possible, the Congress was playing an unusually active part in spurring a reluctant Chief Executive to exploit a degree of political latitude he had probably considered impossible to achieve.

In recent years a remarkable number of other initiatives concerning economic policy have emanated from Congress. Considering the arcane nature of international economic relations, one might be surprised to learn that some of the most astute thought on economic policy has come from members of Congress, normally known as generalists rather than experts in such a specialized field. But the long history of the Ways and Means Committee and the more modern experience of the House Foreign Affairs and Joint Economic committees are marked by distinctive contributions to America's role in the world economy. The ancient view of narrowly focused, local interests as the dominant factor in congressional approaches to foreign economic policy tells a great deal less than one needs to know about Congress's behavior. Former chairman Wilbur Mills of the Ways and Means Committee played a pivotal role in U.S. trade and overseas investment policy. His genius lay in deriving workable and constructive accommodations from the welter of claims and pressures which develop in these areas.

The House Foreign Affairs Subcommittee on Foreign Economic Policy, chaired of late by John Culver of Iowa, has been an important source of forward-looking proposals on issues where executive leadership has been halting or uncertain. Building on extensive and learned hearings on a range of related topics, this group has recognized that, despite the real problems created by the rapid evolution of the European Common Market, the United States should resist protectionist urges and keep up the pressure for long-term trade liberalization. To bolster the country's capacity to meet the requirements of multilateral economic diplomacy, in 1972 the committee invited the executive to join with Congress in designing a basic new grant of trade negotiation authority. The body has given a proper emphasis to relations with the advanced industrial nations, but it has also pressed for enlightened efforts to link trade and development assistance by inclusion in the Committee of Ten—the key monetary planning unit of the industrialized nations—of at least two representatives from the less developed countries.

The Joint Economic Committee Subcommittee on International Economics has authored comparable suggestions to induce the executive to pursue the liberalization of international trade. Under Chairman Henry Reuss, this subcommittee has proposed several devices to curb the extraordinary balance-of-payments deficits which the United States has suffered in the last few years. It contemplates discretionary authority for the President to impose tariff surcharges, subject to legislative override, to elicit necessary adjustments in foreign exchange rates to eliminate the deficits. It has called for all industrial nations to abolish tariff barriers over the next one to two decades, and has underscored the necessity to coordinate "voluntary" trade restrictions—particularly quotas on goods exported to the United States by low-cost suppliers—with internationally agreed criteria for aiding industries damaged by import competition. The subcommittee has also staked out its clear sense of responsibility for the problem of the developing nations by proposing generalized tariff preferences for manufactured goods from such countries.[24] Legislative recommendations of this kind, in a period of rising domestic concern over foreign competition, are striking instances of Congress prodding the President to resist precisely those pressures to which Congress itself has reputedly been vulnerable.

To discuss these dimensions of Congress's role in foreign policy is only to scratch the surface of one of the most complex elements of our government. It is, however, to suggest that the possibilities for constructive congressional involvement go well beyond the familiar responsibilities for advice and consent to treaties, confirmation of ambassadors and other senior appointments, and authorization and appropriation of funds for specific foreign programs of the United States.

The functions mentioned here overlap and interact among themselves and with others. They defy simple prescriptions and neat procedures. No one can expect Congress to devise explicit formal methods for asserting its control over the myriad aspects of American foreign policy. While improved exercise of its formal powers is to be desired, Congress must recognize that the volume and velocity of international politics require an executive with ample capacity to act for the nation. Events will not always await the building of a consensus which is the distinctive trait of legislative action.

But it is not too much to believe that the astute individuals who serve Congress will become more sensitive to the full range of influences, both formal and informal, which their institution has on foreign policy. For those who would enhance congressional participation in these crucial decisions and processes, the opportunities are many and the need is great.

---

[24] Report of the Subcommittee on Foreign Economic Policy, Committee on Foreign Affairs, U.S. House of Representatives, *New Realities and New Directions in United States Foreign Economic Policy*, 92d Cong., 2d Sess., Feb. 28, 1972; also see the subcommittee's hearings, *The International Implications of New Economic Policy*, Sept. 16 and 21, 1971. In addition see the Report of the Subcommittee on International Economics, Joint Economic Committee, U.S. Congress, *A New Initiative to Liberalize International Trade*, Mar. 8, 1973.

VIII. *Ultima Ratio: Congress and the War Powers Issue*

The traditional phrase has varied renderings in English, each redolent with nuance and implication. *Ultima ratio regum*—the

last resort, the final answer, the ultimate argument of a king—war. War is, of course, the last resort of any government, regal or otherwise, which proclaims its sovereignty and insists on prevailing in a dispute with another state. In a special sense, war is also the "ultimate argument" within the American republic.

No disputes between Congress and President strike so close to the heart of representative government as those concerning the so-called "war powers" issue. No other disputes threaten more profoundly the legitimacy of the nation's employment of military force to support its foreign policy. No other disputes have so preoccupied the legislative and executive branches in recent years. And no disputes are more difficult to resolve in accord with both constitutional precepts and contemporary pragmatism. It is no overstatement to say that on a satisfactory accommodation of this issue hangs the integrity of self-government. For the cardinal test of a republic is its capacity to make sound provision for its gravest decisions—the decisions to risk the lives of its citizens in violent conflict for reasons of state.

The dilemmas of democratic war-making run deep; they recur periodically in American life. Lincoln captured one facet of them when he addressed Congress on July 4, 1861: "Must a government of necessity be too strong for the liberties of its own people, or too weak to maintain its own existence?" The question was not rhetorical. It had engaged the most intensive deliberations in the constitutional convention, as the drafters there convened began to wrestle with the problem of devising a government potent enough to maintain its sovereignty but restrained enough to avoid the kingly wars which had drained the lifeblood of England for the whims of a monarch.

The constitutional history of this issue is richer in curbstone opinion than in conclusive authority; it is nevertheless clear that the original war powers doctrine was bent toward reserving to the Congress the great decisions of war and peace.[1] In this realm even more than most, the President was to be an executive chained to the means and ends approved by the legislature. To be sure, the Chief Executive held explicit authority as Commander-in-Chief of the nation's armed forces, but the types and scale of those forces were matters to be determined by Congress. Beyond this explicit grant of authority to command such forces as the legislature placed at his disposal, the President's "share" of the war-making power rests more vaguely upon his general authority as the country's executive agent and more specifically upon his role as the principal representative in foreign affairs.

These presidential powers, however, were purely instrumental in nature. Circumscribing them were firmer and more precise grants of power to the Congress, particularly the power to provide for the common defense, to declare war, and to raise and support an Army and Navy. Furthermore, the Constitution bound the legislature to re-examine its dispositions for the armed forces at least every two years, by forbidding any appropriation to support an Army for a longer period. The charter-writers of 1787 shared a determined skepticism of standing armies; no President would be able to transform himself into a despot by ready access to a permanent body of troops. Even the militia could be organized, equipped, and mobilized only on the sufferance of the legislature. Coupled with these powers were the broad authority to make all laws necessary and proper to carry out the enumerated powers, not only of Congress but of all branches of government, and the flat prohibition on any federal expenditure except in accord with appropriations made by law. Precious little latitude existed for presidential profligacy or recklessness. Thus the initial terrain on which Congress and the President shared the war powers quite evidently gave the high ground to the legislators.

Lest there be any doubt as to how the remaining ambiguities of constitutional language should be resolved, further evidence of the founders' intent

[1] The scholarly literature on this subject has grown quite enormous, especially during the period of the Vietnam engagement. Already a classic exposition of many aspects is Arthur M. Schlesinger, Jr., *The Imperial Presidency* (Boston: Houghton Mifflin, 1973). Among other notable efforts are "Congress, the President, and the Power to Commit Forces to Combat," *Harvard Law Review*, vol. 81, no. 8, June 1968, pp. 1771–1805; W. Taylor Reveley III, "Presidential Warmaking: Constitutional Prerogative or Usurpation?" *Virginia Law Review*, November 1969, pp. 1243–1305; and a useful paper by students of the Yale Law School prepared in May 1970, "Indochina: The Constitutional Crisis," published in Committee on Foreign Relations, U.S. Senate, *Documents Relating to the War Power of Congress, the President's Authority as Commander-in-Chief and the War in Indochina*, 91st Cong., 2d Sess., July 1970, pp. 73–119.

abounds. James Madison's notes on the debates during the Philadelphia convention reveal that there was extended discussion concerning where best to entrust the war power, culminating in a series of motions aimed at refining the early provision, which had empowered Congress "to make War." Members of the South Carolina delegation were wary of this formulation, considering the legislature too slow to handle a question which might require speed. To the dismay of some, Pierce Butler proposed vesting the power in the President, "who will have all the requisite qualities, and will not make war but when the Nation will support it."

The delegates rejected that idea, as well as suggestions that the war power be allocated to the Senate alone. Roger Sherman, among others, thought the original phrase should remain intact, since "the Executive should be able to repel and not to commence war." Elbridge Gerry, who for a time was to withhold his support of the resulting Constitution on the grounds that it gave too much power to the President, joined Madison in offering the amendment which caught the nuance the convention was seeking: They moved "to insert 'declare', striking out 'make' war; leaving to the Executive the power to repel sudden attacks."

In short, the records of the constitutional convention indicate that the congressional power to declare war, undergirded by the several related legislative controls over the armed forces already mentioned, was the pre-eminent authority over decisions regarding United States involvement in hostilities. Only in the narrow range of contingencies in which battle was thrust directly and immediately upon this country did the executive retain authority to hold the attackers at bay, pending legislative determination of the scope of belligerent actions the United States would take. It is an exceedingly dubious argument to contend, as few do, that this reservation of fundamental power to the Congress meant only that the legislature would approve declaration of war.[2]

The substance of the power granted made Congress responsible for deciding whether or not, as well as when and to what extent, the United States would expend its blood and treasure in violent conflict with another state. This blanket authority embraced not only wars which were formally declared but also limited, informal conflicts—what the Supreme Court once termed "imperfect wars." For even imperfect wars run the risk of escalation into vast drains on a nation's resources, and the founding fathers felt that those kinds of collective risks should be collectively assessed. A modern sophisticate, looking back on the war fevers which have erupted periodically in American history, may question the theory that wars should be harder to get

[2] The ablest exponent of this limited view of the power to declare war is Terry Emerson, "War Powers Legislation," 74 *West Virginia Law Review*, 53 1972, reprinted in the *Congressional Record*, July 20, 1973, pp. S14166–S14184. Emerson is legislative assistant to Senator Barry Goldwater, the principal opponent of war powers legislation.

into if Congress holds the ultimate decision. But there can be no question that this was the theory on which the authors erected the Constitution. And the theory finds recent vindication in the powerful congressional opposition to U.S. involvement in both the First and the Second World Wars.

The early presidents understood the basic guidelines quite well. John Adams chose not to respond to French depredations on American shipping until he had obtained specific congressional authority and fuller means to do so. The Franco-American imbroglio of 1798 prompted Congress to make suitable statutory arrangements and to create both the Department of the Navy and the Marine Corps to enable the President to cope with the threat; it did not, however, declare war, confirming both branches' understanding that congressional powers over military hostilities were comprehensive. In pursuing this course, Adams was acting on the counsel of no less an activist than Alexander Hamilton. Contrasting with his normally expansive views of executive authority, Hamilton's judgment in this instance stressed the need for executive deference to the legislature: "In so delicate a case, in one which involves so important a consequence as that of war, my opinion is that no doubtful authority ought to be exercised by the President."[3]

In 1801 Chief Justice Marshall aligned the judiciary with the evolving practice by ruling that the "whole powers of war" belong to Congress. And later that year Thomas Jefferson bound the U.S. Navy to such tight instructions that American sailors actually freed a Tripolitan marauder after disarming it, in spite of the fact that Tripoli had already declared war on the United States. Jefferson's first message to Congress indicated the stringent limits under which he felt the Constitution placed him: "Unauthorized by the Constitution, without the sanction of Congress, to go beyond the line of defense, the vessel, being disabled from committing further hostilities, was liberated with its crew. The Legislature will doubtless consider whether, by authorizing measures of offense also, they will place our force on an equal footing with that of its adversaries." It is fair to conclude that the balance of authority for such decisions was never an issue between Federalists and Republicans, or among the several branches of government during the opening years of the republic.

The vigor of this doctrine persisted through much of the nineteenth century. When President Polk swerved from it in his troop deployments at the outset of the Mexican War, moving forces into disputed territory claimed by both Texas and Mexico, he precipitated an uproar in Congress. The House of Representatives, in a resolution commending General Taylor for his leadership in the conflict, approved an amendment stating that "the war was unnecessarily and unconstitutionally begun by the President of the

---

[3] Hamilton's letter to the Secretary of War, May 17, 1798, quoted in Francis D. Wormuth, "Vietnam War: The President vs. the Constitution," in Richard Falk (ed.), *The Vietnam War and International Law* (Princeton, N.J.: Princeton, 1969).

United States." In order not to detract from the commendation of Taylor, the language was subsequently deleted from the resolution, but it undoubtedly caught the drift of opinion in Congress, where Polk's victory did not silence the rebukes his unilateral acts had generated. Among the supporters of the amendment had been John Quincy Adams and Abraham Lincoln. In a famous letter of the time, Lincoln, in particular, reiterated the common understanding that presidential wars were anathema to the Constitution:

> Allow the President to invade a neighboring nation whenever he shall deem it necessary to repel an invasion, and you allow him to do so whenever he may choose to say he deems it necessary for such a purpose, and you allow him to make war at his pleasure. . . . Kings had always been involving and impoverishing their people in wars, pretending generally, if not always, that the good of the people was the object. This our convention understood to be the most oppressive of all kingly oppressions, and they resolved to so frame the Constitution that no one man should hold the power of bringing oppression upon us.[4]

The entire purpose of the constitutional provision was, to paraphase an earlier commentary, to shift decisions on war from those who spend to those who pay.

Ironically, Lincoln's own later ordeal as President brought major qualifications to the very principles he had enunciated in 1848. Considering a challenge to Lincoln's proclamation of a blockade of the Southern ports, the Supreme Court's *Prize Cases* ruling (1863) not only recognized the President's broad power to wage *defensive* war against invasion or rebellion but decided that the President was *the sole judge* of when such defensive war had been thrust upon the United States. This was a major development in the gradual expansion of the Constitution-makers' dictum that the President should be empowered to repel attacks. It also highlighted a major gap in the war-making provisions, a gap which has persisted until the present day.

Without careful and exact arrangements for concurrent or at least subsequent congressional appraisal of the President's judgment of when an attack requires the United States to invoke forceful means of self-defense, the Chief Executive is left with a leeway over acts of war which was utterly unintended by the founders, no matter how advantageous it may have seemed to later proponents of a strong executive. It is largely through this portal—a kind of open door for the President to determine which hostile acts, accomplished or impending, demand measures of self-defense—that the Chief Executive has greatly enlarged his influence in this realm while that of Congress has partially atrophied.

All this may seem ancient history, but it provides a set of important benchmarks for evaluating the contemporary moves to restore a larger mea-

---

[4] Quoted in Committee on Foreign Relations, *Documents Relating to the War Power of Congress*, p. 89.

sure of congressional participation in decisions involving the risk of war. Though familiar to consititutional historians, this context is little known to many citizens; it even seems foreign to some ranking members of Congress and the executive, who have become inured by modern strife to a more generous view of presidential prerogatives.

Before turning to the experience of recent times, one needs to make a few further observations concerning the record of the nineteenth century. Lincoln's exploitation of executive power was undoubtedly the high-water mark of presidential assertiveness. Yet the fact that Court and Congress tolerated most of his actions in the twilight zone of legislative-executive powers is of mixed significance. It hardly constituted an abdication of war-making authority by the men in the Capitol, as the insistent legislative demand to share key decisions throughout the conflict indicated. The heightened power of the Lincoln Presidency depended uniquely on the circumstances of *civil* war, with the Chief Executive deriving added constitutional authority from federal obligations to maintain the union, to stifle insurrection, and to guarantee each state a republican form of government. The Civil War unquestionably amplified presidential power but under criteria not precisely applicable to the international arena in which the war powers normally function.

A second, more general comment is in order concerning the numerous incidents in which various presidents have employed military force abroad without prior congressional approval or subsequent sanction. It is a commonplace in arguments for a broad construction of the Commander-in-Chief's war powers to cite these incidents as compelling precedents. State Department sources have enumerated more than 160 such cases, the majority of which occurred in the nineteenth century; Terry Emerson catalogues 199 instances. But the bulk of these episodes hardly qualify as anything more than showing the flag or protecting the lives and property of American citizens. If for no other reason than the fact that the President lacked sufficient forces in being to enter sustained hostilities, only modest ventures were supportable without resort to the Congress. The volume of such incidents is impressive; their weight is not. It is fair, then, to characterize the first century and a quarter of legislative-executive relations as generally faithful to the intentions of those who drew the war powers provisions of the Constitution.

"A page of history," Justice Holmes once said, "is worth a volume of logic." Quite true, but on the crucial question of the allocation of war powers one must read the page of history more closely than has been customary in the era of global war. History and constitutional logic were consonant until growing international responsibilities generated unprecedented stresses on the United States' institutional arrangements for decisions regarding the use of force abroad. The serious divergence between practice and principle is a phenomenon of the twentieth century.

AN END TO DEFERENCE?

For all their preoccupation with checks and balances, those who drew the Constitution fully appreciated that the sought-for primacy of Congress could not be assured by mere "parchment barriers." A certain dynamic tension was inevitable, and nowhere more probable than in the grave matters of state touching the war powers. The *Federalist* papers acknowledged that the first law of nations, as of men, was the law of survival and that, unless the Constitution established sound and workable procedures to protect national security, it would invite open or subtle evasion by one or another branch. Hamilton and Madison shared the opinion, it seems, that such encroachments might well come from the legislature, perhaps by intruding in the tactical decisions and operations of the designated Commander-in-Chief. The Continental Congress had displayed inclinations in this direction during the War for Independence, and a number of state legislatures had already demonstrated an overblown tendency to grasp for executive prerogatives.[5] Accordingly, the authors of *The Federalist,* quoting Thomas Jefferson's notes on the Virginia experience, called attention to the hazards of congressional despotism.

Yet their larger fear, as was true of others who came to Philadelphia that year, was of an executive bent on aggrandizement and operating under the combined exigencies and opportunities of a state of war. Even the most well-intentioned President might succumb to the temptation to short-circuit strict constitutional channels in order to meet presumed threats to national security. The Civil War and Reconstruction appeared to confirm successively both the tendencies perceived by the Federalists, with President and Congress competing to determine the conduct of war and the conditions of peace. Since 1900, however, the pendulum has oscillated less and swung more sharply toward executive dominance of the war powers. Many relatively minor episodes illustrate the tendency of presidents to resort to the use of military force with only token obeisance to the need for congressional concurrence. But the most telling and instructive examples involve five different chief executives and the crucial international challenges of their administrations: Wilson and the measures preliminary to U.S. entry into the First World War; Franklin Roosevelt and his prewar maneuvers of 1939–1941; Truman and the Korean action; Kennedy and Cuba, both in 1961 and 1962; and Johnson's conduct during the intensification of the Vietnam conflict.

Obviously, none of these men was a villain usurping power lawfully

[5] It is the experience of the Continental Congress's interference with General Washington which perhaps most impresses Senator Goldwater; see his statement "The Founding Fathers and the War Powers," *Congressional Record,* July 19, 1973, pp. S14140–S14142. Also see the Senator's article "The President's Ability to Protect America's Freedoms: The Warmaking Powers," *Arizona State University Law Journal,* vol. 3, no. 3, 1971, pp. 423–449.

entrusted to a coordinate branch of government. The verdict of history may well be sympathetic to all of them, concluding that their fundamental policies and most of their decisions were of enduring value to national security. Most attempted in some fashion and in some degree to consult with Congress and to enlist its support for steps involving acts or risks of war. Each of these men, however, through convenience they chose to call necessity, used methods of doubtful constitutionality. Considering that Wilson was a professional scholar of the Congress and that all the others save Roosevelt were men who had served in the Senate, it is remarkable that they all chose to claim the maximum scope for presidential authority over national decisions to threaten or to employ armed force. One cannot explain their actions on the assumption that they were ignorant of congressional prerogatives.

The cynic might infer that to know Congress is to despise it. The dispassionate observer might rather conclude that, knowing the difficulties of achieving a legislative consensus, these presidents were not confident they could persuade Congress quickly enough that the particular international situation warranted the urgent measures and high risks which the White House considered necessary. In other words each President judged that the foreign crisis he perceived required the concentrated planning and action of a vigorous executive, not the diffuse and unpredictable deliberations of a legislature. Each may have been right in that judgment, but it is a dangerous habit of mind to inculcate in the presidents of a republic.

To be sure, Wilson at first sought legislative authorization for his planned measures of defense against German submarine attacks. A Senate filibuster frustrated his effort to win approval of a program to arm American merchant ships, whereupon Wilson did so on his own authority. Justifiable though it seems in some respects—particularly in light of recent evidence that Berlin was in fact moving to seek victory through unrestricted submarine warfare against belligerents and neutrals alike—its true significance stands out only in Wilson's later admission that he knew the action was "practically certain" to draw the United States into the war. One may fairly ask whether the President ought not to have framed his initial request for legislative authority in terms of that possibility. If that was the expectation, should not the Congress have determined whether the enforcement of the neutral rights of the United States was worth the likely price of a hot war with Germany? One apt if incomplete answer is that a Senate filibuster was a totally inappropriate device for opponents to use in preventing the Congress from reaching the issue. Wilson had already grown so impatient with Congress that he found the inconclusive outcome a sufficient justification for claiming the right to decide the issue himself. The claim might have been disputed, as indeed it was by some members of Congress, but only Congress acting as an institution could have levied an effective counterclaim. Its failure to do so, and the President's willingness to resolve the constitutional ambiguities in favor of his own power to act, marked a serious tilt in the institutional equilibrium.

That tilt was accentuated by Roosevelt's conduct in 1940 and 1941. Extremely sensitive to the isolationist currents running in Congress and the country, FDR betrayed a grievous lack of confidence in the constitutional mechanisms for shaping national policy toward belligerent situations. Among historians of the period, even his ardent admirers lament the President's deviousness during those months, arguing that he should have taken to the people his case for a firm policy toward the Axis powers and close association with Great Britain.[6] There is good evidence that public opinion, especially after the fall of France, was well ahead of the President and receptive to an accelerated program of preparedness. Roosevelt, however, was unsure of his ability to persuade the Congress and chose to evade the obligation to consult by undertaking a number of unneutral acts which greatly increased the likelihood that the United States would be drawn into the war. On his own authority he entered an executive agreement to trade overage destroyers for certain base rights on British territory; he decided to relieve British troops by dispatching American forces to Iceland; and finally he directed an undeclared war of hunter-killer operations against German submarines in the Atlantic. These measures were strategically prudent but constitutionally offensive.

The President's sense of the Nazi threat may have been keener than that of Congress, and his program to meet it may have been wiser than any Congress would have approved. Yet applause for the results ought to be muted by concern for the procedures. The harder but healthier course would have been for the President to attempt openly to persuade the Congress that his perception of the dangers to the United States from a German victory was an accurate one and that his prescription to cope with them was an appropriate one. After Pearl Harbor, Hitler resolved Roosevelt's political dilemmas by rashly declaring war on the United States. Had the German Fuehrer avoided this act of folly, it is an intriguing question whether and how Roosevelt would have pursued his strategic emphasis on the European theater. At the very least, to act on the scale required, the President would have had to deal with the Congress more forthrightly than before. In the event, the tumult of war utterly obscured the serious and fundamental questions of constitutional balance which the practices of 1939–1941 were raising. The impact of Roosevelt's expansive interpretation of the office dwarfed that of Wilson's.

One further aspect of FDR's exploitation of the war powers deserves note. Just as he reinforced the Lincoln precedent and extended it in unparalleled degree to the conduct of international hostilities on presidential au-

---

[6] Typical of those generally supportive of Roosevelt's actions but critical of his political tactics are William Langer and S. Everett Gleason, *The Challenge to Isolation* (New York: Harper, 1952) and *The Undeclared War* (New York: Harper, 1953). For a summary assessment of the President's supporters and critics on this point, see Frye, *Nazi Germany and the American Hemisphere, 1933–1941*, pp. 1–14.

thority, so, too, he capitalized on the discretion conferred by the *Prize Cases* by declining to enter conflict with some countries even after they had declared war on the United States. For some months Roosevelt simply ignored the declared states of war with Bulgaria, Hungary, and Romania, all of which had followed the German lead on December 13, 1941. It was not until June 1942 that the President sought formal congressional declarations against these states, and then principally as a diplomatic gesture to assuage the Soviet Union. Without explicitly outlining the constitutional basis for doing so and without benefit of congressional consultation, FDR had in sequence chosen to wage an undeclared war and not to wage a declared one.

Roosevelt's exercise of discretion in these respects was perhaps the decisive model for the chief executives who followed, though each added facets to executive claims to use force abroad without congressional authorization. President Truman and his advisers advanced various rationales for the Chief Executive's decision to commit American forces to repel the invasion of South Korea. It was not a "war," but a "police action"; it was an engagement stemming from obligations under the United Nations Charter, one of the international and domestic laws which the President is constitutionally bound to enforce; it was merely a limited conflict which the President was empowered to conduct in carrying out the broad foreign policy of the United States. And before hostilities ended, the Secretary of State was asserting that Congress had no constitutional basis for interfering with the President's alleged authority to use the armed forces for such foreign policy purposes as he considered necessary.[7]

In crucial ways Korea was the "tip-point" in the balance of authority for controlling the nation's belligerent activities. Previous conflicts had eventually brought forth congressional declarations authorizing the military effort, even if initial measures had been taken on presidential authority alone. President Truman, however, neither sought nor obtained explicit congressional authorization for the Korean action. Granted the powerful arguments against a formal declaration of war, the Truman Administration was not so witless it could not have requested authorization in some more appropriate form. Indeed, such was the proposal of Senator Watkins of Utah, who advised the President and his colleagues in that fateful June of 1950 that the Commander-in-Chief should have asked for suitable congressional authority to meet the Korean situation. No one rose to press the point, although Senator Robert Taft was soon arguing that "the President simply usurped authority when he sent troops to Korea to carry out the resolution of the United Nations in an undeclared war."

The Administration decision not to seek congressional approval seems to have been based on nothing more substantial than the view of Secretary

<hr>

[7] See Glenn D. Paige, *The Korean Decision* (New York: Free Press, 1968), pp. 146–156, 262–268, 333–336.

Acheson and other presidential advisers that legislative debate on the issue would be inconvenient and possibly inconclusive at a time when the United States needed to convey an impression of unity and determination. Acheson expressed special concern for the morale of U.S. forces in the field. Taft and others later acknowledged that, if asked, they would have approved the President's course, but the Congress's failure to insist that it be formally consulted seemed to be a tacit acceptance of the executive claim to sufficient authority. One can well appreciate that the tension and peril of the day obscured what might be dismissed as procedural niceties, and one can conclude that the American role in Korea was an important contribution to international peace and security. Nevertheless, in constitutional terms it is difficult to exaggerate the debilitating effect of the experience: for the first time the President of the United States sustained a major and costly war over a lengthy period without benefit of legislative authorization.

In spite of the growing popular disaffection with the war, an attitude which dominated the 1952 election campaign, Truman's decisive action to intervene in East Asia remained an admired model for later chief executives. Global war, limited war, cold war had bred an American preoccupation with tough presidential leadership to meet overt and covert threats to national security. In that preoccupation there was progressively less room for a meaningful congressional role on issues of war and peace.

The mixed results achieved in Korea had appeared relatively worthwhile when viewed as an effective rebuff to outright aggression. There was no such comfort in assessing the decision by President Kennedy to underwrite the invasion of an unfriendly neighbor by a refugee army. The fiasco at the Bay of Pigs in April 1961 left most Americans too stunned to describe the President's action for what it was, a clear violation of international and domestic law and a dubitable assertion of executive power not only to respond to attack but to initiate hostilities, albeit through intermediaries, against another state. Had the move succeeded, it is doubtful that many U.S. citizens would have complained. Given the disastrous end of the venture, there should certainly have been a searching reappraisal of the arrangements which led to such hazardous decision-making within the secret recesses of the executive branch. Kennedy himself later noted that the press might have saved the nation from a great mistake if the *New York Times* and other papers had not refrained (at the President's own request) from exposing the preparations for the Cuban assault. The irony is that the President did not seem to consider that wider consultation with the Congress might also have dissuaded him from the folly of early 1961. There could be no starker testimony to the failure of the separation of powers than this attitude. When a President looks not to his presumed institutional peer, but mainly to extragovernmental forums for checking executive excesses and mistakes, the psychological cement of constitutional government has substantially dissolved.

Success or failure of an international policy cannot be the test of its constitutional propriety. The Cuban missile crisis of 1962, generally considered the highlight of the Kennedy Presidency, illustrates that point and others. The prospect of ultimate catastrophe, a strategic nuclear exchange, loomed over the United States. While maneuvering to avoid war, the President took a number of steps which might have precipitated it, including particularly the decision to quarantine Cuba. In the fashion of the admired vigorous leader, Kennedy made his decisions with negligible consultation with Congress, belatedly informing the legislative leaders of the course chosen by him and his executive advisers. The circumstances of October 1962 are generally considered a virtual prototype of the kind of situation requiring the qualities normally attributed to the executive: secrecy, speed, decisiveness, firmness. It is probably fair to say that most Americans, including those in Congress, perceived the Soviet installation of missiles in Cuba as an emergency in which the nation's trust had to repose in the President, for good or ill. It is difficult to believe that an anguished or alarmed debate on Capitol Hill would have been as persuasive to Premier Khrushchev as the definite and forceful measures taken by President Kennedy.

Nevertheless, seen in hindsight and with the perspective of a decade, several facts appear larger and more important than they did at the time. In spite of the apocalyptic language which surrounds much of the discussion of the crisis, at least some of those who served in the Executive Committee ("Ex Comm") which counseled the President claim that the focus of concern was a *conventional* war which might erupt over efforts to force the Soviet Union to disengage. To be sure, there was deep apprehension that any conflict might escalate to the nuclear level over a period of time, possibly because of Soviet countermeasures against Berlin, where the United States was in no position to enforce its rights by exclusively conventional means. But no one was seriously considering a strategic assault to disarm the Soviet missile forces; nor, in view of American nuclear preponderance, did the Ex Comm believe that Moscow would initiate a strategic exchange. Undoubtedly, the President was wary of the possibilities of nuclear war through miscalculation, and the mere thought of those possibilities infected the proceedings with acute anxiety that Armageddon was at hand. But the concrete measures in prospect were the application of conventional force in the Caribbean and precautions against conventional reprisals in Europe.

Several other facts merit attention. Robert Kennedy later entitled his chronicle of the crisis *Thirteen Days*, a caption which makes the point that the decisions involved were not taken under the stress of immediate action.[8] Days passed and deliberations were extensive among the small circle of participants, a factor stressed by the Kennedy memoir in language which is

---

[8]See Robert F. Kennedy, *Thirteen Days: A Memoir of the Cuban Missile Crisis* (New York: Norton, 1969). See also Sorensen, *Kennedy*, pp. 667–718.

almost a quintessential description of—a legislative committee proceeding. The former Attorney General also commented on the length of time available for debating the options, adding that, "perhaps surprisingly, on most occasions of great crisis it is." The President did not act for six days, but even when the decision was taken, he did not expose the problem to congressional leaders until a short while before he addressed the nation on October 22.

Seized by the urgency and gravity of the situation, such leading senators as Richard Russell and J. William Fulbright pressed the President to take stronger action than the quarantine he contemplated. Having rejected direct military action against the missile installations, Kennedy later mused that the reaction of the congressmen under the shock of the intelligence on Soviet deception was quite similar to the first instincts of those in the executive, most of whom had also inclined initially toward air strikes on the missiles or similar proposals. It is quite plausible that fuller and wider discussion among members of Congress, particularly if faced with specific recommendations from the President, would have elicited a consensus in favor of the type of cautious response selected by the Chief Executive. As it was, even during the week after the Congress and the country learned of the Russian missiles and before the crisis was resolved, the legislature played no part.

This is no revisionist view of the Cuban missile crisis, which was a notable American success in international politics. Precisely because it was successful, the episode has received less critical examination than it warrants as a case study in domestic decision-making. If the situation evolved over many days and if the questions involved choosing the risks the nation would bear in advance of an actual outbreak of hostilities, is it inconceivable that the Congress might have convened in executive session and conducted its own debate on the policy alternatives? Perhaps the process would have been merely pro forma and the Congress would have rallied quickly behind the President's exact course. On the other hand, the Congress might have come to favor other stances—an offer to remove U.S. missiles from Turkey in return for Soviet dismantling of the Cuban facilities or a decision to tolerate Soviet missiles on the island, both possibilities which had enjoyed some support in the Ex Comm at one time or another. Certainly some congressional debate over the price the country should pay to pressure the Soviets to back down might well have occurred even after the President had adopted the quarantine on October 22. At that time he had alluded to the prospect of further measures if the Soviets did not respect the U.S. demands, but those further measures were not specified. The Congress might then have weighed which measures to endorse. The plain fact is that members of Congress did not seem eager to claim part of the responsibility the President had assumed in defining national policy.

Without presuming to suggest a cure for Congress's own reticence to assert its authority to consider such momentous issues, one may conclude this review of the missile crisis with two brief notes. First, the mythology of the Cuban encounter should not blind us to the fact that there was ample time for more extensive consultation with the Congress. In this respect the confrontation was not unique, and it is far from obvious that the Congress should have been excluded from considering the problem. Second, had the outcome been a diplomatic or military disaster, one may be sure that the President would have been endlessly damned for risking so much on his own authority. The incident brings home the truth that time and again in American history political pragmatism has deified results over methods. Much of presidential practice has acquired a Lincolnesque gloss, through which the man in the White House consoles himself with the conviction that means really are not as important as ends, and that "if the end brings me out wrong, ten angels swearing I was right would make no difference." There is truth there, but also temptation.

It would be too facile to say that the disasters of unilateral presidential decision-making which were avoided in Cuba descended upon President Kennedy's successor as he came to grips with the problems of Southeast Asia. The opportunity for and degree of congressional participation in the Johnson Administration's decisions regarding Vietnam were much greater than had been the case in the Cuban episode. Opinions differ as to how far and how genuinely the Congress shared the burden of committing the United States to what became a major war. Senator Barry Goldwater has identified more than twenty instances in which congressional authority was engaged in support of U.S. steps in Southeast Asia; most of these involved appropriations to support U.S. troops in the field and are of questionable significance as expressions of congressional policy, since legislators understandably feel constrained not to oppose supplies for armed forces once they are committed to battle. Mr. Johnson himself stressed not only the congressional endorsement of the Gulf of Tonkin resolution in August 1964, but the approval of the May 1965 supplemental appropriation bill which he had specifically identified as a test of legislative support for expanded military measures.[9]

A number of senior congressmen, including Chet Holifield of California, claim that they were in no way deceived by the far-reaching implications drawn from the Southeast Asia resolution, and that they had approved the language with their eyes wide open to the large-scale hostilities which might ensue. Others, notably Chairman Fulbright of the Senate Foreign Relations Committee, later came to feel they were actually misled as to the facts of the incidents of the Gulf of Tonkin which precipitated the action on the resolution. It seems that few congressmen actually expected that their votes in August 1964, intended to bolster the President in a posture of deterring the

[9] See Johnson, *The Vantage Point*, pp. 112–119, 150–153.

North Vietnamese from enlarging their activities in support of the conflict in South Vietnam, would actually serve to underwrite a massive expansion of the U.S. military role there. When Under Secretary of State Nicholas Katzenbach later characterized the resolution as a "functional equivalent" of a declaration of war, he only enflamed the budding congressional opposition to the U.S. effort in Vietnam.

Paradoxically, even the eventual repeal of the resolution may have been counterproductive from the standpoint of establishing congressional authority in the area; the confused legislative history of the repeal effort provided some support for President Nixon's claim that he was entitled to pursue his program in Southeast Asia entirely on his own authority as Commander-in-Chief. The method of repeal did not afford definitive evidence that the President's only remaining authority, as Senator Cooper contended, was to withdraw U.S. forces from the region. Professor Alexander Bickel and others suggested that Congress might have been wiser to set a terminal date for the resolution and couple it with a proviso obliging the President to seek an affirmative authorization from the Congress for continuing hostilities thereafter. Such an approach might have encountered much the same difficulty and executive antipathy as other attempts to set a fixed date for U.S. disengagement from Vietnam, but as it is, the muddied legislative history of the Tonkin repealer may have done more harm than good in adding fuel to presidential claims of capacious authority to carry on hostilities without benefit of legislative authorization. Well before the resolution's repeal, President Nixon had abandoned it as a basis for his policy in Vietnam and had undertaken secret bombing raids and incursions into Cambodia without advance notice to Congress, much less consultation.

Mr. Nixon defined the problem he faced as one in which he found himself as Commander-in-Chief with large forces already engaged and in which he claimed sufficient authority to protect his troops during disengagement. Yet even if one accepts the contention that the President could protect his forces by attacking enemy sanctuaries in a neutral state unable to enforce its neutrality, it strains reason to argue that the Chief Executive could wage hostilities for several years in order to protect the U.S. forces engaged at the beginning of that period. If this was the principal remaining justification for the President's maintenance of forces in Southeast Asia, it was feeble indeed. But other justifications are too vague or sweeping to provide sound constitutional guidance. One may admire the President's program of orderly disengagement from Southeast Asia and still insist that it ought to have proceeded under more explicit congressional authority.

Throughout the long process sketched here, one witnesses the utter degeneration of legislative-executive collaboration on decisions in the realm of war powers. It is impossible to read this record without concluding that the fluid and informal processes of communication between the branches, which might have sufficed to weld them together as a national decision-making mechanism, have long since withered into impotence. While such informal means of collaboration are valuable in many other ranges of national policy, they appear totally inadequate in matters of war and peace. In fact they may serve only to disguise executive dominance.

One needs to emphasize that the problem is not exclusively or even primarily an aggressive inclination on the part of the executive. It is no less a question of the long-standing willingness of Congress to stand aside, to permit its own prerogatives and responsibilities in this field to take second place to those of the executive. It appears that if a solution is to be found which revives the constitutional equilibrium designed by the founders, formal arrangements must be made to insure that the executive does not pre-empt the vital decisions in this area and that the Congress is both appraised of the need for decisions and obliged to act upon that need.

TOWARD A NEW EQUILIBRIUM

Mr. Justice Jackson once described the government's war powers as a twilight zone in which the President and Congress each hold some distinctive authority but also share a number of less well-defined powers. In simplest terms, the problem is that the President has been employing his powers in the twilight zone to the full, while Congress has rarely and hesitantly used the powers which are clearly its to apply. Thus the recent imbalance between the branches may best be corrected not by assaults on the executive, nor by congressional incursions into areas which were exclusively intended for the other branch, but basically by the use of existing powers which properly accrue to the Congress but which Congress has been accustomed to neglect. For Congress to act wisely in this twilight zone, it must meet both the dictates of the Constitution and the demands of a complicated and changing international environment. It must, in short, devise ways of serving both security and the Constitution, for to fail either would be to undermine both.

From these twin criteria one can deduce several general requirements which congressional rejuvenation of the war powers must meet. Any scheme must permit timely and flexible executive action to meet any emergency, but it must insure that the pressures of a crisis do not become a pretext for prolonged military action without benefit of legislative debate and authorization. Speaking broadly, any practicable scheme must also seek to guarantee that Congress will have the information and opportunity to anticipate, if possible, and to act upon, in any event, the broad range of military contingencies which this country may face. In brief, Congress should engage its war powers without disengaging those of the President. Lest this prove merely a euphemism sanctioning the unfortunate habits of the past, the Congress must re-establish the central principle that it is the custodian of constitutional authority to commit the armed might of the United States to protracted conflict.

A modern metaphor may convey as well as any the essential features of the arrangements envisaged here. Recognizing the awesome dangers of unauthorized use of nuclear weapons, the United States has long followed the so-called "two-key system" for safeguarding its weapons of mass destruction. The purpose is to insure that no nuclear weapon in the American inventory can be fired without the carefully timed and coordinated operation of separate locks by at least two officers. Thus even if an unbalanced or malicious individual gained access to nuclear weapons, he could not detonate them without the active and voluntary cooperation of someone else. Two other aspects of U.S. nuclear controls reinforce this effort to prevent unauthorized use: (1) so-called permissive action links (PAL) render weapons inoperable without positive and explicit authorization from higher authority, and (2) in the event certain systems are readied for firing, the well-known "fail-safe" procedures require that attacks be canceled unless the President issues final and affirmative orders to proceed.

These concepts find a close analogy in the original design of the Constitution. The war powers of the United States government were encumbered with a kind of "two-key system" also, since even before the advent of nuclear technology the decision for or against military action was an issue of utmost gravity. The simple four-cell matrix in Figure 2 illustrates the design.

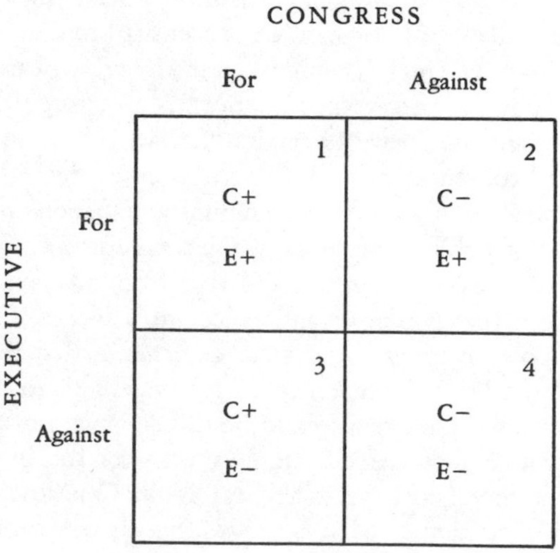

CONGRESS

	For	Against
For	1 C+ E+	2 C− E+
Against	3 C+ E−	4 C− E−

EXECUTIVE

FIGURE 2. THE DECISION FOR WAR

The intended effect of the Constitution was to limit the engagement of American military power to situations in which both Congress and the President agreed that it was necessary, i. e., cell 1. When both branches opposed the use of force (cell 4), the question would obviously not arise. In the situation described by cell 3, even if Congress favored the use of force, the Constitution-makers saw to it that the President as Commander-in-Chief could not be compelled to use the Army and Navy against his better judgment. It is cell 2 that describes the deviant situation which seems to have recurred, namely, one in which the President's affirmative decision to use force has been sufficient without a definite and matching authorization by Congress.

Here is where the "two-key system" of the Constitution has malfunctioned. Only the Congress can remedy the defect, and it is incumbent upon it to do so. To push the metaphor somewhat further, the Congress is also constitutionally obliged to create a kind of "permissive action link" to assure its primacy in releasing American force for prolonged combat and to forge a ."fail-safe" system in which any initial executive commitment of forces is subject to review—and if need be reversal—by systematic congressional action.

An earlier chapter has discussed the habit of deference which Congress acquired regarding executive action in national security policy. That habit understandably persisted so long as the President's track record in foreign affairs was marked by success; but the ordeal of Vietnam blighted that record and shattered the customary deference to presidential dominance. The breakdown of the substantive consensus on Vietnam spread to other policy areas, and the collapse of substantive consensus brought a collapse of the procedural consensus which has prevailed in the years of executive monopoly of the war powers. Before the American people forge a new substantive consensus on their role in world affairs, they will probably have to shape a new procedural consensus as well. Redefinition of the national interest and the national mission in an altered community of nations hinges directly on the restoration of public confidence in the ways foreign policy decisions are made. Such confidence can scarcely derive from the spectacle of endless friction between the legislative and executive branches. Particularly in the field of war powers, many citizens are demanding that the Congress keep better tabs on the President. Even if one is sympathetic to the intentions and undertakings of the United States in Southeast Asia, he must reckon with the plain fact that most Americans now consider the intervention both a political and a moral mistake. The heat is on Congress to safeguard the nation against repetition of what is viewed, rightly or wrongly, as a presidential error.[10]

In the past, legislative attempts to gain control of national commitments,

---

[10] Both the Gallup and the Harris survey data reveal this trend; a summary of some

including commitments to use force, have foundered on unpromising concepts. As a caution to those seeking workable guidelines in this area, one does well to examine two of the most far-reaching initiatives of the last generation. Both failed of adoption when proposed as amendments to the Constitution, but they exemplify the extremes to which Congress may be tempted.

The first of these was the so-called Ludlow amendment, a scheme designed to curtail the nation's capacity to employ force by requiring a national referendum before war could be declared. Introduced by an Indiana representative in December 1937, the plan was seen by the Roosevelt Administration as a grave threat to cripple the President's capacity to carry on the nation's foreign relations. Secretary of War Stimson denounced the idea, convinced that potential aggressors would see it as "a further demonstration that American foreign policy was in the end dependent on a political campaign."[11] In a letter to the Speaker of the House of Representatives, President Roosevelt strongly opposed the amendment as impracticable in application and dangerous in result. "I fully realize that the sponsors of this proposal sincerely believe that it would be helpful in keeping the United States out of war," he wrote. "I am convinced that it would have the opposite effect."[12]

Attempts to kill the plan in committee were unsuccessful, but opponents were able to defeat the measure on the House floor by a vote of 209 to 188. The strength of the isolationist vote on the bill did not escape the notice of German diplomatic observers, who interpreted the episode as a further indication that the United States would be unlikely to intervene in any European conflict. There can be little question that passage of the Ludlow amendment would have permanently weakened the capacity of the United States to act vigorously in world affairs.

A later and more sophisticated congressional initiative involving the country's foreign policy processes provoked a fierce political struggle during the Eisenhower Administration. The proliferation of U.S. international commitments through both treaty and executive agreement had aroused a host of constitutional questions. Among the most serious were those touching the respective roles of legislature and executive in undertaking international obligations for the United States and the relationship of international agreements to provisions of federal and state constitutions.

Many members of Congress and the public had come to view with suspi-

---

relevant surveys appears in Seymour Martin Lipset, "Polls and Protests," *Foreign Affairs*, vol. 495, April 1971, pp. 548–555. On the complex relations between public opinion and voting, see Benjamin I. Page and Richard A. Brody, "Policy Voting and the Electoral Process: The Vietnam War Issue," *American Political Science Review*, vol. 66, September 1972, pp. 979–995.

[11] Henry L. Stimson and McGeorge Bundy, *On Active Service in Peace and War* (New York: Harper, 1947), p. 313.

[12] Quoted in Oscar Theodore Barck, Jr., and Nelson Manfred Blake, *Since 1900: A History of the United States in Our Times* (New York: Macmillan, 1952), p. 605. The plan's sponsor, Louis L. Ludlow, was a Democrat.

cion the growing reliance on executive agreements as compared with formal treaty arrangements. In particular Republican critics of the Roosevelt and Truman administrations pointed to executive agreements made at Malta and Potsdam in 1945 as alleged instances of unwise policy and outrageous procedure. Generally condemning the substance of those agreements, these critics also charged that they violated the spirit of the Constitution by denying the Senate the opportunity to review them. There was a growing fear in some quarters that presidents might resort increasingly to purely executive procedures, relegating the treaty mechanisms to the status of a "historical relic." Many feel that fear has been more than vindicated by subsequent practice on the part of the executive.

At the same time prominent members of the bar were calling for a constitutional amendment to restrict even the treaty-making power. The American Bar Association expressed concern that, unless the treaty processes specifically were constrained, they might be used to impose reforms on the states or to abridge the constitutional rights of American citizens. In April 1952 John Foster Dulles, soon to be Eisenhower's Secretary of State, seemed to confirm these fears when he told an ABA meeting that treaties "are indeed more supreme than ordinary laws, for congressional laws are invalid if they do not conform to the Constitution, whereas treaty law can override the Constitution." Dulles's remarks went further:

> Treaties, for example, can take powers away from the Congress and give them to the President; they can take powers away from the state and give them to the federal government or to some international body, and they can cut across the rights given the people by the constitutional Bill of Rights. . . . This extraordinary power seems to have been deliberately intended by our founders in order to give the federal government untrammeled authority to deal with the international problems.[13]

Stated so starkly, without reference to the countervailing factors that impede use of the treaty power for such purposes, this doctrine generated a groundswell of apprehension within the legal profession.

After simmering through much of the postwar period, pressures to restrict the treaty-making power and to limit the use of executive agreements came to a head in the Eighty-third Congress. When the new Congress convened for the first time on January 7, 1953, Senator John Bricker, a Republican of Ohio, joined by sixty-two cosponsors, submitted Senate Joint Resolution 1, a proposed constitutional amendment dealing with these issues. Asserting congressional authority over executive agreements, the bill also declared that any treaty provision conflicting with the Constitution

[13] Quoted in Eisenhower, *Mandate for Change, 1953 to 1956*, pp. 279–280; see also pp. 277–308 and *Congress and the Nation*, vol. I (Washington, 1965), pp. 110–113, on which this discussion draws heavily.

would be without effect in the United States and that treaties could become effective as internal law only through legislation "which would be valid in the absence of a treaty." An amended version, similar to a text drafted by the ABA and introduced by Republican Senator Arthur Watkins of Utah, was reported favorably by the Senate Judiciary Committee on June 15.

The fight over the Bricker amendment represents a high point of institutional friction between Congress and the executive. Like the Ludlow amendment this initiative sought to establish permanent procedural constraints beyond those already affecting executive conduct of foreign relations. The concerns which motivated its sponsors are not easily relieved, but the extended discussion of the plan in 1953–1954 gave the Senate and the country an opportunity to weigh broader considerations than the theoretical possibility that treaties and executive agreements might provide a means for destroying the Constitution. Qualifying his remarks of 1952, Secretary Dulles emphasized that the treaty power had not in fact been abused and that the proposed amendment was far too drastic a remedy for an evil that had not yet materialized. Mr. Eisenhower recalled that under the Articles of Confederation, the central government had been virtually impotent to carry on a coherent foreign policy; he feared that the Bricker plan would do much to restore such a condition. A distinguished minority of the Senate Judiciary Committee, including Senators Wiley, Hennings, Kefauver, and Kilgore, delivered a stinging critique of the recommended amendment, declaring that it would leave the United States only partially sovereign.

The Eisenhower Administration was willing to accept a simple amendment invalidating any executive agreement that did not accord with the Constitution, but the President and Secretary Dulles were adamantly opposed to the far-reaching provisions of the Senate bill. Various attempts at compromise proved futile, and one of the epic struggles of the Eisenhower years ensued. When Senate Joint Resolution 1 and several alternative proposals came to a vote in February 1954, it became clear that a majority of the Senate favored more sweeping changes than those acceptable to the Administration. The decisive test came on February 26 when a version offered by Senator Walter George of Georgia failed by a single vote (60 to 31) to win the necessary two-thirds approval.

Both the Ludlow and the Bricker initiatives were excessively rigid notions which certainly threatened to do serious damage to the country's capacity to function in international affairs. They bear only the grossest resemblance to the more refined instruments advocated in recent years.

Gradually, during the latter years of U.S. involvement in the Southeast Asian war, congressional discussion of how best to address these problems has gained in sophistication. Many members remain apprehensive about their institution's capacity to deal constructively with the war powers issue, but an evident consensus emerged in Congress that some action must be taken. This conviction resounded across a large part of the political spectrum, and was most striking among some members who provided consistent support of U.S. military efforts in Vietnam. Thus proposals touching the balance of power over a national commitment to armed conflict came from such diverse sponsors as Congressmen Fascell, Zablocki, Findley, Bingham, and Anderson, and Senators Javits, Stennis, Taft, Eagleton, and Spong, to mention a few.

The common theme of most such proposals has been that Congress cannot rely upon the formal declaration of war as its only device for participating in the processes of military engagement, and that it must avoid being placed in the straitjacket represented by a request to vote provisions for forces already committed to battle. Indeed, one of the keenest lessons of recent years has been the futility of trying to use the appropriations power to control or limit hostilities once they have begun. Like nuclear weapons in war, the cut-off of funds is too powerful to be used in all but the most extreme case of estrangement between Congress and the President—a degree of estrangement, one notes, which not even Vietnam induced.

Following the Cambodian incursions of U.S. and Vietnamese forces in May 1970, for several years a number of legislators made intense efforts to cut off funds for continuing the war after a certain date, but a succession of such attempts died aborning. A general policy declaration propounded by Senator Mansfield did survive as an amendment to the fiscal 1972 military procurement authorization bill, but the President emphatically rejected it as a nonbinding expression with which he disagreed and would not comply. Senator Brooke and others managed to attach a fund cut-off in the Senate version of the 1973 Military Procurement Act, designed to end the American role in Southeast Asian hostilities within four months provided U.S. prisoners of war were returned. The provision failed in conference. Only after the Vietnam ceasefire, with fierce fighting developing in Cambodia and revelations of undisclosed American bombing there even prior to the 1970 assaults on the North Vietnamese sanctuaries in that country, did the House come to join the Senate in enacting a firm date to terminate U.S. participation in the fighting. Even then, though the President agreed to abide by the bombing cut-off on August 15, 1973, Mr. Nixon bitterly denounced the congressional action as the virtual betrayal of a friend in distress. Although hailed as a major legislative departure in applying the power of the purse, this section of the Second Supplemental Appropriations Act of 1973 came so late in the course of U.S. involvement in Indochina that it offered an uncertain omen of future congressional willingness to jerk the pursestrings when American forces were directly engaged on the ground in active hostilities.

The lingering need is to devise regular procedures to insure that Congress will meet its responsibilities to assess the wisdom and propriety of using force in particular instances. Accordingly, in spite of executive testimony that Congress should not tamper with the original vagueness with which the

Constitution cloaked the war powers, there developed a substantial thrust toward codifying for the first time the balance of authority between the branches and toward defining precise mechanisms by which Congress can make its power felt at appropriate intervals before and after forces are sent into battle.

The legislators involved are under no illusions that an easy panacea can be found. Congressman Dante Fascell, the highly respected author of the original House proposal to clarify legislative and executive authority in this area, argued persuasively that a whole network of mechanisms and attitudes must be developed to insure that Congress plays a proper and constructive role in the ultimate issues of national security. Fascell and his colleagues have presented a powerful case for the contention that "the final arbiter of the war powers is the Congress." But they have not asserted a narrow institutional claim. Their premise has been the prudent one that, in Congressman Fascell's words, "consultation, common counsel and continuing accountability are essential to viable foreign and defense policies." In that context, the congressional impulse is not to imprison the President in counterproductive statutory chains, but to liberate the Congress from the misguided notion that its own powers should remain dormant while the Chief Executive exploits his to the utmost.

The serious congressional students of this issue have found themselves plunged into a thicket of the most intricate questions of constitutional law and procedure. What kinds of threats short of a direct attack on the United States is the President warranted in repelling on his own authority? Can the President legitimately define such threats for himself or only with the concurrence of Congress? Once such threats are defined, perhaps on an ad hoc basis, does the President have blanket authority to determine the nature and scale of U.S. response? One careful study by the *Harvard Law Review* reaches the judicious conclusion that any U.S. response to an attack on a foreign state, e. g., a NATO ally, constitutes a decision to commence war and hence is constitutionally reserved to the Congress. This view seems to square with the assurances Secretary Acheson gave to Congress in April 1949 that the provisions of the NATO treaty in no way contemplated "automatic war" and that the Congress would have final say in the matter. But comparing that pledge with presidential practice in other areas of the world underscores a central truth concerning legislative-executive relations: the Constitution sometimes facilitates acts it does not legitimatize.

Congressional examination of the larger issues of constitutional authority has led to more concrete questions of procedure. As a practical matter, how can Congress control premature or excessive executive action in an international crisis? Even more troublesome, how can the legislators guard against incremental involvement of U.S. military power in a potential or slowly evolving conflict? Can Congress specify a sensible and workable threshold above which the United States will not go without explicit legislative authorization? Mindful of McGeorge Bundy's wise observation to the House Foreign Affairs Committee that "the war power does not pass exclusively to one branch or to the other merely because the armed forces are engaged," how can Congress make sure it has suitable opportunities and procedures for frequent re-examination of any initial authorization of the use of force? And to perform any of these functions, what methods are available to guarantee that Congress is in a position to make knowledgeable judgments of these several situations?

Extensive floor debate in both houses and prolonged hearings in the House Foreign Affairs and Senate Foreign Relations committees have probed such questions in a depth unmatched in U.S. history.[14] Out of these thorough and cautious proceedings have emerged a number of complementary approaches to key aspects of the problem: (1) congressional access to essential information on which to base decisions concerning the use of force, (2) congressional supervision of precrisis commitments, and (3) congressional review of crisis decisions taken by the executive to employ U.S. armed forces.

The entire matter of congressional access to sensitive information bearing on U.S. foreign relations has been neglected to the point of scandal. Few members have backgrounds in such areas as technical, political, or military intelligence, and contrary to the standard executive charges that Congress is a leaky sieve not to be trusted with genuinely sensitive material, many congressmen are too nervous with such information to handle it carelessly. Occasional leaks in the past have been built into a myth of congressional disregard for safe handling of classified information that has discouraged candor between the branches. In fact, security records of such bodies as the Armed Services committees and the Joint Committee on Atomic Energy have been exemplary. And it is exceedingly doubtful that anyone could identify a pattern of congressional leaks of classified data which caused demonstrable harm to national security.[15] For that matter, the frequent suggestions by anonymous spokesmen of the executive branch that congressmen tend to leak sensitive information for political advantage is more fear than fact. The implication is almost ludicrous compared to the recurrent instances

---

[14] For example, see the Hearings before the Committee on Foreign Relations, U.S. Senate, *War Powers Legislation*, 92d Cong., 1st Sess. Covering the same ground but representing a significantly divergent approach was the House Committee on Foreign Affairs; see Hearings before the Subcommittee on National Security Policy and Scientific Developments of the Committee on Foreign Affairs, U.S. House of Representatives, *War Powers Legislation*, 92d Cong., 1st Sess., and the hearings before the same committee entitled simply *War Powers*, 93d Cong., 1st Sess. See also U.S. House of Representatives, 92d Cong., 1st Sess., Report no. 92–283; and U.S. House of Representatives, *War Powers Resolution of 1973*, 93d Cong., 1st Sess., Report no. 93–287.

[15] See Foreign Affairs Division, Legislative Reference Service, *Security Classification as a Problem in the Congressional Role in Foreign Policy*, prepared for the use of the Committee on Foreign Relations, U.S. Senate, 92d Cong., 1st Sess., December 1971, especially pp. 25–31.

of selective disclosures by members of the executive branch, including disclosures through Administration allies in Congress.

One is closer to the truth in characterizing Congress as intimidated by, rather than casual about, classified data. The result has been that members, including some in positions of major responsibility for overseeing the agencies dealing in secret data, have shied away from treating such information. A classic case was the former Senator, who in many years of presumably supervising the Central Intelligence Agency, more than once declared, "I don't know, and what's more, I don't want to know." Fortunately, that peculiar attitide is fading. Congress is left, however, with few members who have the time or personal resources to cope with the analysis of substantial portions of the relevant information. Furthermore, only a handful of legislative staff personnel are cleared for the sensitive data.

Despite these handicaps, both the Armed Services and the Foreign Affairs committees of the two houses have grown more alert and demanding in terms of the information they expect to receive regularly from the executive. A healthy skepticism has developed toward the intelligence community and its product, although members of the principal committees report that the most reliable information they receive comes consistently from the director of the CIA. Before completing his term of office, Senator John Sherman Cooper sought to take the process one step further by offering legislation to guarantee that the Congress obtain as a matter of ordinary routine the major facts, findings, and reports produced by the Agency. The Senator's proposed amendment to the National Security Act of 1947 has an uncertain prospect, but its basic concept has much appeal in the Capitol, where many members continue to feel that they are spoon-fed only what the executive chooses to reveal, and that they often do not even know which questions to pose in order to reach the critical issues.

The Cooper bill responded directly to the sense of manipulation experienced by his colleagues, an experience scathingly described by Senator Stuart Symington. Symington has himself fought to limit total expenditures on intelligence activities to $4 billion a year, partly as an effort to compel the executive to provide Congress with a more detailed accounting of its efforts in this field and to oblige the executive to share the products of this gigantic enterprise with Congress. Furthermore, revelations of White House attempts to manipulate the CIA to cover the Watergate debacle have heightened congressional determination to impose closer surveillance on the Agency and its practices. There is wide concern over the Agency's illegal connection, albeit under top-level executive pressure, with domestic political activities. Nothing could have done more to breathe life into the dormant Senate Subcommittee on Central Intelligence and to confirm the increasingly active disposition of Chairman Nedzi's House subcommittee.

The disclosure of the Pentagon Papers has not been fully digested by the Congress, but they certainly amplified legislative determination to speed classification procedures and to seek new methods by which Congress can regularly penetrate the inner recesses of the intelligence community. Senator Edmund Muskie has advanced an attractive draft of legislation to revise declassification procedures, shifting the presumption toward early declassification and the burden of proof toward those who would propose retaining classifed labels on particular data. At the same time, Muskie's plan contemplates improved legistative access to information which remains classified.

It is evident that none of these steps would resolve the fundamental problems stemming from the sheer bulk of secret information developed in the executive branch. Congress could move rapidly from starvation to glut, unless means are found to discriminate among the innumerable reports and documents that might become available to legislators. The principal surety here perhaps lies in the new expectations which congressional demands for secret information should create; responsible officials of the executive branch should acquire a heightened sense of the need to keep Congress informed of key studies and reports bearing on current decisions. Presuming that such officials also have an interest in amicable and constructive relations between the branches, they should be increasingly sensitive to the fact that the shortest path to political friction is for one partner to try to snow or gull the other with information that either overwhelms or misleads. It will take a learning process of some duration for Congress to get the feel of what is available and of what it wants in the way of additional information. Whether or not additional formal arrangements are enacted to improve the flow of critical information to the Congress, recent months have seen a decided enhancement of the aggressive attitude which Congress must have in order to obtain and analyze such information effectively.

A special aspect of the information problem concerns the issue of "executive privilege"—a category relating to information which the President may constitutionally deny to the Congress on the grounds that it is personal counsel to the Chief Executive. The theory of executive privilege has long been respected by Congress, in the sense that members agree that a certain confidentiality may reasonably attach to the intimate advice received by the President. But there has been a troubling tendency to expand the notion of privilege to cover a vast and ill-defined body of information developed inside the bureaucracy, including all sorts of studies and planning papers which are in no sense personal to the President. Many such papers illuminate options open to the United States and might well afford an improved basis for congressional participation in the choice of major policy alternatives.

The momentous Supreme Court ruling of 1974 against Mr. Nixon's claim of unbridled authority to assert privilege over information in his possession, though acknowledging that such claims have special force where issues of national security are involved, made clear that they must be weighed against competing interests of a constitutional nature. The Court's opinion paves the way for Congress, if it chooses, to press for less capacious executive interpretations of what is privileged material and what is properly accessible to congressional use, either confidentially or openly. Even before the extreme claims of privilege surfaced in connection with the Watergate scandals, Senator Ervin and others had begun pressing for a strict construction of the concept of privilege, holding that it can only be invoked by the President and that it must be related to a specific body of information. Studies by the Government and General Research Division of the Library of Congress found nineteen instances of privilege claims during the first Nixon term, reportedly the most frequent rate of usage by any Administration.

Several incidents in the foreign policy field have sharpened congressional concern on this matter. During much of 1971, the Foreign Relations Committee sought to obtain a five-year military assistance plan reputedly prepared by the Defense Department. First told such a document did not exist, the committee was later informed that the materials in question were merely contingency planning documents which did not represent Administration policy and hence could be of no interest to the Senators. When the Comptroller General eventually ruled that the committee had authority to cut off funds for DOD military assistance programs unless the documents in question were forthcoming, or unless the President invoked executive privilege, the Department solicited a directive from the President specifically ordering that the material be withheld on the grounds of privilege. The episode was not reassuring, either in terms of the Defense Department's credibility with the Congress or in terms of the scope of the executive claim of privilege.

This contretemps came in the wake of another disillusioning experience in which the executive branch had kept Congress in the dark and flouted the fundamental spirit of the constitutional relationship between the branches, the Cambodian incursions of 1970. One can share the President's concern not to risk premature disclosure of the operation for fear of losing the advantage of surprise and increasing the hazards to American and allied troops. Yet it is a telling measure of the estrangement between President and Congress that while the governments of Cambodia and South Vietnam had advance notice of the U.S. decision to attack the North Vietnamese sanctuaries, the Congress had none. In late April 1970, only days before the incursions, Secretary of State William Rogers had evaded attempts by the Foreign Relations Committee to pin him down on the drift of Administration thinking about the rapidly degenerating situation in Cambodia. To be sure, there was no basis for challenging the Secretary's reluctance to describe which advisers were putting forward what proposals to the President, but it is an odd and perverse view of the privileged nature of intra-executive deliberations to hold that Congress should remain ignorant of the fact that the President was planning to send U.S. forces across an international border, albeit one which the North Vietnamese were violating with impunity. An observer infers that Mr. Rogers's failure to signal this possibility to the committee, at the very time Saigon and Pnom Penh were consorting with

Washington on the project, reflects less a concern for possible security leaks than a decision to pre-empt the Congress and deny its key committees even the opportunity to raise questions or express views to the President. Incidents of this sort offended many congressmen who were supporters of the President's decision to attack the Cambodian sanctuaries.

More general issues of executive privilege arose in connection with the extraordinary shift of influence over foreign policy from the Department of State to the National Security Council during the years 1969–1973. As the role of the Assistant to the President for National Security Affairs grew during the Nixon years, many congressmen began to feel that it was imperative to gain greater legislative access to the information developed at NSC level. However, the President's Assistant, Dr. Henry Kissinger, chose not to appear officially before congressional committees, although he was willing to meet members of the House and Senate committees informally and off the record. Given the unique importance of the NSC apparatus, Chairman Fulbright and others contended that Dr. Kissinger should appear in formal session, closed if necessary and subject to the invocation of executive privilege regarding specific elements of NSC counsel to the President.

The distance between the branches on this issue was illustrated by the committee's difficulty for many months in obtaining the background interviews which Dr. Kissinger accorded members of the press from time to time. Representatives of foreign news media, including the Soviet press agency, TASS, took part directly in these press conferences, but ludicrously, the NSC for a period denied the Foreign Relations Committee transcripts of these backgrounders. The problem was belatedly resolved, but until early 1972 committee members still lacked the opportunity which reporters had of questioning Dr. Kissinger in his role as the NSC director. Largely because they respected his achievements and services to the nation, members were unwilling to threaten to cut off funds for the burgeoning NSC staff as a means to compel Dr. Kissinger to comply with their request for his appearance. The immediate dispute became moot in August 1973 when Kissinger became Secretary of State. Although he retained his title as a Presidential Assistant, he was subsequently available to testify officially as the Cabinet officer directing the Department of State.

In the interest of accountability, however, and recognizing that future national security assistants are unlikely to hold office simultaneously as Secretary of State, there is much to be said for Congress pursuing a proposal advanced by Senator Charles Percy. This approach calls for a change in the National Security Act to give the Assistant to the President for National Security Affairs a statutory "second hat," in analogy to the twin functions long borne by the Science Advisor to the President, who also served as the statutory director of the Office of Science and Technology prior to its dissolution. The theory is that under those circumstances, the national security Assistant could appear before Congress in his statutory capacity. Unless a more forthcoming attitude emerged in the White House, however, even this statutory innovation could well end in frustration and friction.

So long as the National Security Council system functions as it has in recent years, this is likely to be a central issue in the legislative quest for improved information on foreign policy and national security. Without debating whether the President's Assistant actually eclipsed the Secretary of State as a policy-maker during the Kissinger-Rogers duumvirate, the strengthened NSC apparatus obviously played an unprecedented role in filtering, analyzing, and coordinating the policy output of the bureaucracy. Its study memoranda and other documents could provide Congress with one of the most convenient handles on the entire range of foreign policy questions. The questions addressed through the NSC apparatus are, after all, matters of national and government-wide concern; they are not the personal property of a privy council. In groping for a harmonious working relation between the branches, more cooperation on this front is crucial.

The task of restoring trust is a joint responsibility, and Congress must make clear that it will not abuse confidential exchanges to browbeat executive spokesmen or to reap political windfalls on particular issues. But neither side will be able to demonstrate its trustworthiness in this particular realm so long as the entire domain of NSC operations is insulated from congressional observation. The reasonable course would seem to require some opportunity for Congress to interrogate and consult with the Council's director and some sharing of those NSC studies and materials which constitute, not personal advice to the President, but the definition of problems, programs, and policy alternatives for the nation.

Turning to the problem of precrisis commitments, the executive has certainly undertaken many of these obligations in recent years without either the knowledge or the consent of the Congress. A number of clandestine commitments became known during the important investigations of the Symington Subcommittee on United States Security Agreements and Commitments Abroad. As hard as it is to believe, the practice had arisen that secret agreements concluded by the executive with other governments were normally withheld from the Congress. Thus the Senate has had no opportunity to evaluate whether certain executive agreements might better have assumed a treaty form and to express such a judgment to the executive. Given the preponderant usage of the executive agreement form, the result has been not only a dilution of the Senate's treaty power but a major inroad on the Congress's war power as well. A number of members have pointed out that the political judgment regarding U.S. participation in the defense of South Vietnam would have taken on a different light to the Congress if it were known that other countries in the region—notably Thailand and South Korea—were contributing to the effort only under the inducement of certain dubious executive agreements.

A straightforward and promising remedy was offered by Senator Clifford

Case, building on an effort two decades ago by Senator William Knowland. In order to permit the Congress to form an independent judgment on the merits and propriety of undertakings made by secret executive agreements, Senator Case's plan requires the Secretary of State to transmit to the Congress the text of any international agreement, other than a treaty, to which the United States is a party. Transmittal is to both the Senate Foreign Relations Committee and the House Foreign Affairs Committee, which are bound by an appropriate injunction of secrecy to be removed only by the President.[16] Despite Administration opposition, the Senate overwhelmingly approved the plan; on the House side the executive relaxed its effort to defeat the measure and final enactment came late in the Ninety-second Congress. Early experience with the measure suggests that it can operate harmoniously and that it will prove an extremely valuable innovation. It avoids the pitfalls of the old Bricker amendment, but by alerting the Congress to executive practice, it reaps comparable benefits.

The Case plan is a simple and workable scheme to implement the earlier National Commitments resolution, passed by the Senate in 1969. That expression of the sense of the Senate was not binding, but it made clear the view of a majority of senators "that a national commitment by the United States results only from affirmative action taken by the executive and legislative branches of the United States Government by means of a treaty, statute, or concurrent resolution of both Houses of Congress specifically providing for such commitment." At that time the Senate did not really come to grips with the varieties and degrees of "commitment" which the United States might assume, but its main concern was obviously to prevent unauthorized and secret engagements which promised the use of American military force to support a foreign state.

Not only had the Foreign Relations Committee been enflamed by Under Secretary of State Katzenbach's reference to the Tonkin Gulf resolution as the "functional equivalent" of a declaration of war, but it had been acutely disturbed by Secretary Rusk's discussion of certain economic and military assistance programs in terms which, to the committee, seemed to imply the most far-reaching obligations to the further defense of recipient states. Rusk undoubtedly had a more discriminating notion in mind, but by that time senators were taking no chances on being locked into large commitments by the relatively tiny half-steps of foreign aid. The National Commitments resolution grew out of those sentiments, but even its principal backers soon considered it ineffectual. Unless the Congress knows what executive agreements exist and what they involve, there is no realistic way for it to be sure

---

[16] See *Transmittal of Executive Agreements to Congress,* Senate Report no. 92–591, Jan. 19, 1972, and Senator Case's statement before the Subcommittee on National Security Policy and Scientific Developments, Committee on Foreign Affairs, U.S. House of Representatives, *International Executive Agreements,* June 19, 1972, pp. 2–10.

the country is not being committed unilaterally by the President. The Case proposal ought to remedy that astonishing ignorance; it could be the decisive step in positioning Congress to assess what, if any, action it should take to enforce or to alter understandings reached by the executive. It should also induce a wholesome prudence on the part of the executive officials responsible for negotiating such sensitive accords. Prominent members of the Senate Armed Services Committee share the suspicion that U.S. commitments may have grown beyond wise proportions and that the United States must re-evaluate these undertakings to bring American defense obligations in line with its tightening military capabilities.

In addition to the attempt to penetrate the problem of commitments around the world, some congressmen are gravitating to other types of controls over precrisis decisions which might lead to U.S. military action. There is now a widespread appreciation that, while fully respecting the necessity for presidential authority to meet rapidly developing threats to security, executive actions can thoroughly box in congressional options before any question of actual commitment to battle is presented to Congress. This is true whether or not there is some understanding, formal or informal, public or private, with another government. Of particular importance is the disposition of U.S. military manpower in various strife-torn sectors of the globe. Troops in the field can be a lightning rod, conceivably attracting fire in a period of tension and thereby engaging the U.S. interest with an intensity that circumstances might not otherwise justify. Thus, having for the first time set numerical ceilings on the armed forces in 1971, Congress is moving to maintain closer scrutiny over the size and deployment of U.S. forces overseas.

The kernel of the problem here is evident to both branches of government. On occasion, exploitation of executive agreements to achieve goals the administrative branch was not prepared to espouse overtly had descended into a kind of crude gamesmanship. A former chairman of the Joint Chiefs of Staff, General Earl Wheeler, explicitly confronted the advantages of such arrangements in avoiding the difficulties of a treaty association with Spain. In an internal memorandum of 1968, the general pointed out that "by the presence of the United States forces in Spain the United States gives Spain a far more visible and credible security guarantee than any written document." To speak more precisely, those forces to which he referred were to be deployed to Spain, of course, according to a written document, a classified agreement negotiated exclusively by the executive branch. Disclosures of this attitude and the practices accompanying it greatly fortified senatorial determination to get a handle on the whole problem of precrisis commitments undertaken by the President on his own authority.

One plan to deal with this matter, developed in conjunction with independent experts and congressional authorities and endorsed by the prestigious Committee for Economic Development, would provide for an annual military manpower authorization for each service plus a broad authorization of the numbers of forces to be deployed to designated geographic areas. The President could, of course, shift forces between regions if necessary, but the plan would require him to report promptly to the Congress whenever any such redeployment occurred. The great advantage of this kind of procedure is that it would regularize congressional review of the scale and deployment of U.S. armed forces, permitting the Congress to join with the President in an orderly annual review of where troops are in relation to potential trouble spots. In this manner Congress could convey to the President its own sense of whether certain deployments are worth maintaining, or whether the risks of particular installations of U. S. forces overseas exceed our interest in that theater. Congress could form a firmer opinion for itself as to whether it really would be prepared to support hostilities in a region if they erupted—and the question of whether Congress would really be prepared to bite the bullet is, needless to say, of considerable importance to any President in allocating U.S. forces abroad.

Rather than having each congressional attempt to deal with such questions take on the appearance of a confrontation with the executive—as in the case of the recurrent Mansfield amendment on NATO force levels—such an annual manpower review would provide Congress an opportunity to make modest periodic adjustments in the guidelines for overseas deployment. Legislation to create an annual manpower authorization procedure could also put an end to the harrowing and unnecessary disputes which recur each time the Congress faces a decision on reviving selective service or revising the all-volunteer Army. The measure contemplated here could also make provision for whatever standby draft authority might be required for each succeeding year, permitting the nation to pursue its preference for volunteer service with adequate contingency arrangements to meet any manpower deficit that might persist.

Senator Fulbright has put forward a related measure which would require monthly reports by the President on the disposition of U.S. forces around the globe. The frequency of such reporting would insure that significant redeployments would come to Congress's attention promptly, improving the chances for timely legislative debate on impending confrontations abroad. Offered as a floor amendment in 1973, the Fulbright bill received less consideration than it warrants, and one surmises that it will attract extensive hearings in the future.[17] Together with the concepts already outlined here, the Arkansas Democrat's proposal represents a promising evolution of congressional thought about ways to couple legislative oversight with ample executive authority to deploy forces as need be. The Armed Services Com-

[17] See Committee for Economic Development, *Military Manpower and National Security* (New York, 1972); see also Senator Fulbright's interesting amendment in the *Congressional Record*, July 20, 1973, pp. S14194 ff.

mittee in the Senate has already begun to scrutinize manpower and deployments, and the time is ripe to systematize these procedures more thoroughly.

If these ideas for close congressional scrutiny of all executive agreements and for regular legislative authorizations of the size and deployments of the armed forces come to fruition, the Congress will have obtained an important handle on some of the crucial dimensions of "precrisis commitments." None of these plans, however, would insure that Congress has the decisive say in involving the United States in military hostilities. In short, there would still remain the question of what function, if any, the Congress could fulfill after a crisis erupted.

It is on this question that the most intensive congressional efforts have concentrated, resulting in a rich set of proposals to give further statutory elucidation to the distribution of war powers. Beginning in 1970 the House and Senate committees have held thoroughgoing hearings, seeking to find a formula which would insure that Congress is not bypassed in the crucial decisions to commit U.S. military power. Congress had addressed many aspects of these issues in the prolonged deliberations of 1969 and 1970 concerning the so-called McGovern-Hatfield and Cooper-Church amendments which sought to limit the use of American forces in Indochina. Each of these two plans, though markedly different in scope, touched the fundamental question of whether and how the legislature could make its putative authority over war effective. While Congress did not enact a binding provision to set a final date for U.S. disengagement from the Vietnam conflict, as the McGovern-Hatfield plan and its variants sought to do, it did levy explicit prohibitions on the introduction of U.S. ground troops into Laos or Thailand.[18] Later it passed a statutory reiteration of President Nixon's commitment not to reintroduce American troops into Cambodia after the May 1970 incursions were completed. The animated debates over these proposals set the stage for more far-reaching efforts to insure congressional participation in future decisions to engage American armed forces in hostilities.

Initial steps to set a framework for legislative engagement in future contingencies came in the House of Representatives. Following extensive hearings in the Foreign Affairs Subcommittee on National Security Policy and Scientific Developments during the Ninety-first Congress, the House passed H. J. Res. 1355 on November 16, 1970. The subcommittee chairman, Congressman Clement Zablocki, offered a nearly identical measure in the Ninety-second Congress as H. J. Res 1, and after further hearings it was duly passed in August 1971. Incorporating the contributions of many House members and independent witnesses, H. J. Res. 1 carefully refrained from challenging the President's constitutional authority. Indeed the resolution

[18] In addition to the hearings and reports on war powers previously cited, a convenient reference is American Enterprise Institute, *The War Powers Bill*, Legislative Analysis no. 19, 92d Cong., Washington, Apr. 17, 1972.

specifically recognized his power "in certain extraordinary and emergency circumstances . . . to defend the United States and its citizens without specific prior authorization by the Congress." The bill did, however, strongly assert the Congress's own powers and provide that in any case of emergency use of military forces without prior congressional authorization the President should promptly report in writing to the House and Senate, explaining the circumstances, grounds, and probable scope of his activities. By requiring such a report as soon as possible, it was hoped that at the very least Congress would have an occasion and an opportunity to conduct its own deliberations and reach its own decisions on the wisdom of the course undertaken by the Chief Executive. The reporting procedure, which President Nixon had reportedly indicated a willingness to accept, seemed a sensible first step toward reviving dormant congressional authority in this field. It did not guarantee that Congress would in fact take any action on the basis of such a report.

Gradually, a more ambitious approach evolved in the Senate. Building on the original bill by Senator Jacob Javits, a remarkable coalition of senators came to favor legislation that defined the broad contingencies under which the President could use military force without advance congressional authority and prescribed a mechanism by which, if hostilities were to continue beyond a period of thirty days, the Congress would be obliged to provide such authorization. Lacking affirmative legislative action, the President would be required to disengage U.S. forces. The opponents of the measure also proved to be an unusual alliance. Senators Goldwater, Gurney, Hruska, and McGee, among others, were joined by a number of prominent private authorities—Eugene Rostow, George Ball, James McGregor Burns, and Arthur Schlesinger, to mention a few. They were matched against equally prestigious and more numerous constitutional and political professionals who endorsed the purposes and provisions of the Senate war powers bill—Alexander Bickel, McGeorge Bundy, Arthur Goldberg, and others. A reasoned and illuminating debate occupied the Senate for two weeks preceding the key vote on the measure; on April 13, 1972, it passed overwhelmingly, 68 to 16, with many other senators being recorded in support of the bill. Particularly when weighed against the determined executive campaign to defeat the plan, the outcome testified to the conviction of most senators that additional arrangements are needed to guarantee that Congress meets its own responsibilities to make the fundamental decisions regarding future military contingencies. As John Stennis sadly noted, "With all deference, I do not think we have been living up to that responsibility."

During the Ninety-second Congress the two houses were unable to reconcile their divergent approaches to the war powers issue, the House preferring its simpler reporting arrangements, the Senate supporting its more elaborate provisions for mandatory action. But the prolongation of the violence in Southeast Asia and the enduring concerns which had arisen on the Hill kept the question alive in the Ninety-third Congress, and there was noticeable movement toward common ground between the two houses. In some respects, it seemed that the more the members studied the problems, the more determined they became to enact strong legislation. Thus, having conducted dozens of hearings and thrice passed an earlier war powers bill, on July 18, 1973, the House of Representatives approved a far more ambitious measure comparable to the Senate plan, though differing from it in essential respects. Approved in the face of an explicit veto threat by a vote of 244 to 170, the bill contemplated the termination of any presidential use of force abroad within 120 days unless Congress specifically authorized its continuance. Going beyond the Senate bill, it provided firm arrangements to guarantee that any one member of either house (as opposed to the upper chamber's reliance on cosponsorship by one-third of either body) could force a vote by both the House and Senate on a resolution sanctioning the President's action. Despite constitutional objections by a number of members, the House went even further than the Senate in providing that by concurrent resolution not subject to veto Congress could at any time order the disengagement of U.S. forces.

The fundamental presumption of the House thus came to match that of the Senate, namely, that the President should not be able to employ forces on a sustained basis unless Congress affirmatively moved to endorse such action. The key test in the House debate came on this issue, when Congressman Whalen, who eventually supported the bill, moved to reverse the presumption and to authorize the President to continue hostilities unless Congress disapproved his action "by the passage of a resolution appropriate to the purpose." The Whalen amendment failed by the narrow margin of 200 to 211, revealing that many members were troubled by the tough committee approach. The central concern appeared to be the impression that to require congressional approval to sustain further hostilities meant that the President might be forced by congressional inaction to reverse a grave commitment. Yet under the provisions of the bill, with generous arrangements to insure that Congress faces the issue, it is inconceivable that Congress would not act, if by that term one means it would not vote upon the question. Moreover, in the words of Congressman Paul Findley, "Inaction has been the traditional way by which the Congress has rejected unwise policy, not only in the foreign field, but in the domestic field as well." After all, if Congress does not approve the President's recommendations to subsidize housing or to share revenue or to move the capital to the hinterland, the housing is not subsidized, the revenue is not shared, and the seat of government remains in Washington. In the immediate aftermath of the formidable House action, the Senate overwhelmingly passed an updated version of its own bill, opening the way to an early conference to consolidate the congressional position.[19]

[19] See *Congressional Record*, July 18, 1973, pp. H6231–H6284, and July 20, 1973, pp.

The resulting compromise legislation promised to be a decisive turning point in the history of legislative-executive relations. While extending the President's authority for independent action to a sixty-day period, the measure established strict procedures to insure that Congress would be constrained to act, either to validate or invalidate any extended employment of American military power. The expected veto action of President Nixon was framed in terms which seemed oblivious to the refinements which the act had incorporated to meet the concerns of those anxious not to paralyze the Chief Executive in a crisis; in fact, the veto message was composed even prior to receipt of the final version of the legislation and seemed strangely disconnected from its actual provisions. Without sacrificing substance, the legislators had actually been so generous in their respect for presidential authority that a principal sponsor of the original plan, Senator Thomas Eagleton, felt obliged to oppose enactment, as did a number of other previous supporters. Nevertheless, on November 7, 1973, preponderant and bipartisan majorities of the two houses overrode the veto and carried the War Powers resolution into law.

To gauge the wisdom and propriety of the arrangements envisioned by the war powers legislation, one needs to take account of the real concerns which have troubled the critics. Their objections rest on both constitutional and pragmatic grounds. Some fear that the measure seeks to extend congressional power so far as to impinge on authority legitimately exercised by the President as constitutional Commander-in-Chief. To afford Congress an explicit opportunity to reverse a presidential commitment of troops—"a sixty-day veto"—struck Senator Sam Ervin as creating, in effect, 535 commanders-in-chief. In his view Congress retains ample control of the President's use of the armed forces through its control of the pursestrings, however difficult it may be to pull those strings tight when hostilities are actually under way. Yet the allegation that the act infringes on the President's authority as Commander-in-Chief appears to confuse the President's acknowledged strategic and tactical control of military force with an exclusive claim to shape the objectives for which such forces are to be employed. The proponents of the

S14159–S14227. In the course of the Senate debate, Senator Robert Griffin offered an ingenious alternative to the Javits-Stennis-Eagleton approach; Griffin's proposal would have coupled a mandatory reporting requirement for any use of force with an expedited mechanism for Congress either to approve the engagement or to prohibit the expenditure of any funds beyond a specified date. The Griffin formulation enjoyed the considerable advantage of focusing legislative action on an undisputed constitutional power, that of appropriations, and would have avoided many of the controversial features of other bills which were subject to the charge that they affronted the President's authority. For the President's veto message and the final debates see *Congressional Record*, Nov. 7, 1973, pp. S20093–S20116, H9641–9661. A notable overview and analysis of the tensions between presidential and legislative claims to war power is Louis Fisher, *President and Congress: Power and Policy* (New York: Free Press, 1972), pp. 175–235.

War Powers Act developed a case sufficiently persuasive to a vast majority of their colleagues that decisions on these larger objectives are properly and primarily a prerogative of the Congress. And they consistently confirmed that no statute could pretend to diminish the President's constitutional powers; it could only provide "necessary and proper" means for Congress to apply its own.

In his extensive critiques of the proposal, Senator Barry Goldwater articulated the most expansive view of the President's powers as Commander-in-Chief and the most restrictive interpretation of Congress's authority in these realms. Stressing that even in the eighteenth century declarations of war had become obsolete, he contended that the founding fathers must have known that in conferring on the legislature an intentionally feeble and ceremonial authority. Goldwater also invoked Lincoln's famous dictum that "measures otherwise unconstitutional might become lawful by becoming indispensable to the preservation of the Constitution through the preservation of the Nation." However cogent that doctrine may have been at a certain level of abstraction or in the context of a civil war, it persuaded few senators in 1973. When faced with a claim that to save the law, the President might have to break the law, they heard a horrifying echo: "To save the village, we had to destroy it." It would not wash in an era of Vietnam abroad and Watergate at home.

Through the maze of constitutional argument one perceived that most opponents were alarmed by pragmatic considerations of international politics. By setting new and formal procedures for Congress to control the use of the nation's military capabilities in times of crisis, would the act undermine our network of alliances? Would it nullify such policies as those expressed in the Middle East resolution of 1957 and similar documents? Would it destroy the credibility of the American deterrent at crucial moments? Would it enfeeble the President by placing him in a procedural straitjacket? In short, might the War Powers Act become, through the cruel perversity of politics, the "War Provocations Act," as many thought the neutrality acts of the nineteen-thirties had proved to be?

The legislative history should go far toward quieting those apprehensions. Clearly, the advocates of war powers legislation are under no illusions that it will restrain an American President from acting vigorously to meet what he considers threats to the security of the United States or to the safety of its military personnel and other citizens abroad. The record of debate invariably clarifies the law in the direction of maximum reasonable latitude for effective presidential action during a crisis.

The real effects of such legislation are likely to be twofold. First, by making advance provision for timely congressional deliberation on any commitment of U.S. forces to hostilities, it should enhance the likelihood of genuine consultation between the branches on these grave issues. The President will know that he faces an early accounting before the Congress and will presumably display even greater prudence than otherwise in taking risky action involving actual or potential conflict at arms. But far from debilitating the deterrent power of American military capabilities, these arrangements should signal to potential adversaries that when the President does act, he does so with clear expectations that Congress will be with him. Second, by requiring Congress to render a judgment on the case within a fixed period, it should guarantee that the legislature meets its profound obligation to make a collective decision before the United States sustains a substantial international conflict.

No machinery can insure wise action, and the requirement that Congress act within sixty days or some other fixed period distressed a number of thoughtful students. Some worry that a President might be so inhibited he would evade certain confrontations where the United States might better be served by firmness. Others speculate that, facing a possible sixty-day deadline, the President might actually conduct a fiercer and more violent war in hopes of ending it abruptly. And some remind us that Congress has often been the eager hawk among the branches, raising the possibility that the legislature could press the Chief Executive to more forceful action than might be constructive. Judgments will differ as to how likely these tendencies are to materialize, and as to how serious they are compared to the obvious hazards of persisting in legislative-executive habits which impede, if they do not preclude, meaningful congressional participation in decisions of this character.

The straightforward requirement that the President report to Congress any hostile use of the military ordered on his own authority is a solid contribution to genuine collaboration between President and Congress simply because it provides an element of accountability for executive disposition of force. Yet one wonders whether, without a target date for action on its own part, Congress could be depended on to face the hard task of weighing and judging these critical issues. Perhaps the most vital function of the sixty-day time frame is to compel Congress to meet its own responsibilities—not as a constraint on the President, but as a fulfillment of its own constitutional mandate. It is evident that Congress, as well as the man in the White House, can reach its decision foolishly or recklessly. But surely in a republic the most foolish decision is for Congress not to decide at all. With persistence in the several lines of action discussed in this chapter, Congress has a unique chance to forge a panoply of instruments to guide the country's precrisis commitments and its basic decisions regarding which crises merit the risk of prolonged hostilities.

In his summation to the Senate after years of effort on the war powers problem, Senator Jacob Javits phrased the matter wisely. "What we are trying to do," he said, "is . . . to bring about an end to the guerilla warfare between Congress and the President in which Congress has been constantly bested, with such tremendous tragic cost to our country, before such a violent reaction developed as to really sweep away Presidential authority." There is the insight on which a constructive War Powers Act must rest. The President's authority to protect the nation has been jeopardized by the bloody experience of the last decade. It can be revived not by assertive claims of unbridled executive power; it is precisely such power which has fallen into disrepute. To revitalize the Presidency as an agency of national security requires, rather, the rejuvenation of legislative-executive collaboration, from which can flow wiser and more willing grants of essential democratic support.

A process has begun which, if nourished thoughtfully, can invigorate a government which division has threatened to enervate. No congressman— no citizen—should be content with anything less.

IX. Conclusion: A Marriage of Trust and Tension

"Principles without programs are equal to platitudes." The phrase belongs to George Bernard Shaw; the thought applies to many realms of human action. Erected on a body of contending principles, alternately contradictory and reinforcing, America's system of governance is threatened frequently by the paralyzing lotion of platitudes. Yet Shaw's aphorism captures but part of the truth. Great principles lose their content not only by having no programs for concrete action but also by serving too many programs of divergent character and purpose. The vaunted flexibility of the American constitutional tradition grows suspect in the eyes of some because it accommodates a dominant President in one era and a strong Congress in another, *laissez faire* capitalism in one age and wage-price controls in another, naive professions of disinterested internationalism at one moment and tough-minded expressions of dollar diplomacy at another.

In certain respects that very suspicion represents an enduring insight of the American political faith, a doctrine which distrusts power and disdains impotence. One of the secrets of the system's prolonged vitality is its insistence on thoughtful skepticism rather than thoughtless deference toward public figures and public affairs. As the preceding chapters have intimated, one can sensibly view the efforts to rejuvenate the Congress as the rebirth of an essential agnosticism concerning the wisdom of unfettered executive supremacy in the fields of national security and foreign policy. It is important, however, to distinguish this agnosticism from the overt hostility toward presidential power which occupants of the White House often claim to perceive in Congress's attempts to assert its own authority in these fields.

In adapting the nation's tenets of limited government and individual liberty to a modern environment which demands effective and potent public institutions, the task remains that foreseen by the founders who envisaged a federal republic stretching over a continent and attaining considerable weight in the international arena: to strike a prudent balance of trust and tension between the governed and the governors, and among the several branches of government themselves. Unlike the constant intragovernmental stresses of domestic politics, the issues of national security and international affairs were for too long relatively immune to the flux of political competition between Congress and the President.

Vesting too much trust in the superior competence of the executive, the legislature failed to induce the tension which the Constitution contemplates as a necessary ingredient to the system's overall effectiveness. By contrast, successive Presidents, while protesting their respect for legislative prerogatives, scarcely disguised their aversion to active congressional participation in the large decisions of world politics. In executive eyes, as Congressman F. Edward Hebert once said, Congress seemed "an unnecessary evil." Thus the trust reposed in the President by the Congress was repaid by singular mistrust of the Congress by the President. It is this dangerous and corrosive imbalance which contemporary congressional initiatives promise to remedy.

Several points need to be made in this connection. A stronger Congress does not mean a weaker President. As exemplified repeatedly in these pages, an alert and energetic legislature can, in fact, enhance presidential authority and power in a number of crucial respects. It is almost a truism now to observe that by serving as a medium of domestic consensus, Congress can in fact facilitate the nation's diplomacy. Furthermore, by multiplying the political eyes and ears of the government, Congress can serve as a creative filter for the countless issues which contend for the attention and energy of top policy-makers. In foreign affairs no less than in other areas, the President and his political associates in the executive branch are spread thin, able to assess only a fraction of the myriad problems which arise in the nation's business. An economic division of labor, not to mention the dictates of self-government, argues for active congressional participation in identifying issues for consideration by policy-makers and in outlining candidate programs for action. In addition to matters perceived to be important by the chief executive and the bureaucracy, problems which meet the test of significance in the halls of Congress may often prove to be vital questions which have been obscured in the congested channels of executive decision-making.

Judge John Sirica has put it well: "While the Constitution diffuses power the better to secure liberty, it also contemplates that practice will integrate the dispersed powers into a workable government. It enjoins upon its branches separateness but interdependence, autonomy but reciprocity." To nourish this kind of mixed relationship requires a dynamism too long absent from congressional deliberations and decisions on national security affairs. The hopeful augury of latter years, amidst the gloom of the Vietnam ordeal and acute friction between White House and Capitol, is that such a dynamism is feasible.

A wag once formulated three laws of political dynamics similar to those of physics. First, if there is an issue, there will be a politician to exploit it. Second, if there is no issue, there will be a politician to create one. Third, if there is no politician, the system may be said to be at rest.

The notions are not really facetious. In fact they speak quite directly to the flaw which marked much of American decision-making during the Cold War, namely, the comparative insulation of national security questions from debate and evaluation in the political arena. Thanks to both the President and the Congress, and to drastic transformation of the world scene, the Cold War mold has been cracked. Issues once considered too delicate for politics are moving back into the arena where public choice can be subjected to the cross-cutting values and objectives appropriate to a pluralistic nation. This is too basic and too affirmative a transition to be built merely on disillusionment with executive decision-making, although such a reaction has clearly fueled recent trends. In the long run the new balance of legislative-executive power should be seen as intrinsically sounder than a distorted reliance on executive dominance, a reliance built on mistaken premises and unreasonable expectations.

To manage the new relationship beneficially will require statesmanship of a high order in both branches. The advent of Gerald Ford to the Presidency brought to the White House an unusually sympathetic disposition toward the Congress, its traditions, and its values. Similarly, Congress continues to give voice to its respect for the necessity of a vigorous Presidency. It is learning to address questions of national security in a far more discriminating fashion than previously. The prospects are good that future legislative action will be less categorical, with more fluid devices to engage congressional authority at frequent intervals.

It is fashionable to disparage the tradition of bipartisanship as an enfeebling one, a pattern which enervates the Congress by granting too much leeway to the Chief Executive and which deprives policy of the fruitful critiques bred by a reasonable partisanship. Those are important truths, but one of the most wholesome aspects of the resurgent Congress is the way in which it has kept those truths in perspective. The most active legislative participants have not lost sight of the need to mute partisanship in proportion to the gravity of the issues. There remains through much of the legislature an implicit understanding that the object of a more competitive and partisan debate on national security is, ultimately, collaboration between the parties and between the branches. So long as members are determined to restore vitality to the consideration of these issues, while abjuring vindictiveness, it may well be possible to correct the weaknesses of the older tradition of bipartisan foreign policy while retaining its affirmative thrust. Politics will no longer stop at the water's edge, but when its sails abroad, sophisticated congressional leadership can do much to insure that it is a discerning and productive enterprise.

To draw harmony out of potential discord will require more than sleight-of-hand conducting by the President. As difficult as genuine collaboration between the branches is, it is imperative that the managers of America's foreign affairs accept the responsibility for maintaining meaningful consultation with Congress. The currency of legislative-executive relations is no longer carte blanche. A creative foreign policy must rouse itself from the defensive attitudes permeating the executive establishment and aspire to forging an alliance with the legislature even sturdier than those ties which function internationally. It is hardly too much to expect that the President and the national security bureaucracy should understand that for Congress to grant broad discretion to the executive in foreign affairs is not to approve every exercise of that discretion. And it is not unrealistic to believe that a mutual respect for the independent opinions of each branch, especially when they differ, can pave the way to a far stronger consensus in the broad lines of policy.

This volume has attempted to detail some of the ways in which Congress can serve the President's interest no less than its own. Vigorous congressional involvement in the ongoing affairs of national security can often be the key to the balance of power within the bureaucracy. For example, during the 1960s the Defense Department undertook extensive diplomacy concerning base rights and military deployments in foreign countries. Despite Foggy Bottom's attempts to participate, in Spain and elsewhere the State Department was virtually excluded from the process of base negotiations. Such compartmentalization hardly served the goal of presidential control of crucial foreign policy decisions. Embryonic commitments were evolving without adequate policy guidance from either the White House or the Capitol. Only after congressional intervention was the State Department even able to obtain copies of the relevant documentation. In theory a President could have cured this kind of problem, but the demands of controlling so vast a bureaucracy exceed the capacity of any President and of any White House staff. An active Congress can do much to facilitate political control of the bureaucratic balance of power.

From the presidential standpoint, this kind of congressional intervention should be welcome. It need not be viewed as an assault on the President as a political figure or on the executive branch as such. A healthier perception would see both Congress and the President as the political agents of the American people, seeking to establish adequate means for directing the bureaucratic instrumentalities. To build this kind of perception on a shared basis will require not only a shift of Congress from the passive to the active mode, but a moderation of the imperial attitude which has marked the Presidency in modern times. The Churchillian tendency to construe every challenge as a threat to the essential prerogatives of the Presidency has long since become counterproductive. Surely Presidents must resist encroachments on the necessary powers of the office, but they ought to display a decent respect for the necessary functions of the legislature as well.

In equipping the American government to operate in the international environment, the evident decay of the domestic consensus on foreign policy is a serious liability. It is a liability which neither President nor Congress can overcome alone. The likely cure lies in their collegial action to revive a wholesome framework for legislative-executive relations. A new substantive consensus on the nation's place in the world awaits the establishment of a new procedural consensus.

One blunt observer from Capitol Hill, reviewing the wreckage wrought by Vietnam and the malignant experience of Watergate, put the case with typical force: "People look at the Executive and say we don't trust those bastards. They look at the politicians in Congress and say we don't trust these bastards. The only question is can we trust *these* bastards to keep *those* bastards honest." A raw but relevant perspective.

In a period of waning confidence in governmental institutions generally, it is doubtful that the policies espoused by those institutions will win easy acceptance by the citizenry. If the institutions themselves are to regain credibility and the policies they produce are to acquire popular support, the old images of an abject Congress and an assertive President steering the Ship of State according to secret whim must change. It is through active participation in national security affairs by the Congress that presidential leadership stands the best chance of regaining momentum. Review of executive foreign policy plans and concurrence by the Congress in the basic elements of the President's policies offer the most practical approach to restoring national confidence in America's global role. The strong congressional and popular support for the openings to the Soviet Union and China, for strategic arms control and for similar initiatives, demonstrates that such collaboration is still possible.

Perhaps the most problematic task for Congress to assume in this altered context is to penetrate national security issues early enough to have significant influence. If the legislature remains dormant until the executive apparatus has generated a firm policy recommendation, all the problems of rigid commitment by the President to a particular stance militate against true collaboration. The entire process solidifies and grows dubious if Congress ignores an impending policy problem until the executive is set in concrete on its position.

It will not suffice to rely on the old axiom formulated by Professor E. E. Schattschneider, "The President proposes, the Congress disposes." That categorical conception of the separation of powers and functions would establish a fence where there should be a bridge. Given the modern growth of bureaucracies to mammoth proportions, today's Congress needs to penetrate the bureaucratic processes well before executive proposals are completed if it is to play a meaningful role in a vast number of policy domains. It has become one of the highest missions of legislative politics to steer bureaucratic politics—to induce program and policy formulations responsive to representative preferences, to discourage premature elimination by the bureaucracy of ideas and options which warrant fuller consideration in the open processes of Congress. This objective calls for timely intervention by concerned legislators, collectively or individually, while the bureaucratic decision-making process is still in process. Normally, this intervention should take the form of inquiry, rather than pre-emptive legislative action, for the congressional task is not to disrupt thorough preparation of executive recommendations, but to insure that such preparation takes adequate account of the sentiments and purposes flowing through Congress.

This is one reason why the concept of individual policy entrepreneurship by members of Congress offers so much. With 535 sentries, bolstered by sufficient staff, there is a good chance that one or another member or committee will detect a burgeoning public problem soon enough to engage congressional interest before final presidential recommendations are devised. Only by early participation in considering such questions can Congress aspire to a proper influence on the bureaucratic processes which bear so heavily on the shape of options and the choice of actions.

In raising this standard for an activist posture by Congress toward the internal proceedings of the executive branch, one need not disregard the special responsibilities borne by those with operating responsibilities. Particularly in the national security field, the civilian and military officials who have direct charge of the foreign policy and defense establishments warrant the thoughtful consideration of legislators concerned with these matters. But Congress should guide its own conduct by the knowledge that those with operating responsibility often disagree among themselves and that, in resolving those disagreements, there is a profound need to bring into play the broader values to which the legislature is most sensitive. High policy is not and must never become primarily a matter of expert judgment or technological calculus, and it serves no national interest for Congress to be unduly reticent about intruding in the deliberations of the executive branch. If members of Congress do not monitor those deliberations aggressively, albeit in good spirit, the hard-won lessons of recent years will go for nought. The great questions of security, strategy, and peace may descend once more into the shadowed crevices of government.

Happily that danger seems relatively remote, given the conjunction of a rejuvenated Congress and the Presidency of Gerald Ford. The behavioral and procedural changes described in these pages give reasonable assurance that Congress will not again slip into a listless demeanor which concedes to the President an unwise latitude for national security policy. The diffusion of national security influence among several committees and subcommittees has given many members of Congress a stake in demanding a role in various programs and policies. Their standing with their peers and their success with their constituents have come to depend, in ways difficult to foresee some time ago and hard to portray even now, on persistent alertness in supervising defense and foreign policy. The newly formed habits of congressional staff promise to sustain their closer scrutiny of such matters. And so far as strategic policy and weapons procurement are concerned, the regular reports on cost and performance trends which the General Accounting Office is now providing will encourage periodic review of the major choices unfolding in this field. Similarly the evident diplomatic leverage derived from initiatives like the Mansfield amendments on NATO troop levels and the Jackson amendments on SALT and trade with the Soviet Union have established such devices as enduring elements in congressional practice. One may expect other comparably sophisticated maneuvers to appear in coming years.

Indispensable to Congress's continuing effort to shape a constructive role for itself are the formal innovations which reinforce the behavioral shifts which have taken place. The novel requirement that the executive branch file all international agreements, classified or otherwise, with the appropriate committees is calculated not only to induce more responsible action by the negotiators but to impel Congress to evaluate diplomatic efforts which were long hidden from view. The Foreign Affairs and Foreign Relations committees will have an institutional imperative to assess such undertakings with a wary eye, lest later disclosure of ill-considered commitments become a rebuke to the committees as well as to the President. The plea of ignorance will excuse no member who fails to meet these added responsibilities.

The War Powers resolution promises to be a cornerstone of the changing structure of legislative-executive relations. Ideally, the final version of this legislation would have enjoyed the cordial support of both branches. Mr. Nixon's unyielding refusal to seek a compromise in this area was probably more symptomatic of the siege mentality which blighted his Administration than of the issues in dispute. Future presidents, one hopes and anticipates, will perceive the real advantages which the act affords to them as well as to Congress. Above all, this legislation guarantees that Congress will have to choose openly and specifically whether to sustain or suspend the use of American forces in a hostile theater. Its provisions insure that this choice will be made without undue haste or endless evasion, the twin hazards to which legislative action is subject under the stress of crisis. Many years and many ordeals may pass before its premises are fully tested, but the act attests to a sturdy conviction that future conflicts involving the United States will find this country either quickly united or promptly disengaged. If there is a sounder prescription for the use of force by a democratic government, no one has yet advanced it.

In mid-1974 the Congress adopted another momentous reform which will have major implications of a different sort. Unlike the War Powers Act, the Congressional Budget and Impoundment Control Act earned generally favorable reactions in the executive branch, which had come to argue that congressional claims to more power over fiscal policy were welcome, provided Congress organized itself to act responsibly in adjusting the balance of expenditures and revenues. Toward this end the Congress has created budget committees with comprehensive authority to help shape budgetary priorities, taking account of both the President's recommendations and those of a new Congressional Office of the Budget. Beginning with 1977 the fiscal year will begin on October 1 rather than July 1, meaning that Congress and its committees will gain added time to evaluate the executive branch proposals. This should end the disruptive pattern of modern times in which congressional budget action was rarely completed by the beginning of the fiscal year, leaving agencies to operate on so-called "continuing resolutions" which destroyed orderly administration.

This measure will have immense importance for every department of government, but especially for the defense establishment and other parts of the national security bureaucracy. The act provides for systematic debate on national priorities early in every calendar year in order to establish guidance for individual legislative committees to apply within their jurisdictions as they review the components of the budget. At the end of the authorization and appropriation cycle, prior to September 15 of each year, a second budget debate will oblige Congress to reconcile projected revenues and expenditures, requiring the members once again to weigh competing claims on national resources at the macroscopic level. These procedures translate into a method for an unprecedented comparison of the different sectors of the budget. In particular, they mean that for the first time there will be a systematic attempt to make trade-offs between desirable levels of expenditures on weapons systems and human resources, on military manpower and urban reconstruction, on overseas bases and mass transit, on foreign aid and domestic health programs. This will not end the complexity of choices in the national security field, but it will force them into competition with other legitimate claims on the budget. The plan also calls for five-year expenditure projections, and the display of such estimates will necessitate far more rigorous judgments about defense and nondefense commitments alike. Like the knowledge that one is to hang on the morrow, the vision of future deficits should serve to concentrate the mind marvelously.

The net effect of this remarkable innovation will be to prevent any tendency for national security programs and expenditures to slide back into their long-privileged sanctuaries, sheltered from general review and evaluation. Even before final enactment of the recent budget reforms, Senator John McClellan's Appropriations Committee had begun to apply many of its principles, setting targets for particular programs early in the year and refining them in the light of economic trends and later actions by authorizing committees and subcommittees. In the lower chamber, when Congressman Melvin Price assumed the Armed Services chairmanship following Representative Hebert's unprecedented rejection by the Democratic caucus in January 1975, Mr. Price pledged to take his cues on defense spending from the new Budget Committee. In the face of these more orderly procedures for allocating public moneys, the Defense Department and related agencies were encountering increasingly stringent oversight. Without a trace of hostility toward essential investments in national security programs, one may still find reassurance in the knowledge that Congress has now devised effective methods for weighing expenditures in this area against comparably vital appropriations for other social purposes.

The movements sketched in these pages have vastly altered the context of legislative-executive relations. One might be tempted to portray the reassertions of congressional authority as a passing phase brought on largely by the personal frictions associated with Lyndon Johnson and Richard Nixon. To be sure, the distinct and highly personal disasters of those presidents played an important part in forging congressional determination to play a larger role. In the perception of many citizens the latter-day extravagances of the Presidency served mainly to debase the coinage of national security, particularly in Mr. Nixon's hollow invocation of security to shroud abuses of the domestic political system. An irony of our age is that presidents obsessed with problems of national security lost their capacity to discriminate among them and, so doing, lost their ability to enlist the support of their fellows. When counterfeit claims abound, genuine security considerations are more difficult to perceive.

Yet the resurgence of Congress is the product of more basic factors than resentment of the idiosyncracies of latter-day presidents. It is the result of the resounding demonstration that the constitutional system itself must be insulated from the perils of an overweening Presidency—most of all perhaps when the incumbent enjoys great popularity. The auspicious signs lie not only in Congress's willingness to assume its essential part in the scheme of governance but in the reviving insight of executive leaders that honest collaboration with the legislature is indispensable to American action in the world at large. On being nominated for the Secretary of State, Henry Kissinger pledged "to bring the Congress into a close partnership in the development, planning, and execution of our foreign policy." In his early months in office, amid the terminal throes of the Nixon Presidency, he made notable strides toward an improved partnership with Congress, but relations remained tense and erratic.

With the inauguration of Gerald Ford as the thirty-eighth President, the restoration of harmony between the branches became a realistic hope. Mr. Ford caught exactly the right nuance in expressing his preference not for a honeymoon with Congress, but for a "good marriage." The foundations for such a marriage are now sounder than at any time in memory. Both partners have learned that, as Nicholas Katzenbach has written, "democracy is too fragile to be divided into foreign and domestic affairs. We cannot give the President a free hand in the one without eroding the whole of the governmental system that all policy seeks to preserve."

There will no doubt be fierce disputes over the prerogatives of the two branches, as there will be over the wisdom of particular policies. But Congress and the President will endure those stresses with heightened awareness that each has the power and the will to fulfill its constitutional mandate. That is the prerequisite to the mutual respect on which legislative-executive cooperation must rely. In that knowledge lies the true bedrock of American security.

Index